RON PAUL

A LIFE OF IDEAS

Edited by Brian Bagnall
Co-edited by Stephanie Murphy
Designed by Hayden Sundmark
Printed in the United States of America

Library and Archives Canada Cataloguing in Publication

Horner, Christopher C

Ron Paul : a life of ideas / Christopher Horner, Karen Kwiatkowski.

ISBN 978-0-9738649-4-6

1. Paul, Ron, 1935- . 2. Presidential candidates--United States.
3. Presidents--United States--Election--2008. 4. United States--Politics
and government--2001-. I. Kwiatkowski, Karen U. II. Title.

E901.1.P38H67 2008   973.931092   C2008-904587-4

VARIANT PRESS
143 Goldthorpe Crescent
Winnipeg, Manitoba
R2N 3E6

This is an unofficial biography. Ron Paul and anyone related to
Ron Paul do not sponsor, authorize or endorse this book.

FOREWORD

Lawrence Lepard is a venture capitalist and investment manager who, in 2007, spent a significant amount of his own money to purchase full-page ads in USA Today and the New York Times (see Appendices for the text to these ads).

Almost 20 years ago I first became aware of Ron Paul while I was reading an editorial that spoke about how we have over 500 elected representatives in Washington, DC and to the author's knowledge there was only one truly honest one. I have forgotten the author, and the statement may have contained some hyperbole, but nevertheless it caused me to investigate Ron Paul. Clearly there was something different that made this man stand out in a crowd. My investigation opened a new world to me. By background, I was not particularly political in nature. My training and experience were in business and investing and my general view of the Government was that if it left me alone and taxed me less, then it was good. However, I was not blind to the problems that our country faced and I was fairly certain that the existing political structure was not getting the job done. Time passed, I learned more about Dr. Paul and then I met him at an economic conference in New York. That was it, I was hooked. You cannot meet and spend time with this decent, honest man and not conclude that his heart is in the right place. What a rarity in the political arena: a self-effacing, honest man who calls them as he sees them regardless of the consequences. A man who values principles rather than political preening. Surely no one with these characteristics could survive in Washington, D.C. , and yet he has. This survival has occurred in spite of both political parties doing everything in their power to make Dr. Paul just go away. That alone should tell the reader something. If both political parties hate this man, isn't it possible that he has them figured out and that they are protecting their interests and not the interests of We The People?

Fast forward a few years and I am at home on a Saturday afternoon. I receive a telephone call from Tom Lizardo, Ron Paul's Congressional Chief of Staff. I have never met Tom but he explains that he is calling supporters of Dr. Paul to assess if we would be willing to support Dr. Paul if he made a bid for the Presidency. Recognizing that the odds were long I said yes, the message was so good that who knew what would happen. It was worth the risk, even if only to spread the message. If Dr. Paul was willing to make the effort then the least I could do was support him. The message and the man deserved to be supported. I had no idea where the Campaign would lead, but I knew it would be interesting. The truth has a funny way of making itself known.

What occurred was nothing short of amazing. Who knew that an obscure Congressman from Texas could generate such grassroots enthusiasm and support? Did he win? Of course not, in the traditional sense. But in the non-traditional sense he hit a grand slam home run. I personally believe that what occurred with the Ron Paul Presidential bid will ultimately come to be compared with Martin Luther's nailing of the Theses to the door of the Church in Witenburg, with the Internet playing the role of Gutenberg's press.

People are waking up. The U.S. Federal government is a big part of the problem; not the solution it claims to be. As we are told more and more lies, and reality does not correspond to what the Government has told us, people are becoming aware that the Emperor indeed has no clothes. They can try to kill or slander the messenger, as Rudy Giuliani did in the first debate with Dr. Paul, but the unintended consequences of this action are to draw attention to the message. What beautiful irony. I am convinced that the Divine Power has a fabulous sense of humor. Since these kinds of changes take time, I suspect that it will be a while before we have a Ron Paul majority in Congress or a Ron Paul like candidate in The White House. But I have little doubt that it will happen. In the great sweep of human history progress is always being made. To existing politicians I say, "read em and weep", this is the future, you can either get in tune with it or become a political dinosaur.

Long live the peaceful revolution,

the Freedom Revolution.

LAWRENCE LEPARD
WELLESLEY, MASSACHUSETTS
July 8, 2008

www.thefreedomrevolution.com

CONTENTS

CHAPTER 1

LAND OF THE FREE

PRE-1935

Progressives

The central bank is an institution of the most deadly hostility existing against the Principles and form of our Constitution.

THOMAS JEFFERSON

Sometime around 1880, Ron Paul's great-grandfather and his 14-year-old son, Caspar, risked their lives to make a perilous journey across the Atlantic Ocean. They were traveling from Schlüchtern, a small town in the Hesse state of the German Empire, to the United States of America. His descendents presume that he left his wife and other children in Germany because he lacked the money to bring them, intending to send for them once he was settled in America.[1]

The Pauls landed in New York and made their way to rural Pennsylvania, which contained a large population of the famous Pennsylvania Dutch. They felt at home - the small town in which they settled shared a congenial similarity to Schlüchtern - and they decided to stay. Then, just six months later, Caspar's father died and Caspar was left to fend for himself in a new country where he knew virtually no one. It is unknown whether Caspar ever saw his mother and siblings again.

While the precise circumstances that motivated the Pauls to immigrate to America are not recorded, history offers some clues. Germany was still far behind the US in industrialization in the 1870s, so wages and living standards were higher across the ocean. The Social Democratic Party, guided by Marxist philosophies, was rapidly gaining power and would become the most powerful party in the Reichstag by the early 1900s. In fact, Germany had one of the largest governments in the world at the end of the 19th-Century, having implemented health care in 1883, accident insurance in 1884, and old-age and disability insurance in 1889, all of which were taxpayer-funded.[2]

By contrast, the United States in which Caspar Paul found himself was freer than Germany at the time, and much freer than the United States of 2008. Taxes at all levels of government consumed just 5% of the gross national product.[3] There was no federal income tax or Social Security, and the average person had no contact whatsoever with the federal government, save for using the Post Office.

There was no Child Protective Services Agency to put Caspar into foster care; instead, there were orphanages and charitable organizations, usually run by churches, which helped him cope without his parents. There was a small federal Immigration Agency, but Caspar was in no danger that it would deport him back to Germany. In these days before the Interstate Commerce Act of 1887 and the Sherman Antitrust Act of 1890, there were very few regulations dictating how Caspar must operate a business; since the country's currency was soundly backed by gold and silver, there was no inflation to speak of either. And there were no child labor laws to prevent the teenaged Caspar from earning a living. He was undoubtedly heartbroken, poor, lonely, and scared, but he was free.

However, numerous changes were occurring in America around the time of Caspar Paul's immigration. The American Civil War, fought when the Confederacy attempted to secede from the United States, had ended in 1865, the year before Caspar's birth on August 3, 1866.

The Civil War wasn't only about slavery; it ultimately was about who was supreme – the federal government, or the states. The Union victory in 1865 settled that question and marked a transformation in the laissez-faire federal government of 1787. At that time, political power was mainly vested in states and localities, and the federal government existed mainly to settle disputes between them and to deal with foreign governments. However, with the end of the Civil War, there emerged a powerful and overarching national government.

Caspar Paul's grandson, Ron Paul, would later state that Abraham Lincoln did not have to start a war to get rid of slavery. "Six-hundred-thousand Americans died in the senseless Civil War," he said. "No, he should not have gone to war. He did this just to enhance [the federal government] and get rid of the original intent of the Republic."[4]

The Civil War also introduced other unprecedented expansions of government into American society, such as subsidies to big business; an income tax; conscription; suspension of free speech and habeas corpus; and fiat (non-precious metal backed) paper money. While most of these measures were repealed after the war, all of them would eventually return – some permanently.

While the America of 1865 wasn't as free as the America of 1787, it was still arguably the freest country on earth. And, after the death of his father, Caspar Paul worked to overcome his unbearable grief and make the most of his new environment, which he undoubtedly saw as a land of opportunity.

Caspar ended up in the small town of Green Tree, Pennsylvania. There, he met a local woman named Sophia Ziegler, with whom he attended church. Although Sophia was born American and raised in Pennsylvania, her parents Johann and Gertrude were also from the Hessen state in Germany.[5] During the American Revolution, thousands of Hessian soldiers had fought against the framers of the United States Constitution. Ironically, these immigrants of Hessian descent were now enjoying the society that some of their forebears had attempted to crush.

Farming was all Caspar knew from his old homeland, so he worked to earn a living through truck farming. It involved growing fruit or vegetable crops on a large scale, and then transporting them to sell in other regions where an unsuitable climate prohibited their growing.[6]

He eventually added a dairy to his operation, selling milk and eggs from his basement, because it provided a source of income in the winter months.[7]

Sophia and Caspar married on May 4, 1899. The couple had four sons: Herbert, Howard Caspar (born August 19, 1904), Louis, and Arthur; and one daughter named Estella.[8]

....

As Caspar and Sophia operated the farm and dairy, the America they knew was undergoing major changes, one of which was the passage of the Progressive Package of 1913.

The Progressive changes were introduced over a period of about thirty years, starting in the 1890s, and involved the merger of numerous disparate factions – all of whom were looking to use government to achieve ends that they had failed to bring about through voluntary exchange and persuasion.

The Progressive Package had numerous elements, including alcohol prohibition, women's suffrage, and the strengthening of the Jim Crow segregation laws. But three aspects in particular induced a massive increase in the power and force of government, and from local and state governments to the federal government.

Ron Paul would one day convey his assessment of the Progressive legacy when he said, "The big government nanny-state is based on the assumption that free markets can't provide the maximum good for the largest number of people. It assumes people are not smart or responsible enough to take care of themselves, and thus their needs must be filled through the government's forcible redistribution of wealth. Our system of intervention assumes that politicians and bureaucrats have superior knowledge, and are endowed with certain talents that produce efficiency. These assumptions don't seem to hold much water."[9]

The first prong of the Progressive attack on American liberty was the Sixteenth Amendment, which gave Congress the power to tax citizens' incomes. Progressives had been lobbying for an income tax for a few decades before it was passed. There were several rationales behind their support of the income tax: the government needed more revenue; the government was too reliant on tariffs (which many Americans felt burdened them as consumers while shielding businesses from competition); and the rich should be paying more, because they could afford more.

So the income tax was largely sold to Americans with the logic that it was a tax increase for the rich and a tax cut (it reduced tariffs) for the poor and middle class.

This quickly proved to be untrue: in 1913, the first year the tax was collected, the bottom rate was 1% on incomes up to $20,000 ($424,601.38 in 2007 dollars), and 7% at the highest level. By 1918, at the height of World War I, the top rate had skyrocketed to 77%. Since 1917, the tax rate has never been below 24%; it reached its high of 94% in 1944.[10]

In addition to raising everyone's tax burden and giving the federal government a virtually unlimited source of revenue, the income tax also further consolidated federal power over the states. It gave the federal government the ability to dictate state laws by attaching conditions to federal funds. For example, the National Minimum Drinking Age Act of 1984 required states to raise the legal age for purchasing or publicly possessing alcoholic beverages to 21 as a condition for receiving 100% of their federal highway funds. By 1988, all 50 states had enacted the required legislation.[11]

Caspar Paul's grandson, Ron Paul, would one day work in Congress to repeal the Sixteenth Amendment and, as he often said, "replace it with nothing." He expressed this view when he wrote, "Could America exist without an income tax? The idea seems radical, yet in truth America did just fine without a federal income tax for the first 126 years of its history. Prior to 1913, the government operated with revenues raised through tariffs, excise taxes, and property taxes, without ever touching a worker's paycheck."[12]

A second aspect of the Progressive Package of 1913 was the Seventeenth Amendment, which changed the method of electing US senators from being elected by state legislatures to being elected by the state's citizens through a direct vote.

Movements for this change had occurred sporadically throughout the 19th-Century, largely with the argument that it would end the deadlocks that sometimes prevented state legislatures from choosing senators (45 deadlocks occurred in 20 states from 1891-1905, and Delaware didn't send a Senator to Washington from 1899-1903).[13] Proponents also claimed it would reduce alleged bribery and corruption in choosing senators.

But opponents, both at the time and later on, argued that the original method was part of the elaborate system of checks and balances the founders placed throughout various levels of government. They believed that almost everything the government did was potentially destructive, so deadlocks were desirable.

They also argued that the original method of electing senators made the senators beholden to their states - state legislatures had often instructed senators on how to vote - which was another check against potential federal tyranny. A case in point was the Virginia and Kentucky Resolves of 1798, in which the state legislatures urged their senators to oppose the Sedition Act, which made it illegal to criticize the federal government.

James Madison, a founding father and instrumental author of the Constitution, argued that structural barriers, rather than just enumerated powers, were necessary to keep the federal government in check. He argued, "The appointment of senators by state legislatures gives to state governments such an agency in the formation of the federal government, as must secure the authority of the former."[14]

Even Alexander Hamilton, who lobbied for seven years to amend the Articles of Confederation because "we need a government of more energy," and who wanted a permanent president who would appoint all state governors and have sole veto power over all state legislation, believed that the selection of Senators by state legislatures would be an "absolute safeguard" against federal tyranny.[15]

Ron Paul, in his characteristic agreement with the founding fathers, would later call for a repeal of the Seventeenth Amendment.[16]

The third major aspect of the Progressive Revolution was the Federal Reserve Act, which gave the United States a central bank, the Federal Reserve. The origins of the Federal Reserve Act are complicated, but they began with the Panic of 1907, in which loan retractions led to numerous bank and business failures, and the stock market plunged 50%. It was the fourth such panic in 34 years.[17]

Many businessmen became wealthy by providing goods and services in the relatively laissez-faire environment of 19th-Century America. They had acquired their fortunes by creating products that customers wanted to buy – the voluntary nature of these transactions had forced them to make their customers happy, or else they would stop buying.

Unfortunately, some among these businessmen wished to use the power of government to protect themselves from competition and pad their profits. They began agitating for a central bank - which would be under their ownership and control - by exploiting public fear and confusion over the latest panic. They manipulated public opinion through their relationship with intellectuals and opinion-makers, who convinced average people like the Pauls that a central bank was for their own protection because it would be a lender of last resort that could prohibit bank and business failures.[18]

But, as economist Murray Rothbard notes, banks should be no less subject to suffering the consequences of unsound business practices than should any other business. When bank runs and business failures occur, it is a natural consequence of bad choices by the owners. Though painful, failures encourage other businesses to be careful with their investments and lending, and they encourage consumers to patronize businesses with good reputations and sound finances.

It didn't happen immediately, but eventually the Federal Reserve Act made it possible for the government to increase the money supply by creating money which was not backed by gold or silver. The Federal Reserve did so not by printing paper dollars (the Treasury is responsible for currency), but by loaning money to private banks at cheap interest rates, thereby increasing the amount of credit in the overall economy and potentially encouraging irresponsible lending by bankers.

With the power of "the Fed," as it was nicknamed, the government could raise money without overtly raising taxes, while levying the hidden tax of inflation by slowly increasing the money supply and devaluing the dollar.

Another stated goal of the Federal Reserve was to stabilize US currency. The statistics speak for themselves on whether the Fed accomplished this goal: from 1913, the year the Federal Reserve was created, to 2007, the dollar's purchasing power decreased by approximately 95%.[19]

Before the creation of the Fed, inflation was not inevitable; a reverse inflation calculation reveals that what cost $1 in 1800 cost $0.57 in 1913. So, in the century before the creation of the Federal Reserve, the purchasing power of the dollar not only didn't erode - it nearly doubled.

The explanation that Federal Reserve detractors gave for these statistics was that, in contrast to paper money that governments can print with abandon, any commodity that naturally evolves into money, such as gold, must be valuable and finite. That way, the money supply cannot increase faster than the amount of real wealth created by economic growth.

In addition to giving government virtually unlimited revenue, fiat money also benefits politically connected industries, namely in the financial sector, because they have access to newly created money first, before the rest of the economy suffers from the increase in the money supply. This gives them time to spend or invest it while it's still worth more. In this way, argued opponents of the Fed, inflation is an insidious wealth transfer from the poor and middle class to the wealthy and politically-connected.

As Caspar and his sons were growing their dairy business, President Woodrow Wilson led the United States into the international conflict that became World War I. Some historians have noted that it is likely that the US government couldn't have afforded to enter the war without the Federal Reserve. During the war, the money supply doubled, and the national debt rose from $1.2 billion to $24 billion by 1920.[20]

In addition to the horrors of the war, including leaving over 10 million people dead, there were many unforeseen consequences of the United States' involvement. Ron Paul has made the argument that the Federal Reserve enabled US entry into World War I.[21] He and others have said that this set off a domino effect that led to the horrors of the Holocaust, World War II, Stalin's purges, and the Cold War. As the argument goes, WWI helped spur the Bolshevik revolution in Russia in 1917. And the devastating economic sanctions imposed on Germany by the Treaty of Versailles helped Hitler rise to power in 1933 by exploiting the lingering resentment over the outcome of the war and by promising to cure Germany's economic ills.

Paul, an outspoken proponent of peace and foreign non-interventionism, expressed this view when he said, "The first World War was sold to the American people as the war to end all wars. Instead, history shows it was the war that caused the 20th century to be the most war-torn century in history. Our entry into World War I helped lead us into World War II, the Cold War, the Korean War, and the Vietnam War. Even our current crisis in the Middle East can be traced to the great wars of the 20th century."[22]

The Great War, as it was known, was followed in the United States by a depression in 1920. This depression, however, ended in about a year when the government responded by reducing taxes and expenditures, and allowing wage rates to fall without intervening.

By the 1920s, Caspar and Sophie were advancing in years, and they decided it was time to pass the family business to their children.

Herbert, the oldest, didn't want to work in the family dairy. Instead, the budding entrepreneur opened up his own Agway store, part of a chain of stores selling farm supplies. He eventually had four children. Estella, the only child to get a college education, would become a teacher.

This left Howard (the second oldest), Louis, and Arthur to inherit the family dairy and farm land. They expanded the basement dairy their father had started into home delivery, initially using horse-drawn delivery wagons. As their business grew and technology advanced, they eventually came to own a modern dairy and twenty refrigerated trucks.[23]

As the Pauls' business grew, the Fed created an artificial boom from roughly July 1921 to July 1929, increasing the money supply by about 65% and repeatedly injecting the economy with cheap, easily available credit.[24]

One insidious effect of a centrally-regulated money supply is the boom-bust cycle. The boom is brought about when the central bank artificially lowers interest rates. The availability of "cheap credit" causes mal-investment (unsound investments) motivated by misleading economic indicators. This false prosperity causes people to feel wealthier short-term. As a result, politicians are motivated to pressure the Fed to lower rates, especially around election time.

As the money supply grows faster than economic output, people bid against each other for scarce resources using their borrowed money acquired by the new availability of cheap credit. Eventually, prices and interest rates begin to rise, which indicates that more projects have been started than current resources allow. Those questionable projects are soon abandoned, which causes the liquidation of the mal-investment through layoffs and foreclosures. This represents the bust portion of the business cycle.

If the Fed tries to forestall the bust by continuing to lower interest rates, it risks causing hyperinflation or even runaway inflation, which equates with the devaluation of the currency. This compounds the problem in the long-term, but it seems better in the short-term than the politically unpopular response of allowing unsound businesses to fail and to liquidate their assets.

Ron Paul explained his view on the business cycle when he said:

> Since the creation of the Federal Reserve, middle and working-class Americans have been victimized by a boom-and-bust monetary policy. In addition, most Americans have suffered a steadily eroding purchasing power because of the Federal Reserve's inflationary policies. This represents a real, if hidden, tax imposed on the American people. From the Great Depression, to the stagflation of the seventies, to the burst of the dotcom bubble, … every economic downturn suffered by the country over the last 80 years can be traced to Federal Reserve policy. The Fed has followed a consistent policy of flooding the economy with easy money, leading to a misallocation of resources and an artificial boom followed by a recession or depression when the Fed-created bubble bursts.[25]

With the creation of the Federal Reserve, the entire economy was placed in the hands of a few powerful men. No longer was this power self-regulated by the free market; it was regulated centrally. And if there was one important lesson the world learned from 20th century experiments in socialism, it was this: centralized regulation doesn't work.

In response to economic problems of the 1930s, the Federal Government issued a law that made it illegal to own gold, and then confiscated gold from private citizens. This, they thought, would increase demand for paper money and provide a solution to the country's economic woes. The Paul family, along with all Americans, was forced to give up the gold savings they had worked so hard on the farm to earn, in exchange for pieces of paper.

Most Americans gave up their gold because they were afraid not to. But as Ron Paul explained:

> The Founders of this country, and a large majority of the American people up until the 1930s, disdained paper money, respected commodity money, and disapproved of a central bank's monopoly

control of money creation and interest rates. Ironically, it was the abuse of the gold standard, the Fed's credit-creating habits of the 1920s, and its subsequent mischief in the 1930s, that not only gave us the Great Depression, but also prolonged it. Yet sound money was blamed for all the suffering. That's why people hardly objected when Roosevelt and his statist friends confiscated gold and radically debased the currency, ushering in the age of worldwide fiat currencies with which the international economy struggles today.[26]

But many people of the time, limited in their understanding of economics and desperate for a remedy, believed their government was acting in their best interests.

During the tumultuous time of the Great Depression, the Paul brothers began families and continued to operate their dairy. Louis married and had one child. Arthur also married and had one child.

On October 23, 1929, twenty-five-year-old Howard married a woman named Margaret Dumont. They had met in a social group called Luther League, part of the Lutheran church they both attended. Margaret's parents, Joseph and Lena, were both locals born in Pennsylvania. Margaret eventually became the bookkeeper for the Paul brothers' dairy.[27]

Because the Pauls were self-employed, they managed to weather the bust caused by the Federal Reserve. While others found themselves without work, the Pauls managed to keep the dairy running. But they would also have to live through the Great Depression, which would continue for more than ten years - despite, and perhaps even because of, intervention on the part of the federal government.

CHAPTER 2

LIFE LESSONS

1935-1950

Welfare State

We contend that for a nation to try to tax itself into prosperity is like a man standing in a bucket and trying to lift himself up by the handle.

WINSTON CHURCHILL

R onald Ernest Paul was born on Tuesday, August 20th, 1935, the third of what would be five Paul sons born to Howard and Peggy Paul in the 1930s. Ron joined older brothers Howard William "Bill" and David Alan, and an extended family at the Green Tree, Pennsylvania dairy farm. This included his paternal uncles, Louis and Arthur Paul and his grandmother. The family would soon be complete with the births of younger brothers Jerrold Dumont and Wayne Arthur.

As the son of a German immigrant, Howard Paul was, in a sense, a refugee from the sophisticated German socialism created under Prussian Chancellor Otto von Bismarck specifically to bind the individual to the state, cradle to grave. The extended Paul family, and all five boys, worked hard from an early age, busy with school and church. Years later, Ron's wife of fifty years observed that his was not "a family that played a lot. Everything was serious."[1] It might be seen by some as ironic that this was the origin of the man who would one day become perhaps his country's greatest advocate for freedom and liberty. His conservatism is the conservatism of the founding fathers who, like his grandfather, rejected a powerful centralized government in the Bismarck model.

Howard and Peggy Paul were active Lutherans, and Howard hoped that all of his sons would grow up to be Lutheran ministers. In fact, Ron's older brother David later became a Lutheran minister, in Michigan, and his younger brother Jerrold became a Presbyterian minister in New York. Ron recalls that he briefly considered becoming a Lutheran minister, but eventually decided on a different path of service.[2]

The St. Stephen Evangelical Lutheran Church that serves Green Tree, Pennsylvania today explains Lutheranism as "not in competition with other Christians" and that "the Holy Communion is the family mean where pardon, peace and joy are present in the deepest sense." Ron Paul recalls that "what influenced me most in my family and upbringing ... was the work ethic and church. It was faith-based. We spent a lot of time at our church and that was part of our routine."[3]

Over the years, Ron would marry and raise his children in the Episcopal Church. He recalls, "As the years went on both of us became more annoyed with the liberalization of the Episcopal Church and it didn't fit us." Much later in life, in line with the Lutheran embrace of all Christianity, he attended Baptist services.

"Some evangelicals get a little bit annoyed because I'm not always preaching and saying, 'I'm this, I'm this, and this.' I think my obligation is to reflect my beliefs in my life," he explains. "I like the statement in the Bible that when you're really in deep prayer you go to your closet. You don't do it out on the streets and brag about it and say, 'Look how holy I am.' If a person has true beliefs and is truly born again, it will be reflected in their life."[4]

As a child, the Paul family emphasized church, work and study – in a community where these were indeed the shared values. Years later, Paul explained how his politics are in line with his religious values. "We want government, but we want self government, or local government, or family government. But we don't want the nanny-state to tell us how to deal not only with economic matters, but also in the area of virtue. If you think the nanny-state is okay to make the society more fair economically ... the conservative comes along and says, 'Well, we're going to legislate virtue.' It's the same issue and we're trying to put this issue of freedom back together again. It's not two parts: economic freedom and personal freedom. There's only one freedom."[5]

These words are significant, because of what was happening to Americans during Ron's childhood. About two years before he was born, FDR signed emergency executive order 6102, suspending the right of private American citizens to own gold. Most adults recalled, with some concern, a similar gold grab by an American President bent on global war, and Wilson's legal vehicle for gold confiscation, the *Trading with the Enemy Act* of 1917. Many average Americans saw this as confirmation that government, once again, could not really be trusted on issues of money.

Nearly coinciding with Ron Paul's birth, John Maynard Keynes produced his own child or sorts; a formalized guideline for the government interference in and management of the economy, and a bible for FDR and subsequent presidents who would seek to "do something" about the American economy. Keynes' *The General Theory of Employment, Interest and Money* was released in early 1936 to great welcoming by the Roosevelt administration. A few Americans opposed Keynesianism, such as the journalist Garet Garrett. However, Garrett acknowledged the impact of Keynes' work, saying,

"Probably no other book has ever produced in so little time a comparable effect. It has tinctured, modified, and conditioned economic thinking in the whole world."[6]

Garrett, writing ten years after the publication of Keynes' book, explained how Keynesian economic theory facilitated socialism in America. "For the planned society they were talking about, the socialists were desperately in need of a scientific formula," he explained. "Government at the same time was in need of a rationalization for deficit spending. The idea of welfare government that had been rising both here and in Great Britain — here under the sign of the New Deal — was in trouble. It had no answer for those who kept asking, 'Where will the money come from?' It was true that government had got control of money as a social instrument and that the restraining tyranny of gold had been overthrown, but the fetish of solvency survived and threatened to frustrate great social intentions."

As described by Garret, the political and economic tension of this timeframe was focused on government's proper role in monetary policy, economic and social justice, and the vast new overreach of American government interference and control of everyday life. Ron Paul would spend his adult life battling these overweening and ravenous forces for government intervention at home and abroad. Long before that, however, Ron witnessed the results firsthand of this kind of state-dominated society.

In 1936 and 1937, the Works Progress Administration came through Allegheny County and conducted detailed inventories as part of the WPA Home Survey Project. These government surveys, conducted to provide employment during the depression, required the inspection of every home and business, including the Paul farm, recording "construction material, number of rooms, baths, floors, heat, age, roof, plumbing, plaster, interior trim, condition, workmanship, basement size, laundry, sewer, rent value, special features, size, cubic construction, u. value, garage cars, const. material, size, condition, value, paved street, transportation factor, school factor, district trend, transition, lot size, solid ground, topography, acreage, a. tillable, owner, address and remarks."[7]

This process must have seemed quite a government intrusion on the privacy of average people in Green Tree in 1937. They might have wondered how those WPA drafters and note-takers employed by the federal government were paid. Of course, it was in paper money printed by a centralized American government, unrestrained by a commodity-backed currency. Those Americans who actually produced something of value for their community, like the Pauls and their neighbors, lost out with this arrangement as the value of their savings decreased.

When Ron Paul was four years old, a number of streets in Green Tree were paved, courtesy of WPA labor.[8] To the local residents, this was seen as visible progress; something positive.

Ron's childhood was spent in an era that had hope and even happiness, despite real concerns over economics and looming war. These were uncertain times, as Americans hoped to avoid another war in Europe, even as Washington, D.C. seemed bent upon it.

Even during the Depression, there were icons and entertainment. These sights, sounds, and events helped shape his perceptions. It was the era of big bands led by Glenn Miller and Tommy and Jimmy Dorsey, and jazz greats such as Duke Ellington and Count Basie. It was the era of the underdog racehorse Seabiscuit, who captivated Americans for several years through 1940 with his drive and toughness.

It was the heyday of radio. Radio news and entertainment had blossomed, connecting Americans with each other and the world in a way that had never happened before. Through it all, because no one expected their government to do everything for them, people helped each other.

Ron's earliest memories include happily sharing his room with his brothers. His brother David recalls they "grew up in a house with five boys in one bedroom."[9] In 1940, Ron joined his brothers at his first paid job. Unlike the hard work done by government bureaucrats in the WPA, creating and collecting federal records on the interior trim and construction materials of homes and businesses of Allegheny County, five-year-old Ron worked in the basement of their four bedroom house alongside his brothers, checking hand-washed milk bottles for spots, "earning a penny for every dirty bottle they spotted coming down a conveyor belt."[10]

Paul recalls, "We learned the incentive system." The bottles were washed by Ron's uncles, and one uncle was a little more careless than the other in this duty. "We liked to work for that one uncle, because we got more pennies."[11]

In 1940, politically bending to the popular American antiwar sentiment of the day, Franklin Roosevelt said, "I have said this before, but I shall say it again and again and again; your boys are not going to be sent into any foreign wars."[12] But the Pauls would soon learn they could not believe everything they heard from the federal government.

Ron was halfway through his first year in school when news came of the Japanese attack on Pearl Harbor, and the US entry into the Second World War. So began the wartime economy in the United States, complete with government rationing of food and commodities, the common use of government ration tickets, and government issued stickers, edicts and required approvals for a wide variety of human enterprises that only months before had operated freely, without the helping hand of an all-wise government bureaucrat.

In 1942, Roosevelt established the War Production Board, the Office of Price Administration and other government bodies to oversee federally mandated production goals, and price controls throughout the economy, including the important agricultural sector. Young Ron observed his father duly affixing a government issued sticker to his car windshield, with authorization numbers to match his government issued ration tickets for gasoline; he observed his mother checking her ration book with its stamps for the family's various food and sundry needs.

Because the Pauls ran a dairy, and delivered milk, butter and cheese directly to local customers, the onerous hand of the nationally managed economy reached into the Paul household on a daily basis, in an unprecedented manner. In addition to government concern over the production of dairy products by small farmers, rationing placed a new government burden on all retailers, who were required to collect the stamps for rationed items from every customer.

As with all government rationing, and price controls, it created shortages and misallocations, and those shortages and misallocations fostered a black market – which is to say – the free market, temporarily made illegal by government edict. Merchants in particular were suspect in providing goods outside of the government rationing system, and instead of being celebrated as the backbone of the country, farmers were increasingly suspect by government agents focused on infractions within the complicated command economy of World War II.

Although Ron was far too young to begin forming political beliefs, the events around him were shaping his values. Those values centered on freedom. "I claim that I was born with it," he later recalled. "I think a lot of us are born with instincts that we'd like to be left alone in our privacy, and my instincts were there. I think I was conditioned over the years by our educational system and what our government tells us … that you're a strange person because you believe that."[13]

Ron Paul's future political beliefs had their start in the differences he and his family observed in the 1930s and 1940s between real work on the dairy, government interference with private enterprise, and Depression-era government make-work in his hometown of Green Tree. Decades later, he discussed counterproductive federal farm policies, and the "ridiculous" National Animal Identification System (NAIS). "I typically don't trust big government," he said, pointing out that NAIS was "another national mandated expensive program that may benefit some large farmers at a cost to the small farmers" and was another "example of a problem that didn't need solving."[14]

He believed that government has a misconstrued idea of what rights are, and asks, "Where does the government get the power to regulate or transfer material things? Is the government productive? No! The government is destructive and gets in the way of individuals who want to take care of themselves."[15]

During his early childhood, Ron was learning about hard work, diligence, logical thinking, and perhaps, as his middle name suggests, what it means to be earnest. His later exposure to the long-established economic ideas of the Austrian School, with its opposition to Keynesian economics and emphasis on sound money, must have given logical wings to the ideas and observations he had as a child of the Great Depression, a period extended and made worse for common people through misguided national economic policies of FDR and his successors. In spite of these policies and their counterproductive results, and in part due to the national command economy established and enforced as part of the US involvement in World War II, government grew rapidly, and it never shrank back to its pre- Depression and pre-World War II levels.

Years later, Paul would explain how big government solutions don't work, even as many Americans clamor for government solutions to every problem. He explained, "The big government nanny-state … assumes people are not smart or responsible enough to take care of themselves, and thus their needs must be filled through the government's forcible redistribution of wealth. … A real solution to our problems will require a better understanding of, and greater dedication to, free markets and private property rights."[16]

Green Tree was a small farming, mining and railroad town located two miles southwest of Pittsburg, in Allegheny County. During his formative years, events and conditions influenced Ron's ideas on what is valuable, what is important, and how the world works. Allegheny County had a strong sporting culture which influenced Ron deeply. On his milk route, Paul delivered to celebrated baseball Hall of Fame recipient Honus Wagner, who ran a sporting goods store in Pittsburgh and worked as a hitting trainer for the Pittsburgh Pirates.[17] Baseball was a favorite sport for the local boys, and Paul would continue his love of baseball well into adulthood.

The trajectory of his whole family reflects the values of hard work and service instilled by Howard and Peggy Paul, and their western Pennsylvania community. Ron's older brother Bill became a mathematics professor, eventually becoming the head of the math department at Appalachian State University in Boone, North Carolina. David and Jerrold became ministers, and youngest brother Wayne became a certified public accountant. His father and uncles sold the dairy operation when they retired in the early 1970s, about the time that home deliveries of milk ended.

Ron Paul, like most Americans from the period, had no sense of establishment or entitlement. "He doesn't have any of that in his background," commented his brother David.[18]

Notwithstanding these traditional and liberty-cherishing perspectives of Americans across the country, the warfare-welfare state that had germinated under Woodrow Wilson and blossomed under FDR would continue to grow. This warfare-welfare state would ultimately be embraced and cherished by both the left and right, by mainstream churches and by both public and private educational establishments. Reining in this metastasizing and suffocating growth, breaking these chains on human freedom and productivity, would later become one of Ron Paul's life missions. But before he would run for political office and begin an American revolution for freedom, he would simply run for the joy of it.

CHAPTER 3

HIGH SCHOOL YEARS

1950-1953

Public Education

*Whenever is found what is called a paternal government, there is found
state education. It has been discovered that the best way to ensure implicit
obedience is to commence tyranny in the nursery.*

BENJAMIN DISRAELI

In the fall of 1949, fourteen-year-old Ron Paul entered his freshman year
at Dormont High School in Pittsburgh, Pennsylvania.[1] Known to most of
his friends and classmates as Ronnie, he would eventually become the top
student and athlete in his class.[2]

Ronnie was well-liked by his peers and they persuaded him to run for
president of the student council, a position he had little interest in pursuing
given his calm demeanor.[3] However, young Ron eventually assented and was
subsequently elected to one of his very first political offices.

Family continued to play an important role during Ron Paul's teenage
years. Ron was instilled with a solid work ethic at an early age, due in large
part to the experiences he gleaned from his years at the family dairy—where
he continued to work during high school in addition to holding down a job at
a drug store.[4]

He soon gained a healthy respect for the value of money and learned the
importance of hard work and of living within one's means. These traits would
later manifest themselves during Paul's career as a United States congressman,
where he would often speak critically of Washington's wasteful spending

habits.

Throughout his four years in high school, Ron genuinely enjoyed all academic subjects (except perhaps Latin, which was his most challenging and least favorite).[5] He was also a member of the National Honor Society and graduated high school with honors.[6]

He was equally in his element when it came to sports. The quintessential student-athlete, he played football and baseball and was also part of the wrestling team, but it was in track and field that he truly excelled.

As a sophomore, Ron placed second in the state in the 440-yard dash.[7] In his junior year, Ron was the Pennsylvania State Champion in the 220 and 440-yard dash and placed third in the 100-yard dash.[8] Paul's time in the 100 was 9.7 seconds,[9] which was just shy of the national record and "pretty fast for the early 1950s," according to his future wife, Carol.[10]

Unfortunately, at the peak of his competitive years Ron suffered a serious knee injury during a football game. The injury was so severe it would require surgery to repair a torn ligament and half a year (much of it on crutches) to recover. Although he could walk once again, his knee was not the same. It felt wobbly and weaker than before, a condition that would plague him throughout his adult life.[11] In time, Ron painfully came to accept that his competitive track days were over, although he continued running.

Despite this setback, Ron was able to rehabilitate his knee sufficiently to convince one college to offer him a full track scholarship. Paul did not accept it, however, fearing that he would not be able to regain the speed that accounted for his previous success.[12]

....

The school system in 1950 was far different from the heavily regulated system decades later. Although publicly funded, it was largely left to local parents and teachers to decide how best to educate students. Despite the smaller budgets, it was a system that managed to turn out highly productive, responsible, literate individuals that were among the best and brightest in the world.

Since that time, the federal government has taken control of every aspect of schools, from what teachers are allowed to talk about and how they can discipline students, to the curriculum and tests. Ron Paul would one day fight against federal oversight of America's public schools. As a result of this steadfastness, some of Paul's detractors have alleged that he stood in opposition to public funding of education altogether,[13] though this is a disingenuous claim.

Ron Paul certainly resisted the paternalism inherent to government schooling. When asked to explain how the *states* should handle education, he stated a preference to remove government from the equation. First and foremost, he advocated on behalf of parents and communities, noting that his role as a federal official was to discuss federal policy. "Parental control of child rearing, especially education, is one of the bulwarks of liberty,"[14] he noted. Parents once made decisions about their children's schooling through local school boards, Paul observed, only to see this power systematically replaced by the judicial system and the executive branch of government.[15]

As an advocate of limited government principles, Paul held firmly the idea that public schools function most efficiently when empowered to operate unencumbered by federal regulations. In short, states and localities should be free to make educational decisions best suited to their own needs, not those dictated by the federal government.

Ron Paul advocated the abolition of the United States Department of Education, which he believed was created unconstitutionally when it was formed by the Department of Education Organization Act and signed into law by President Jimmy Carter in 1979.[16]

"The federal government has no constitutional authority to fund or control schools," Paul later stated.[17] "I want to abolish the unconstitutional, wasteful Department of Education and return its functions to the states. By removing the federal subsidies that inflate costs, schools can be funded by local taxes, and parents and teachers can directly decide how best to allocate the resources."[18]

Ron Paul justified his opposition to federally centralized education by deferring to America's parents, who began to home-school their children in greater numbers since the 1990s.[19] To him, this illustrated a growing dissatisfaction and frustration with government schooling among many Americans.

Paul believed parents should receive a tax credit for K-12 educational expenses, regardless of whether or not their children attended public, private, or home-based schools.[20] He defended this by stating, "Washington politicians have imposed a one-size-fits-all model on the nation's schools, to the detriment of parents and local school districts. It is time to correct that mistake by ending the practice of forcing parents to send all of their education tax dollars to the federal government."[21]

He also believed teachers should receive a tax credit, effectively increasing teacher pay without raising federal education expenditures.[22]

In addition to his attempts to weaken the federal stranglehold on academia by returning more money to the taxpayer, Paul likewise rose in opposition to congressional expenditures aimed at increasing the scope of federal management of education at the expense of parents' rights.

Paul also objected to any attempt by the Federal Government to regulate the mental health of children in schools. Such an attempt was made in 2004 by the *New Freedom Commission on Mental Health*, which issued a report recommending mandatory mental health screening of every child in America.[23]

As someone who had spent years practicing medicine, Dr. Paul drew on his own experiences in expressing serious concern over the drugging of youngsters while their brains were still developing, citing a collegial opinion that psychiatric diagnoses are inherently subjective.[24]

Moreover, despite the significance of these apprehensions, Paul nevertheless concluded, "The greater issue ... is not whether youth mental health screening is appropriate. The real issue is whether the state owns your kids."[25]

Ron Paul was not merely concerned about the government's influence over school children but college students as well. Paul expressed opposition to the College Access and Opportunity Act of 2006,[26] namely its provision to establish an *Academic Bill of Rights*.[27]

Though this *Academic Bill of Rights* was advertised as a measure that would allow students in public universities to express opinions contrary to those held by politically correct professors without fear of reprisal, Paul identified it as a natural result of the political correctness that emerged due to the federal funding of colleges and universities in the first place.[28]

The irony was not lost on Paul, who said, "[I]n a perfect illustration of how politicians use problems created by previous interventions in the market to justify new interventions, Congress proposes to use the problem of political correctness to justify more federal control over college classrooms."[29]

Paul explained that despite the supposed good intentions of the *Academic Bill of Rights*, it would, paradoxically, "further stifle debate about controversial topics"[30] in the classroom, "because many administrators will order their professors not to discuss contentious and divisive subjects, in order to avoid a possible confrontation with the federal government."[31]

....

Ron Paul's most high-profile opposition to a federal monopoly on America's public schools was against the No Child Left Behind Act of 2001 (NCLB),[32] which was signed into law by President George W. Bush on January 8, 2002.[33]

Paul expressed distinct opposition to this legislation, condemning it for its unconstitutionality and for escalating federal control over education in the form of increases in both government spending and mandatory testing requirements for states and local communities.[34]

Paul criticized the very foundation of NCLB when he stated, "A better title for this bill is 'No Bureaucrat Left Behind' because, even though its proponents claim [NCLB] restores power over education to states and local communities, this bill represents a massive increase in federal control over education."[35]

Paul thoroughly analyzed the bill and demonstrated its micromanaging intent, noting, "[NCLB] contains the word 'ensure' 150 times, 'require' 477 times, 'shall' 1,537 and 'shall not' 123 times. These words are usually used to signify federal orders to states and localities. Only in a town where a decrease in the rate of spending increases is considered a cut could a bill laden with federal mandates be considered an increase in local control!"[36]

Paul explained that NCLB would lay the foundation for a de facto national exam, as states and localities shaped their own assessments around the "nationally-normed" test in order to save teachers and students the burden of having to prepare for multiple yearly exams.[37] As a defender of intellectual freedom and advocate of fierce intellectual debate, Ron Paul worried that such centralization of thought would lead to a national curriculum characterized by further breakdown in the academic integrity of public schools.[38]

....

Consistent with his opposition to pervasive federal mandates such as NCLB, Ron Paul similarly questioned the concept of federal school vouchers— taxpayer-provided stipends that parents apply to private and parochial schools as a means of removing their children from failing public schools.

At first glance, one might think Paul would have supported federal school vouchers. After all, they provide greater individual control over compulsory education. He even argued before the House of Representatives in September 2003 that state and local governments have the right (under the Tenth Amendment) to establish voucher programs. However, he emphasized that there is no place for them at the *federal level*.[39]

Paul urged Congress to recognize that vouchers are "little more than another tax-funded welfare program establishing an entitlement to a private school education";[40] that they unfairly benefit only a "particular group of children selected by politicians and bureaucrats";[41] and, perhaps most importantly, that because voucher advocates claim that children have a "right" to a "quality" education, "private schools will be forced to comply with the same rules and regulations as the public schools" as bureaucrats subjectively determine which schools provide a "quality" product and which do not.[42]

Recognizing that government funding invariably leads to government control, Paul shared with his colleagues an example of how voucher programs were being targeted for abuse almost as quickly as they were proffered as the solution to ineffective public schooling:

> Some supporters of centralized education have recognized how vouchers can help them advance their statist agenda. For example, [Siobhan] Gorman, writing in the September 2003 issue of the Washington Monthly, suggests that, "The way to insure that vouchers really work, then, is to make them agents of accountability for the private schools that accept them. And the way to do that is to marry the voucher concept with the testing regime mandated by [President George W.] Bush's No Child Left Behind Act. Allow children to go to the private school of their choosing, but only so long as that school participates in the same testing requirements mandates for public schools." In other words, parents can choose any school they want as long as the school teaches the government approved curriculum so the students can pass the government approved test.[43]

Paul's solutions to public education reform focused not on increasing or managing federal control but *resisting* it. He sought to empower parents and teachers to take advantage of legislation allowing them to keep more of their earnings. Unfortunately, these initiatives have been consistently repelled by big-government politicians in both major parties.

....

Ron Paul was lucky enough to benefit from an education developed by the people around him rather than bureaucrats in Washington with no stake in his daily life. Throughout his life he witnessed the American education system, highly regarded world-wide at the time he passed through it, grow progressively worse as it fell under more federal control.

After his knee injury, young Ronnie underwent extensive swimming therapy in high school as part of a rehabilitation program. Paul soon realized he also had the talent to swim competitively.[44] This love of swimming would stay with him for the rest of his life.

Although Ronnie accumulated several impressive scholastic and athletic achievements, it was his personality that most people noticed. Even as a youngster, Paul had about him a quiet magnetism that impressed classmates and teachers alike. He was humble yet confident, a true believer in the adage that in order to gain respect you must first give it.[45]

One person for whom Ron had tremendous respect at this point in his life was a high school history teacher who was drafted into the Korean War and later killed. This troubled Ron tremendously, and because the war took place almost entirely during Paul's high school career,[46] it consequently played an important role in shaping the congressman's opposition toward the military draft, American interventionism abroad, and war in general when it is waged for anything less than the country's immediate defense.[47]

It was the sum of Ron Paul's character and personality that drew the attention of a beautiful schoolmate, Carol Wells. Although a year his junior, the plucky teenager asked Ronnie in 1952 to accompany her to a Sadie Hawkins party on her 16th birthday. He gladly accepted Carol's invitation and they went steady for the balance of their high school days.[48] With his high-school education drawing to a close, Ron Paul was about to embark on his life's journey.

CHAPTER 4

COLLEGE YEARS

1953-1957

Marriage

It is not a lack of love, but a lack of friendship that makes unhappy marriages.

NIETZSCHE

While Ron Paul was growing up in Green Tree, Pennsylvania, Carol Wells was growing up in nearby Dormont, another borough just outside Pittsburgh. She was the only child of William "Bill" Wells, a successful coffee broker, and his wife, who was also named Carol.[1]

Even as a young girl, Carol was the type of person who made everyone with whom she came into contact feel important. She gave the same caring respect to all those she met, no matter what their station in life.

Carol first noticed Ron Paul when he was running at a high school track event. Soon, she noticed much more. She recalls, "I think what impressed me most was that everybody liked him. But he was a serious student and a serious athlete. He spent most of his time doing that. He wasn't one of the big dating crowd."[2]

With Ron preoccupied mostly with studies and sports, Carol took matters into her own hands. Her aforementioned Sweet-Sixteen birthday party on February 29, 1952, was to be a Sadie Hawkins event, where the girls invite the boys. She invited Ron.[3] It was their first of many get-togethers that continued through high school.

After Ron graduated from high school in 1953, he matriculated at

Gettysburg College, but Carol had another year of high school to complete. Fortunately, she could stand outside the school, look up a hill, and see her family's modest two-story house about five blocks away. If she saw that her mother had hung a towel outside, it was her signal that a letter from Ron had arrived.[4]

After Carol graduated from Dormont High, she attended Ohio University in rural, remote Athens, Ohio. There, she majored in Secretarial Studies and Home Economics, and was a marching-band baton twirler and a member of Alpha Xi Delta,[5] a self-described "women's fraternity" founded in 1893.[6] Every day during those college years, just as she did during high school, she sent Ron a letter.[7]

Ron, meanwhile, studied in Pennsylvania at Gettysburg College. He had turned down track scholarships at other schools, including Penn State, because he felt that the aforementioned knee injury he suffered in high school would prevent him from performing at a high enough level to justify taking the money.[8]

He chose Gettysburg because he wanted a small college, and because it was a church-affiliated school. Plus, a good high school friend of his, Richard Lewandowski, had started there a year before.[9]

Gettysburg College, founded in 1832, is in Pennsylvania, near the famous Civil War battlefield and the cemetery where Abraham Lincoln gave his Gettysburg Address.[10] During the war, both the Northern and Southern armies swept through the campus. One of the campus buildings even served as a battlefield hospital for wounded soldiers of both armies. The college garnered additional fame in the years after Ron Paul graduated, when Dwight D. Eisenhower moved to Gettysburg and wrote his memoirs at the college after his second presidential term.[11]

At Gettysburg, Ron was a serious student. Friend Richard Lewandowski's then-fiancée Lois recalls that Ron was "usually seen either going to the library, or coming back to the fraternity house with an arm load of books."[12]

Ron went to Gettysburg with the idea that he might become a Lutheran minister – the same career chosen by his brothers David and Jerrold.[13] However, the politics of the time had a life-altering impact on his choice of career.

"The same events that early on motivated me to go to medical school later motivated me to participate in politics," he later recalled. "Clear memories of the horrors of World War II and the Korean War and the reports of loss of life of family, friends, and neighbors had an impact on me. I knew very early on I never wanted to carry a gun in a war. ... I definitely knew at an early age that I preferred a medical bag to a gun, healing to maiming, life to death."[14]

Ron's athletic career continued at Gettysburg. Always one to make lemons into lemonade, he discovered a new sport – swimming – during therapy for his knee injury. He joined the college swim team. He also continued in track and field as a runner, despite the injury that had hindered his performance in high school.[15]

Not long after arriving at Gettysburg, Ron joined the Lambda Chi Alpha fraternity. Lambda Chi Alpha, founded at Boston University in 1909, later expanded to include more than 300 chapters across the country. In 1928, it was one of the first national fraternities to take a stand against the cruel and often dangerous hazing associated with the initiation practices of many fraternities.[16]

By 1972, the group eliminated pledging altogether, becoming the first national fraternity to do so.[17]

Thus, while the popular perception of fraternities of the era is dominated by the raunchy movie Animal House, Lambda Chi Alpha offered something different at Gettysburg – and that's what attracted Ron. As he recalls, "Every fraternity has a different reputation – some were only sports, some were only playboy types, but Lambda Chi was well-known for academics and having a lot of well-rounded people in a lot of different activities as well as sports. The fact that they represented all the different areas and cared about having good grades, I thought it would be better because I wasn't into the drinking and the things some fraternities were known for."[18]

Of course, it may have helped that activities within the fraternity house were monitored by a fraternity house mother who lived there. And, as for alcohol, Gettysburg College was a dry campus at the time.[19]

High school friend Richard Lewandowski became Ron's big brother in the fraternity. Mr. Lewandowski's wife, Lois, recalls that the fraternity indeed contrasted with the present-day stereotype and that people had more respect for each other back then. For example, Sunday dinners at the fraternity were a special occasion because girlfriends could visit. The men would wear dress shirts and ties; the women would wear dresses, and a fraternity brother would always escort the house mother to the table.[20]

From the outset, Ron was a leader in his fraternity – first, as president of his pledge class, and later as the chapter secretary.[21] Additionally, he became the group's house manager, a job that paid $9.00 a month. Eventually, he became the kitchen steward. He later recalled, "You had to order all the food, plan all the meals; you were in charge of the cooks for three meals a day, seven days a week. I got $43 a month for that and that paid for my food... and the food was good because I got to buy it."[22]

Among Ron's closest friends in the fraternity were Lewandowski and J. Michael Bishop, a fellow biology student who would go on to win the Nobel Prize in 1989 for his research on viruses that can cause cancer.[23] When Ron wasn't busy with his many activities, he enjoyed relaxing around the fraternity house. A pool table provided a favorite form of indoor recreation for the group.[24]

Although Ron had originally aspired to become a minister, his voracious appetite for reading and natural curiosity led him toward biology. As his studies progressed, the prospect of becoming a doctor won out. In his second year, he designed his course schedule to allow him to enter a medical school after college.[25]

In the fraternity house and around the campus, Ron's character was evident to all who came in contact with him. Mrs. Lewandowski recalls that he was not only pleasant and polite, but also an obviously "honorable man." She also notes that Ron blended sociability with honesty. "If you asked his opinion on something," she recalled, "you would know he was telling you exactly what he really thinks."[26]

During Ron's childhood and adolescence, he had earned and saved enough money – selling lemonade, mowing lawns, delivering papers, and helping out in a drug store – to pay for his first year's tuition of $325 plus expenses.[27] The fraternity job paid Ron's rent, and he had a small academic scholarship. However, that still didn't provide him with enough money for all four years of college.

So, in addition to his studies, sports, and other responsibilities, Ron took on more jobs. He delivered laundry, and in his second year he became the manager of "The Bullet Hole," a campus coffee shop, which still existed fifty years later. (The shop was named after the Gettysburg College athletics teams, the Bullets.)[28]

Many of Ron's classmates didn't work nearly as hard as Ron, and they often wondered why he took on so many jobs. As Ron secretly knew, all this work was for a specific goal. He was planning to purchase a very special – and costly – item that would forever change his life.

On Christmas breaks, back in Green Tree, Ron delivered mail as a temporary mail carrier for the US Postal Service. As a Congressman and presidential candidate decades later, he would support eliminating the Postal Service's monopoly on first-class mail delivery and call for competition.[29] The United States Constitution does allow Congress to create post offices – but nowhere says that government post offices or mail delivery services need be a monopoly.[30]

During summer breaks from college, Ron would deliver milk for his father's business, Green Tree Dairy, filling in for regular drivers who had gone on their summer vacations.[31] He retained an intimate connection to the dairy business, as evidenced many years later, when he introduced legislation to abolish stiff penalties on interstate shipments and sales of unpasteurized milk. Some people believe that pure raw milk is healthier than pasteurized milk because raw milk contains enzymes that the pasteurization process destroys.[32] However, Ron never publicly took a position on the purported health benefits of raw milk – after all, it is not a politician's place to tell people what's good for them, even if the politician happens to be a doctor. But he declared before Congress that Americans "have the right to consume these products without having the federal government second-guess their judgment about what products best promote health."[33]

Ron managed to pay his college tuition with his many part-time and summer jobs. However, when he reflected on his experience years later, in 2007, he noted, "College was much cheaper then and the prices are much higher now – due to inflation and other reasons."[34] To help students enjoy the same opportunities he had, Ron Paul would later introduce the *Make College Affordable Act*, which would create a full tax deduction for undergraduate college tuition, reasonable living expenses, and interest on certain student loans.[35]

Despite their separation during college, Ron and Carol stayed in touch. There was no World Wide Web or Internet then, and long-distance phone calls were a luxury. Carol sent daily letters through the post office, and they saw each other whenever they could. Carol would sometimes go to Gettysburg to watch Ron in track meets. One year, she came to visit Ron for his fraternity house party weekend. Another time, Ron went to Athens for the final dance of Carol's sorority.[36]

In the summer before Ron's senior year, the two went on a picnic in Dormont Park near their families' homes. The park's swimming pool was a major center of social activity for young people in the area, and it featured some small hills, which offered a view of the swimming pool below. On Independence Day, people would sit on the hill to watch fireworks launched from the pool's parking lot.[37]

At Ron and Carol's picnic on July 20, 1956, Ron made some fireworks of his own on that hill by proposing to Carol. Carol wasn't surprised by the proposal because they had talked about marriage. But she was surprised by one thing: she thought she would have to wait until after Ron's college graduation before they could afford a ring. Instead, Carol recalls, "I got a lovely diamond," then and there.[38]

Perhaps most young people in that situation couldn't have afforded a ring – but Ron Paul's self discipline, careful planning, and hard work had allowed him to save enough money to buy the ring for that memorable moment.

After Carol enthusiastically accepted Ron's proposal, the couple went to see her parents, who were pleased to hear the news. The next day, Carol's mother held a lunch for Carol's friends to celebrate. Ron's parents were pleased, too, but his father was deeply concerned that marriage would disrupt Ron's studies and that he wouldn't finish college as a result. Carol persistently assured Mr. Paul that his son would finish college in the next semester, but the "old fashioned and very religious" mindset of the elder Paul made him skeptical.[39]

During a break between semesters in Ron's senior year of college, on Friday, February 1, 1957, at 7:30 p.m., Ron and Carol were married. The ceremony was held at the Dormont Presbyterian Church, and attended by more than 300 guests. Snow covered the ground outside for a truly "white wedding."[40] Carol wore a white Chantilly lace gown with a bouffant tulle skirt, popular in that day, and a silk illusion veil attached to a half hat; Ron wore a black tuxedo with a white tie. Carol held a cascade of white flowers; Ron wore a white carnation boutonniere.[41] The bridesmaids, also in white, carried armloads of red roses, and the white-clad flower girl sprinkled rose petals down the aisle.[42]

Ron's brother David was the best man. A fraternity brother of Ron's, Sherick Gilbert, sang "The Wedding Prayer" and "The Lord's Prayer," songs that have remained important to the Pauls throughout their lives.[43]

After the wedding, the group adjourned to a large ballroom at the Dormont New Century Club, where the couple cut into a traditional four-tiered cake with a bride and groom figure on top. A live band entertained, and the newlyweds danced to "When I Fall in Love," a song Doris Day first made a hit in 1952, the year the couple first met.[44]

At the reception's end, guests tossed rice as Ron and Carol got into their car and headed off to Durham, North Carolina.[45] Durham not only served as the location of their honeymoon, but also gave Ron an opportunity to visit Duke Medical School. The newlywed couple had a chance to see the town in which they might soon live. "We decided we liked it," said Carol, and Ron applied so that he could begin studying there the next fall.[46]

Before medical school, though, there was a final semester to finish at Gettysburg. Ron moved out of the fraternity house and into a third-floor apartment of an old Victorian house in town on Carlyle Street with Carol, a move made possible by Ron's extra jobs. Their apartment couldn't be accessed from inside the house; instead, they had to take a spiral staircase outside the house up to their new home. They fastened some bells to a rubber band so that visitors could tug the band from the ground below to let the Pauls know they were there.[47]

Immediately inside the apartment door, there was a living room to the left and a kitchen to the right, with the apartment's only bathroom next to the kitchen. Mrs. Paul recalls that if someone were undressed in the bathroom when visitors arrived, this could create a rather difficult situation, as the unclothed individual had no means of escape.[48]

The house was just down the street from the Majestic Theater. It was a movie theater then, but Ron and Carol didn't go often. ("We aren't big movie people," says Carol.)[49] More than 50 years later, Ron would return to the same theater during his 2008 presidential campaign, where he gave his own "Gettysburg Address" before more than 800 enthusiastic supporters who packed in to hear his message of hope and freedom.[50]

With the rent at their apartment a staggering $50.00 per month,[51] Carol worked through the rest of the school year as a secretary in the registrar's office and also typed papers for professors.[52]

Living in Gettysburg, the Pauls could get anywhere in town by walking. If they needed to travel some distance – say, to Pittsburgh – they had a gift from Carol's grandfather Wells for that: a 1949 Cadillac.[53]

The Pauls knew this was a rare period in their lives; Carol recalls that they "wanted to make time for each other in that time, because we knew it would be more difficult when he started medical school."[54] Ron had a light class schedule, and therefore had more free time than usual.

They chaperoned fraternity events together. Mrs. Paul also attended an evening class with her husband, in which they studied various plays. The professor, she recalls, "had memorized the encyclopedia through the letter 'N,'" but had stopped there on the advice of his doctors that any more would not be good for his mental health. The professor also knew the words of plays they studied verbatim - beginning to end – making the class a great source of entertainment as well as education.[55]

Some 51 years later, Mrs. Paul recalled these few months at Gettysburg as a "fun-filled time" in the couple's life together and a "great beginning."[56]

During this time, Ron Paul began to question what he had learned in his college economics courses. His family background, and his experience of succeeding through his own hard work and self discipline, told him that something was not right about the government's socialist schemes, and he began to look to free-market alternatives.[57]

As Ron Paul's marriage grew, and as he formed his ideas about the proper role of government, he developed ideas on the relationship between government and marriage – which, in his view, should be no relationship at all.

Marriage, after all, was an institution that pre-dated the existence of government. Even now, many people, like him, "associate their wedding day with completing the rituals and other requirements of their faith, thus being joined in the eyes of their church and their creator, not with receiving their marriage license."[58] Indeed, he observed, the state marriage-license requirement was a relatively new invention, originally ostensibly implemented for health purposes or used to enforce laws against interracial marriage,[59] but now just one more example of unnecessary "control of the state" over private matters.[60]

For centuries, if marriages were evidenced by anything beyond verbal vows, it was little more than a reference made on a page of the family bible or in some instances in the records of a church. In short, marriage was purely a private matter in which government had no reason to be involved.

When the government intervened in private institutions, it was often due to the tax code. Many arguments for expanding the definition of marriage to include relationships other than that between one man and one woman were based on tax deductions for married couples. Paul would rather have Americans decide their culture locally, independent of federal politicians and bureaucrats – meaning the federal government should have no role in defining marriage.

Still, according to Paul, state governments were acting within their role under the US Constitution in creating marriage-license requirements. The Constitution provided no role for the federal government in marriage, though, and as far as Ron was concerned, no such role was necessary.

So when conservatives clamored for a "Federal Marriage Amendment" to the Constitution in the early 2000s, to define marriage as a union between one man and one woman, Ron did not jump on the bandwagon. Instead, he warned his colleagues that such federal centralization of the marriage issue was not conservative at all, and could lead to consequences that conservatives wouldn't like.

A constitutional amendment would, he said, disrupt the balance of power between the federal government and the states, "one of the virtues of the American political system," and this in turn would threaten "self-government and individual liberty."[61]

Ron also rejected the proposed amendment because it would concede the left-wing premise that important social questions should be answered by the federal government. As he wrote then, "Ironically, liberal social engineers who wish to use federal government power to redefine marriage will be able to point to the constitutional marriage amendment as proof that the definition of marriage is indeed a federal matter!"[62] And if something as basic and private as the definition of marriage were appropriate for the federal government to determine, what *wouldn't* be appropriate for the federal government to decide?

Building on his early thoughts about marriage, and the day of the vows he had taken with Carol at the Dormont Presbyterian Church, Ron also rejected other federal efforts intended to promote marriage, such as a proposal by President George W. Bush in 2004 to spend $1.5 billion to promote "healthy marriages." Any such federal scheme would necessarily be funded by taxpayer money – and he could not support any law apparently aimed at promoting morality, yet funded in a way he considered to be immoral, by taking money by force from taxpayers.[63]

Besides, he saw out-of-control federal spending as responsible for damaging American families in the first place, through the "soul-destroying welfare system that rewards out-of-wedlock births"[64] – a system that had largely come into being after Ron and Carol grew up and were married, through the efforts of Lyndon B. Johnson and others. From experience with his own marriage and his own family, Ron came to know that, "Healthy marriages are the result of individual conviction and personal responsibility, neither of which can be mandated by the government."[65]

On May 19, 1957, Ron Paul graduated from his final year of college. He was destined to enter medical school, after which he could fulfill his dream of becoming a physician, with Carol by his side. The young couple could scarcely predict the excitement which lay in their future as they embarked on their journey together.

CHAPTER 5

SCHOOL OF MEDICINE

1957-1961

Civil Rights

A people who extend civil liberties only to preferred groups start down the path either to dictatorship of the right or the left.

WILLIAM ORVILLE DOUGLAS

While finishing his bachelor's degree in biology at Gettysburg College, Ron Paul applied to the Duke University School of Medicine.[1] His exceptional grades at Gettysburg aided in his acceptance, but it was his half-hour interview with the dean that impressed the administration with his commitment to becoming a medical doctor. He was accepted, and matriculated at Duke in 1957.

Ron and his newlywed wife, Carol, headed to Durham, North Carolina where they would make their new home. Carol soon found work as a medical secretary. They rented "a tiny little blue frame house" that Carol's grandmother nicknamed "the doll house," due to its quaint dimensions.[2] After settling into their new home they purchased a furry brown and white female collie to live in their spacious backyard.

Duke University was founded in 1838 by a group of Methodists and Quakers. It was later expanded with large endowments from Washington Duke, a tobacco industrialist, and later his son, James Buchannan Duke, an electric power industrialist.[3]

By 1957, the Duke University School of Medicine was among the top five in the entire country. Duke's medical school (like Duke University) was very research oriented. Traditionally, medical students learn the basic medical sciences in their first two years, followed by clinical rotations in their third and fourth years. At Duke, Ron would receive one compressed year of basic sciences, followed by clinical rotations in the second year. This allowed for a third year of medical research, where students take on a small research project.

In many ways, Ron's first year at Duke was not much different from his college years. Much of his time was spent taking copious notes as a professor lectured in front of the class, writing on the chalk board occasionally. There were also many labs, where students did everything from producing viral cultures to dissecting cadavers.

The second year took Ron much closer to his ultimate goal of becoming a physician: Ron and his classmates learned how to diagnose patients. During clinical rotations, they visited hospitals and interviewed patients under the watchful eye of a doctor, who provided guidance and confirmed the students' diagnoses. The students would even analyze blood and tissue samples in an attempt to arrive at a proper diagnosis. It was an exciting time for Ron, who was, for the first time, doing the work of a doctor.

During Ron's second year of medical school, the couple's first two children, Ronald ("Ronnie") and Lori, were born at Duke, in 1958 and 1959 respectively.[4] According to Carol, their well tempered, registered collie helped raise their first two children. The dog even made a financial contribution to the family one Thanksgiving by giving birth to a litter of puppies. The Pauls were able to sell one of the puppies for thirty-five dollars, which gave them enough travel money to drive home so that their extended family could meet their two new infants.[5]

While in medical school, Ron developed a passion for politics and economics. It was ignited by Boris Pasternak's <u>Dr. Zhivago</u>, a gift from his mother Margaret. The book made a case for the threat that big government bureaucracies pose to creativity and liberty.[6]

One person who influenced Ron philosophically was Leonard Read, who established The Foundation for Economic Education (FEE). According to Paul, "He was a very lone wolf after WWII. Everything had become big government and internationalist. He wrote a lot of articles himself and revived some classic articles that were forgotten, like Frédéric Bastiat's 'The Law.' Henry Hazlitt was associated with him and [Ludwig] von Mises as well. Von Mises and the Austrian economists influenced me the most on policy. He was also close to Hayek who wrote <u>Road to Serfdom</u>. Then I read Ayn Rand's books. They all had a strong influence on me."[7]

While Ron Paul was hard at work studying medicine, formulating a political worldview, and starting a family, the country was in the midst of a federal government power grab of unprecedented proportions. It would have a transformative effect on the United States.

At the dawn of the 1960s, few politicians seemed to understand the concepts that Ron embraced. However, during the 1960 Republican national convention, Barry Goldwater, a senator from Arizona, demonstrated his appeal to small-government conservatives.[8] Senator Goldwater would soon have a profound impact on Ron Paul's politics.

Goldwater was famous for his non-interventionist policies. This philosophy resonated with the young Ron Paul, who later observed:

> Freedom works! Free markets supported by sound money, private

property, and respect for all voluntary contracts can set an example for the world – since the resulting prosperity would be significant and distributed more widely than any socialist system. Instead of using force to make others do it our way, our influence could be through the example we set that would motivate others to emulate us.[9]

Segregation and race-based discrimination had a long history in the United States, embraced by some people and backed by federal and state governments. For example, the federal government had maintained a segregated military; the United States Supreme Court upheld state-enforced segregation in public schools until the *Brown vs. Board of Education* decision in 1954. State governments, particularly in the south, were notorious for their "Jim Crow laws," which maintained legally enforced segregation in public places under the pretense of "separate but equal" accommodations.

Nevertheless, following the end of World War II and the start of the Cold War, a new paradigm regarding race relations was emerging in the United States. Politicians attempted to take political advantage of this pre-existing trend. Under President Harry Truman, a Civil Rights Commission was established with the aim of combating racial prejudice in the United States.

On June 11, 1963, President John F. Kennedy introduced the bill that would become the 1964 Civil Rights Act. Kennedy argued for an expansion of federal power by outlining the challenges facing Blacks in the United States. Defining what he meant by "civil rights," Kennedy said:

> It ought to be possible for American consumers of any color to receive equal service in places of public accommodation, such as hotels and restaurants and theaters and retail stores, without being forced to resort to demonstrations in the street, and it ought to be possible for American citizens of any color to register to vote in a free election without interference or fear of reprisal. It ought to be possible, in short, for every American to enjoy the privileges of being American without regard to his race or his color.[10]

Until 1964, civil rights had traditionally worked in tandem with civil liberties. Civil liberties are basic rights and freedoms that are recognized and guaranteed in the Bill of Rights and the Constitution, generally understood as protections for citizens against government abuse of power – for example, the free exercise of speech, assembly, and nonviolent civil disobedience. The latter was a tactic practiced by Rosa Parks and later by the Reverend Martin Luther King Jr. Commenting on the civil disobedience of Rosa Parks, Ron Paul later said that "by challenging the injustice of segregation and refusing to give up her seat, Rosa Parks became an icon for a generation."[11]

The passage of the Civil Rights Act in 1964 defined civil rights as government protection from unequal treatment based on race. As the bill moved through congress, its scope was broadened to include other categories of people besides racial minorities – for example, women and religious minorities. It also created the Equal Employment Opportunity Commission.

The intentions that motivated the passage of the Civil Rights Act were considered noble by most Americans. They were beginning to embrace the view that hating another person based on his race (racism) is wrong. However, there were some who argued against the passage of the Civil Rights Act, not because of racism, but because of a few fundamental objections.

The Civil Rights Act contained a section (Title II) which mandated protection against discrimination for minorities at "Places Of Public Accommodation" or any entity engaged in interstate commerce. It exempted private clubs but did not define what that term meant. In practice, this meant that private businesses which were open to the general public, such as hotels, bars, and movie theaters, would be subject to the provisions of the Civil Rights Act. Opponents of the bill based their objections on this, and argued that it is a violation of the property rights of private business owners to subject them to the provisions of the Civil Rights Act. However morally reprehensible racism may be, they argued, it is not the proper role of government to legislate morality.

Furthermore, they argued that bigoted business owners would be at a natural disadvantage compared to tolerant ones, because they would lose out on all of the business they might get from whatever group they discriminated against. Customers would always be free to boycott a business that they viewed as unfairly discriminatory, as had been a common tactic in the Black civil rights movement.

Opponents of the Civil Rights Act did not object to the abolition of government-enforced segregation or discriminatory laws. Rather, it was the intrusion on the property rights of private businesses and the attempt to legislate morality that drew their criticism.

Senator Goldwater was one of those who opposed the Civil Rights Act, mainly based on objections to Title II. His detractors would be hard pressed to make the argument that he was a racist individual. According to Time Magazine, Goldwater "was the first chief of staff of the Arizona National Guard to desegregate the Air Guard. He was a member of the N.A.A.C.P. in the early 1950s, contributing $400 to the N.A.A.C.P. effort to get the Phoenix school system desegregated."[12] He had been a pioneer in voluntarily desegregating his family's business, a department store, in his home state of Arizona.[13] He also had several black senate staffers. Furthermore, he voted in favor of every Civil Rights bill until the 1964 Civil Rights Act.

Ron Paul was also against the 1964 Civil Rights act, arguing, "Just think of how the government caused all the segregation in the military until after World War II."[14] On private property, he argued that "it's a property rights issue. And this idea that all private property is under the domain of the federal government I think is wrong."[15]

Senator Goldwater described the future 1964 civil rights bill as being "like a three dollar bill—it's a phony." Goldwater said, "there are too many old laws which aren't even working. And there is this above all, the oldest law of all: you cannot pass a law that will make me like you or you like me. This is something that can only happen in our hearts. This is a problem of the mind, not a problem of the lawyer and the Senator. If we believe that our rights come to us from God, when the day comes that we act as if we believe it, all differences of the white and white and the black and black will be wiped off the face of this nation."[16]

That kind of apparent integrity found an unlikely home in politics, as Ron Paul became interested in Barry Goldwater as early as 1960.[17] "I think it really began with Goldwater," said Congressman Paul's brother, Reverend David Paul. Like the senator from Arizona, Ron Paul would go on to adopt a libertarian philosophy, championing privacy, small government, and a clear separation between church and state.[18] Rev. Paul described how "one of my brothers was in the seminary at Princeton, and that's a bit on the other side of Goldwater, you know," he laughed, referring to traditional Princeton politics. "We had some good discussions on what part the church should play, on whether a pastor should march in a peace march, what the government should be doing."[19]

Later, Ron Paul reasserted Barry Goldwater's argument before the House of Representatives that the 1964 Civil Rights Act "was a massive violation of the rights of private property and contract, which are the bedrocks of free society."[20] Paul, like Goldwater, understood that "the rights of all private property owners, even those whose actions decent people find abhorrent, must be respected if we are to maintain a free society."[21]

As a member of Congress sworn to uphold and defend the Constitution, Paul recognized that "this expansion of federal power was based on an erroneous interpretation of the congressional power to regulate interstate commerce. The framers of the Constitution intended the interstate commerce clause to create a free trade zone among the states, not to give the federal government regulatory power over every business that has any connection with interstate commerce."[22] The act was clearly unconstitutional, and a constitutionalist honoring his oath of office would accordingly have no other choice but to vote against the law as Barry Goldwater did in 1964.

In 1963, Kennedy restated of the golden rule in an American context, while recognizing a fundamental injustice that had existed for decades. In his speech the President outlined the racial divide in America and the second class status of millions of Americans on account of the color of their skin. Kennedy underlined his argument asking if African Americans "cannot enjoy the full and free life which all" Americans want, then who would be "content to have the color of his skin changed and stand in his place?"[23] He underlined the need for urgency with a question: "Who among us would then be content with the counsels of patience and delay?"[24]

What have been the consequences of impatience and urgency? Ron Paul answers that "the Civil Rights Act of 1964 not only violated the Constitution and reduced individual liberty; it also failed to achieve its stated goals of promoting racial harmony and a color-blind society."[25] Paul's analysis echoes Senator Barry Goldwater's predictions observing that "federal bureaucrats and judges cannot read minds to see if actions are motivated by racism. Therefore, the only way the federal government could ensure an employer was not violating the Civil Rights Act of 1964 was to ensure that the racial composition of a business's workforce matched the racial composition of a bureaucrat or judge's defined body of potential employees."[26]

Shortcutting the deliberative process and working outside constitutional limits led to a law that worsened racial strife, and not surprisingly increased the power of federal bureaucrats. Ron Paul describes how "bureaucrats began forcing employers to hire by racial quota."[27] He concluded that the policy of racial quotas has "not contributed to racial harmony or advanced the goal of a color-blind society. Instead, these quotas encouraged racial balkanization, and fostered racial strife." Nevertheless Paul concludes that "America has made great strides in race relations over the past forty years" but that "this progress is due to changes in public attitudes and private efforts. Relations between the races have improved despite, not because of, the 1964 Civil Rights Act."

Despite Paul's differences with Martin Luther King Jr. over Title II of the 1964 Civil Rights Act and with King's social democratic political outlook, he has said that he considers King a true patriot. Paul defines the true patriot as one "motivated by a sense of responsibility and out of self-interest for himself, his family, and the future of his country to resist government abuse of power. [King] rejects the notion that patriotism means obedience to the state."

Ron Paul specifically defines King's patriotism in a nonviolent context. "Peaceful, nonviolent revolutions against tyranny have been every bit as successful as those involving military confrontation," he observes. "Mahatma Gandhi and Dr. Martin Luther King, Jr., achieved great political successes by practicing nonviolence, and yet they suffered physically at the hands of the state. But whether the resistance against government tyrants is nonviolent or physically violent, the effort to overthrow state oppression qualifies as true patriotism."[28]

....

During Ron's fourth year at Duke, the medical school focused on preparing he and his classmates for their work as physicians. They had sufficiently developed their diagnostic skills that they would debate different treatments and why they favored one over another.

The responsibilities of parenthood combined with the discipline of medicine meant that Ron was used to operating under pressure. He would not only survive, but thrive in that high stress environment; traits which suited both a medical doctor and a political leader.

Ron Paul received his Doctor of Medicine (MD) degree from the Duke University Medical School in 1961. It was a thrilling graduation. He now had his MD, but he did not yet have a license to practice medicine. For that, he would have to complete one year as an intern at a hospital. Carol, the two boys, their collie, and Ron would soon move out of the "doll house" which held so many happy memories for the young family. Their future was far from North Carolina.

CHAPTER 6

THE INTERN

1961 - 1962

Free Market Economics

An army of principles can penetrate where an army of soldiers cannot.

Thomas Paine

Decades after earning his medical diploma from the Duke University School of Medicine, Ron Paul delivered a commencement address to a group of graduating medical students and congratulated them on "joining the greatest profession."[1] In June of 1961, Paul himself began his career in that greatest profession as a medical intern. After one year, if he performed satisfactorily, he would earn a license to practice medicine.*

Ron Paul was just becoming aware of the problems of government interventionism in his field of medicine when he set out to find a hospital willing to accept him with his freshly-minted medical degree. His grades and personable attitude ensured he would find a good hospital. Ron was immediately accepted at the Henry Ford Hospital in Detroit, which offered one of the nation's oldest and most respected training programs for new doctors.[3] After graduation, Ron and Carol packed up their belongings and said warm goodbyes to their North Carolina friends. The couple loaded up their 1949 Cadillac and drove almost 700 miles along the Interstate 77 with their two small children, Ronnie and Lori, and their collie. After 12 hours they arrived in Detroit, which was at the height of its prosperity. However, the city was soon

---

* Murray Rothbard, the anarcho-capitalist who would later become Ron Paul's mentor and friend, believed government enforced licensure caused an "artificial boosting of demand coupled with an artificial restriction of supply" which caused "accelerating high prices and deterioration of patient care."[2]

to fall into decline, in part due to costly automobile regulations spurred on by activist Ralph Nader.

The Henry Ford Hospital was founded as a philanthropic project in 1915 by the pioneering industrialist whose name it bears, at a time when the great American capitalist was a staunch opponent of America's entry into the First World War. It was a fitting place for the future leading voice of pro-market non-interventionism to begin his medical career. By the time of Ron Paul's arrival, the hospital had grown from a facility able to house and care for 48 patients to a major urban hospital with more than 500 beds on a 20 acre site, more than 20 operating rooms, a 35,000 volume medical library, and a new 17 storey clinic building.

In the early 1960s, a 100 hour or more work week was normal for interns, spent under the supervision of senior doctors. Fortunately, medical interns are paid, unlike interns in some other professions. Ron Paul received a salary of $195 per month.[4]

To supplement their income, Carol ran a dance school from the basement of their home, in which she taught ballet, tap dancing, and even occasionally baton twirling. The income that Mrs. Paul brought in with her private dance lessons was vital given the modest pay her husband earned as an intern. Years later, Carol recalled, "Just to tell you what kind of a budget we were on, the dancing school paid for the newspaper and for extra expenses we had when a month had five weeks!"[5]

At Duke, Ron had learned the breadth and scope of medical knowledge that had been accumulated since the days of Hippocrates, the "father of medicine" from Ancient Greece. At Henry Ford, he put his knowledge to practice. There, he received hands-on training in internal medicine, that branch of the medical arts specializing in the diagnosis and treatment of diseases, especially those of the internal organs. Called *internists* (not to be confused with interns), practitioners of internal medicine are often called "the doctor's doctor," as they are called upon to have an encyclopedic knowledge of the many ailments and maladies that strike the human body. The internist is trained to see and treat the body as a whole, to tackle enigmatic diagnostic problems with an analytical and holistic approach, often having to handle both chronic diseases and the occurrence of multiple ailments at the same time. It was this approach that Ron Paul would later bring to his diagnosis of the political and economic ailments afflicting America.

Ron Paul's keen eye was focused not just on the human body and the many things that can go wrong with it. He perceptively observed his hospital's functioning within the society to which it belonged. He later recalled, "The amazing thing was it was a city hospital and there was no government; there [was] very little insurance and nobody was turned away whether they were illegal or legal, and nobody, nobody was quizzed. If you didn't have the money, you didn't pay, and people came in, and it wasn't that bad. People didn't lay on the side walks. You're more likely to hear stories today of people being neglected in emergency rooms…and dying on stretchers—because we have managed care."[6]

The experience of practicing medicine before the era of managed care remained with him. "Managed care is not market-driven; it's government-mandated," Paul later explained. "It has driven charity out of the system. No more church-financed hospitals and free care for the indigent. Everyone is charged the maximum, and no test is left undone for fear attorneys will be ridiculing us in court alleging our negligence. And if it's not the attorneys, it's the HCFA [Health Care Finance Administration] agents threatening us with fines and prison if we misinterpret any of the *132,000 pages of regulations.* This system artificially pushes costs up, bringing calls for price controls, which only mean rationing and shortages."[7]

It was at this time that Ron Paul's interest in economics and politics began, perhaps as a result of applying his internist's diagnostic approach to the body politic. Like a true doctor, he focused on curing the underlying disease rather than just the symptoms. Despite his exhausting work load and his responsibilities as a husband and father, he found time to read voraciously. Ron's exposure to Barry Goldwater in 1960 had piqued his curiosity about Austrian economics and he soon identified the key books in the field. His previously unfocused beliefs in freedom and individualism soon coalesced around a clear philosophy.

He would later reflect, "Early on and during the '60s as a resident I liked to read other things than just medicine. I became fascinated with economic policy and came across a school of economics called Austrian Economics. It is free market, sound money type of economics. It's a little different than just saying conservative economics because they believe you can't have paper money but have sound money. It also deals with limited government."[8]

The Austrian School of Economics was built on a foundation laid by the fifteenth century Scholastic philosophers of the University of Salamanca in Spain, who discovered that economic laws, such as supply and demand, inflation, and exchange rates, operate within the framework of *natural law.* In other words, economics operates through forces of cause and effect. These Spanish monks defended property rights and free trade, while opposing taxes and government regulation of the economy.

The seed planted by these Spanish monks came to fruition in France in the eighteenth and nineteenth centuries, with economists like Richard Cantillon, Anne Robert Jacques Turgot, Jean Baptiste Say, and most famously Claude-Frederic Bastiat.

Bastiat was one of the first people to observe that socialists often confused free market principles. "Socialism, like the ancient ideas from which it springs, confuses the distinction between government and society," he wrote in 1849's *The Law.* "As a result of this, every time we object to a thing being done by government, the socialists conclude that we object to its being done at all. We disapprove of state education. Then the socialists say that we are opposed to any education. We object to a state religion. Then the socialists say that we want no religion at all. We object to a state-enforced equality. Then they say that we are against equality. And so on, and so on. It is as if the socialists were to accuse us of not wanting persons to eat because we do not want the state to raise grain."

The Austrian School proper was established by Carl Menger, who systematized the thought of his Spanish and French predecessors with his 1871 work, <u>Principles of Economics</u>, whose ideas revolutionized not only the theory of money and prices but the entire discipline. The Austrian School's principles were influential in the Austro-Hungarian Empire, especially in the advocacy of balanced budgets, the gold standard, and free trade, and the rejection of intervention, subsidies, and monopolies.[9]

Austrian economists have observed that throughout the 20th century, the more government subsidized industries, the worse consumers fared. This included attempts to subsidize third world economies with handouts. After reading *Principles of Economics*, Paul concluded that subsidies and handouts were to blame. "Third world countries also lose with these continued government manipulations," he observed. "Agricultural subsidies lead to overproduction, which leads to foreign food aid as a form of dumping. By dumping government-created agricultural surpluses, agrarian economies are artificially kept in a constant state of economic depression. The would-be third world farmer cannot compete with free grain, thus he and his countrymen remain perpetual beggars rather than competitive producers. Also, by keeping food prices high, we keep more of our own citizens dependent on government food stamps, instead of paying fair market prices for food."[10]

Menger also rejected the notion that government must be used to break up monopolies. In a true free market system, as long as an industry is open to new businesses, an *unjust* monopoly can not exist.

If one product dominates a market, there is no reason to act against that product as long as their customers are freely choosing it. "If you are getting big, you are usually getting big because you are doing something good for the consumer," says Paul. "The consumer should be the deciding factor."[11]

A profound influence of Ron Paul would be the Austrian School's greatest proponent of the early twentieth century, Ludwig von Mises, who has been hailed as "the first great modern critic of socialism."[12] He famously said, "Economics deals with society's fundamental problems; it concerns everyone and belongs to all. It is the main and proper study of every citizen."[13]

As Mises instructed, citizen Paul trained his diagnostic eye towards society's fundamental problems. Prior to studying Mises, he took up the study of economics by reading Mises' great student and heir, the London's School of Economics' Friedrich von Hayek, who was later the 1974 Nobel laureate. Hayek's tome, <u>The Road to Serfdom</u>, first published in 1944, introduced Ron Paul to the Austrian School of Economics which he would later unwaveringly promote.

The Road to Serfdom was published when Hayek was considered to be the world's second most famous economist, primarily as a rival and opponent of John Maynard Keynes.[14] Former British Prime Minister Margaret Thatcher was later to call Hayek's book "the most powerful critique of socialist planning and the socialist state which I read at this time, and to which I have returned so often since."[15]

This book, dedicated in friendly jest to "socialists of all parties", had as its central argument that socialism leads inevitably to totalitarianism, a proposition, given the tragic history of the Soviet Union which is now almost universally accepted. But it was a revolutionary observation at the time of its writing, and still so at the time of Ron Paul's reading, when socialism was sweeping the globe, not only in the newly independent nations of Africa and Asia, but also in the West in the form of the welfare state.

Hayek's magnum opus warned against the designs of those whom he labeled the *planners*. It was inconsequential if these planners were of the left or right; both Nazi Germany and Soviet Russia provided Hayek with two powerful examples of the road from collectivism to totalitarianism. In fact, the book was written to warn his contemporaries of the link between these two evils.

Ron then discovered the works of Hayek's teacher, Ludwig von Mises. Of his teacher's tremendous contribution to the field of economics, Hayek said he believed "it is true of all of Professor Mises's works that they were written in constant doubt whether the civilization which made them possible would last long enough to allow their appearance." And the "sense of urgency in which they were written"[16] of which Hayek speaks reminds us of the same sense of urgency that Ron Paul would later bring in his speaking and writing to the defense of the American Republic and the sound economic principles necessary to its survival.

The German economist Wilhelm Röpke said that reading Mises "rendered [him] immune, at a very early date, against the virus of socialism that socialism leads to totalitarianism."[17] Ron Paul the internist would certainly understand Röpke's medical analogy of socialism as pathogen. He had been trained to recognize the maladies that afflict the human body; he now saw in collectivism the main affliction of modern politics.

And indeed, socialism in its various manifestations was the number one killer of people in the 20th century. The Soviets killed 61,911,000 people, Communist China killed 35,236,000, German National socialism killed 20,946,000. In fourth place is imperialism, which killed about 10,214,000 humans. Ron realized that a philosophy that respects the individual is the antidote to such atrocities.

This awareness of the totalitarian nature of socialism led Ron to that towering enemy of collectivism in all its forms, Ayn Rand. She was certainly one of the twentieth century's most popular, influential, and controversial philosophers. An émigré from the nascent Soviet Union, Ayn Rand described herself as a "radical for capitalism." She reached her enormous audience primarily through her works of fiction, her two most famous novels being The Fountainhead (1943) and Atlas Shrugged (1957). Both books were poorly reviewed but became runaway bestsellers. A 1991 Library of Congress and the Book-of-the-Month Club survey ranked the latter as the second most influential book after the Bible.[18]

No one has ever accused Atlas Shrugged of being great literature, but it is an endlessly fascinating book for pointing out all that is great in society and all that is wrong. Very few works of fiction have such a sweeping view, exploring politics, business, and human motivation. Those who read it invariably come away with a different view of the world.

Part of her charm was her ability to pick out the language that Keynesian economists used when their plans to improve society begin to make things worse. In the early stages of failure, her characters play it coy, saying they just need to readjust some variable in the economy. Later, when it is apparent their plans have brought about catastrophic failure, they begin blaming other things - usually speculators, greedy businessmen or the free markets themselves.

Ayn Rand had around her an inner circle of intellectuals that included Alan Greenspan, an economist and part-time jazz musician. Ironically, he would one day become Ron Paul's respected nemesis as Chairman of the Federal Reserve.

Paul later said of Rand's books, "Nobody gave her a review, and anybody who did said it was horrible, horrible, horrible. It was word of mouth and she still sold millions and millions of copies because she was telling the truth and people were anxious to hear it."[19]

The most notorious example of the poor press her books received was this line from Whittaker Chambers' review in the December 28, 1957 issue of The National Review: "From almost any page of *Atlas Shrugged*, a voice can be heard, from painful necessity, commanding: 'To a gas chamber — go!'"[20] It was an odd thing to say of a novel by a woman whose "political philosophy is in the classical liberal tradition, with that tradition's emphasis upon individualism, the constitutional protection of individual rights to life, liberty, and property, and limited government."[21] Rand was greatly offended by the comment, and, by his own account, she never forgave publisher William F. Buckley for allowing it into print.[22]

Long before this review forever soured things between them, Rand, an atheist, had told Buckley, a Catholic, "You are too intelligent to believe in God!"[23] She might have said the same to Ron Paul, as religion is one area Paul disagrees with Rand, a strident atheist. She called her philosophy Objectivism, which required a non-belief in anything supernatural. Paul could not do this, so he considered himself a libertarian instead, which had no such ideological requirement.

Whittaker Chambers' review is emblematic of the rift that was developing between the broadly conservative and broadly libertarian factions within what was then the American right. The conflict might be described as the ouster of the partisans of the latter by those of the former. The conservative-libertarian coalition that characterized the Old Right was coming apart from the stress of the Cold War, and was even more polarized by the time Ron Paul was reading Mises, Hayek, and Rand.

Ron Paul was reading some of the greatest libertarian thinkers at a time when many American libertarians, while firmly anti-communist, were becoming uncomfortable with the increasingly statist and interventionist leanings of American conservatives. It was a division that would outlast the Cold War, and one that would mark the future political career of Ron Paul, as interventionism in foreign affairs had led conservatives to an increasing acceptance of interventionism in domestic economic affairs.

Forty years later, Paul spoke of the depth of economic understanding he acquired during these early formative years:

> Capitalism should not be condemned, since we haven't had capitalism. A system of capitalism presumes sound money, not fiat money manipulated by a central bank. Capitalism cherishes voluntary contracts and interest rates that are determined by savings, not credit creation by a central bank. It's not capitalism when the system is plagued with incomprehensible rules regarding mergers, acquisitions, and stock sales, along with wage controls, price controls, protectionism, corporate subsidies, international management of trade, complex and punishing corporate taxes, privileged government contracts to the military-industrial complex, and a foreign policy controlled by corporate interests and overseas investments. Add to this centralized federal mismanagement of farming, education, medicine, insurance, banking and welfare. This is not capitalism! To condemn free-market capitalism because of anything going on today makes no sense. There is no evidence that capitalism exists today. We are deeply involved in an interventionist-planned economy that allows major benefits to accrue to the politically connected of both political

spectrums. One may condemn the fraud and the current system, but it must be called by its proper names – Keynesian inflationism, interventionism, and corporatism.[24]

World events grabbed the attention of the 26-year-old husband and father at the beginning of an exciting and promising career in medicine. The first year of his residency saw the erection of the Berlin Wall and a year later the Cuban Missile Crisis would put the world on the brink of nuclear annihilation. These two years also saw the quiet escalation of American involvement in Vietnam under President John F. Kennedy.

They were troubled times, but one that would bring happy news to the Paul family. As Ron Paul was nearing the end of his internship, he received news that his wife Carol had been blessed with the couple's third child. In January 1962, Carol bore Ron a son who would forever bear the mark of this fertile period of his father's intellectual development; a son they named Rand.

CHAPTER 7

DRAFTED

1962-1965

Non-interventionism

I hope our wisdom will grow with our power, and teach us that the less we use our power, the greater it will be.

THOMAS JEFFERSON

In the late fall of 1962, a twenty-seven year old Ron Paul was nearing completion of his internship at the Henry Ford Hospital in Detroit, Michigan. Once finished, Ron hoped to continue with his residency where he would practice medicine under the supervision of more senior physicians. His anticipation was tempered by the knowledge that once he and his fellow interns completed the internship process, they might be drafted into the Army as privates. The United States was squaring off with the USSR in the buildup to the Cuban Missile Crisis.

Years later, Paul recalled, "I got the draft notice during the [October 1962] missile crisis. The draft notice said, 'You're going to be drafted and you're going to be sent into the Army unless you want to volunteer. If you volunteer, you can be a captain, you can practice medicine and you can join the Air Force.' I immediately volunteered."[1] Soon, Ron Paul was commissioned an Air Force First Lieutenant.

The Paul family, including four-year-old Ronnie, three-year-old Lori, and a very pregnant Carol, traveled from Detroit to spend Christmas and New Year's with their family in Pittsburg, Pennsylvania. Randall Paul was born in early January, and a few weeks later the young Paul clan was on the road to Kelly Air Force Base (AFB) outside San Antonio, Texas.

As lifelong Pennsylvanians, Ron and Carol were unprepared for the fine weather and wide-open spaces of south-central Texas – and they loved it. The family settled into a rented house, and Ron began service as a medical officer at Kelly AFB, the Air Force's oldest continually active airfield. Only a few years earlier, the B-58 Hustler, the United States' first supersonic bomber, was entered into the inventory. Maintenance responsibilities for this aircraft, as well as F-100 and F-5 fighter aircraft, were assigned to the Kelly Air Force logistics depot. In 1960, the 433rd Airlift Wing (the "Alamo Wing") was activated from a reserve unit and moved from nearby Brooks AFB to Kelly AFB. Four years later, the Alamo Wing would become the first Air Reserve unit to win the coveted Air Force Outstanding Unit Award.[2] Lt. Paul was assigned to the 433rd Medical Group as a flight surgeon, responsible for the medical treatment and certification of pilots, aircrew members, and air traffic controllers.

Exposure to pilots and aircrews, their stories and experiences, and flying with aircrews and medical personnel to various locations inspired Lt. Paul to pursue his private pilot's license. He earned that license during his first year at Kelly AFB, and often flew young Ronnie and Lori in a small plane around the area. Carol even flew with him...once! Ron and Carol also joined a bowling league of doctors, dentists and pilots, and splurged on his and her bowling balls.

Life in Texas was good, with Lt. Paul making $700 a month, significantly more than he had made during his Henry Ford Hospital residency. Even with the increased income and discounted military shopping at the base commissary and exchange, Lt. Paul filled in several evenings a week at a local church hospital emergency room for $3.00 an hour. For the Pauls, working hard and working several jobs were normal.

Carol had helped put Ron through medical school, and the young family was used to frugality. In Texas, for the first time, Carol didn't have to work for a supplemental or even the sole paycheck. She remembered this interval at Kelly AFB as a time of plenty, where they saved and also were able to replace things that they needed, in the expectation of dire finances when Dr. Paul pursued his medical specialty after his term of active duty. It was during this time that Carol first learned the art of cake decorating from a pilot's wife in San Antonio.[3] Years later, she would teach a cake decorating class at Ohio University and would design and author the moderately famous Ron Paul Family Cookbook series.

Life for the Pauls was lively, happy, and — in Carol's words — "so much fun" in San Antonio between 1963 and 1965.[4] However, there were darker forces at work during this era. While Ron Paul was treating patients and working overtime as an intern at a Detroit hospital, the 1961 Bay of Pigs invasion had been launched, and had publicly failed. Havana, as a Soviet-sponsored communist capital in the Western hemisphere, was at best a political thorn in the side of Washington and, at worst, a flamboyant sign that communism was indeed encroaching. The Cold War was heating up.

Most Americans wholly accepted the idea that the United States was the key and primary defender of freedom against an aggressively expanding and dangerous ideology. There was widespread fear in Washington of a domino effect, whereby capitalistic and friendly third world countries would fall, one by one, to communist Soviet or Chinese influences. This viewpoint, embraced by average Americans, was certainly a focus of military strategy and a topic of discussion within Air Force communities like Kelly AFB.

Just months before Paul entered the Air Force, the United States and the American military had participated in an alarming showdown with the Soviet Union over the possibility of Soviet mid-range nuclear warheads stationed off the coast of Florida. If the 1962 Cuban Missile Crisis set the tone for national security thinking before Lt. Paul's enlistment, American military interventions abroad provided the texture of his time on active duty.

In 1963, when Paul joined the Air Force, there were about 16,000 Americans deployed to Vietnam. By 1965, when then-Captain Paul left the active Air Force to serve three more years in the Air National Guard, that number had grown more than ten times to over 184,000. Air Force transport, fighter and bomber pilots were increasingly affected by and serving in Vietnam.

The early 1960s also saw US military interventions, including military air transport operations, in the Congo (then Zaire) and Guatemala. The strengthening of NATO against the Soviet threat in Europe and the expansion of the Vietnam conflict were occurring – even as the first post-World War II-era military aircraft and weapons were rolling off the American production lines, employing many of Ron Paul's neighbors, co-workers, and both military and civilian patients in the San Antonio area.

Lt. Paul's duties as an Air Force flight surgeon in 1963 and 1964 involved certifying Air Force pilots for deployment and, in many cases, redeployment. He often wondered about the eventual fate of these young men.[5] "I recall doing a lot of physicals on Army warrant officers who wanted to become helicopter pilots and go to Vietnam," he told me. "They were gung-ho. I've often thought about how many of those people never came back."[6]

His assigned medical specialty was treating the ear, nose and throat problems of pilots and aircrew, and he was also called upon to assist in the investigation of several aircraft accidents during his time on active duty.[7] These flight surgeon duties took him far from Texas. In fact, he traveled to over twenty countries during his active-duty service, which took him to East Asia, Europe, Latin America, and the Middle East, although never to Vietnam.

At the time, each of these countries was allied with the United States. They stood as bulwarks against communism. In years to come, self-determination movements, conflicts with their neighbors, and domestic political movements would test and challenge the very definition of words like freedom, communism and anti-communism, and the credibility of policymakers in Washington, D.C.

In late 1963 and early 1964, Lt. Paul became involved with the presidential campaign of Senator Barry Goldwater, a small-government Republican known for his strident and bold anti-communism. There was also an Air Force connection, as Goldwater had been promoted to the rank of Major General in the Air Force Reserve in 1962.

Goldwater was expected to face off against President Kennedy in the upcoming election. Lt. Paul met President Kennedy on November 21st, 1963,[8] in San Antonio. The President was in town to dedicate the opening of the new Aerospace Medical Center at nearby Brooks AFB.[9] The next day Kennedy was assassinated and Lyndon B. Johnson assumed the mantle.

At that time, Lt. Paul observed the people running and being affected by foreign wars, as well as the Cold War-driven growth that shaped modern San Antonio. His up-close exposure to the fascinating 1964 presidential campaign and the libertarian Old Right perspectives of Senator Goldwater was complimentary to his Air Force role and duties.

Although Goldwater was against foreign wars, Democrat Lyndon B. Johnson in his infamous "Daisy" commercial insinuated that Goldwater would start a nuclear war. Johnson easily won the election. While disappointing, Paul's association with Senator Goldwater helped refine his views towards the constitutional role of the federal government and the framework of a constitutional foreign policy.

Ron Paul's experiences while in the Air Force honed his common-sense assessment of liberty and what it really means. Perhaps exposure to Texas in the city known for the Alamo contributed to his thinking on the role of the draft. Years later, in philosophical agreement with former Ohio Senator Robert Taft, he wrote "Justifying conscription to promote the cause of liberty is one of the most bizarre notions ever conceived by man!"[10]

As a military officer, Paul took an oath to protect the Constitution, calling for each officer "to support and defend the Constitution of the United States against all enemies, foreign and domestic". Later he would write that, "Legitimate use of violence can only be that which is required in self-defense."[11]

Looking back on those formative years, Paul later stated, "I was in the US Air Force in 1965, and I remember well when President Johnson announced a troop surge in Vietnam to hasten victory. That war went on for another decade, and by the time we finally got out 60,000 Americans had died. God knows we should have gotten out ten years earlier."[12]

Decades later, Paul noted that after US withdrawal, Vietnam became a friendly nation committed to capitalist ideas. He contrasted this history to the US history of economic and political warfare with Cuba, and the failure of American Cuba policy to promote freedom for Cubans or to eliminate a possible threat to US national security. Paul believed that non-interventionism and free trade were more effective than war.

Paul's critics occasionally mistook non-interventionism as isolationism, a philosophy that opposes both military involvement in the domestic, territorial or political affairs of other nations, *and supports* economic self-reliance through trade protectionism.

In truth, non-interventionism recalls the famous advice of Thomas Jefferson: "Peace, commerce and honest friendship with all nations; entangling alliances with none."[13]

In Paul's version of history, intervention in foreign countries, whether overt or covert, actually postponed or prevented democracy and freedom from taking root. The blossoming of real freedom and peaceful relations occurred only after US interventions ceased.

He noted that US interventions, whether in Korea, Vietnam, the Philippines, Central America, Africa and the Middle East, have produced a variety of unintended consequences that have not only prevented liberty for the countries involved, but dangerously affected America's national security situation. The CIA worried for years that blowback from misguided interventions abroad would endanger America. Several attacks in the Cold War and post-Cold War period, ranging from the Iranian hostage seizure in 1979 through the 1982 Marine barracks bombing in Lebanon and to the September 11th, 2001, attacks, reflect this blowback effect. Paul argues that every one of these attacks would have been avoided had the United States followed a free-trade and non-interventionist foreign policy.

Paul's advocacy of non-intervention for so-called humanitarian crises has also been criticized by many on the neoconservative left. During President Clinton's intervention in Kosovo and Bosnia-Herzegovina in the 1990s, Paul articulated what was then the Republican Party position: US military intervention was unnecessary and counterproductive. Again, Dr. Paul's prescriptions would have prevented death and destruction and promoted freedom in the region. He pointed out the hypocrisy that is part and parcel of an interventionist foreign policy, saying, "There are certain countries, like in Rwanda, Africa, we certainly did not apply the same rules to that country as we do to Bosnia and the Persian Gulf and Iraq. We did not do this when we saw the mass killings in the Far East under Pol Pot."[14]

Paul demonstrated a commitment to helping all people in his work at Kelly AFB and on the night shift at the local San Antonio hospital, regardless of religion, race, or nationality. Yet, in line with a philosophy made popular by the American Founders, he states, "The moral and constitutional obligations of our representatives in Washington are to protect our liberty, not coddle the world, precipitating no-win wars, while bringing bankruptcy and economic turmoil to our people."[15]

Ron Paul's experiences – as a flight surgeon, as a commissioned Air Force officer in that critical time of the early 1960s, as a witness to the mistakes of one American interventionist and idealistic president after another – convinced him of the clear and constitutional logic of a foreign policy of non-intervention, and the social, economic and security benefits of freely trading with all countries, allying with none.

CHAPTER 8

RESIDENCY

1965-1968

Abortion

If you don't know whether a body is alive or dead, you would never bury it. I think this consideration itself should be enough for all of us to insist on protecting the unborn.

– RONALD REAGAN

By mid-1965 America was entering into a new era: the Civil Rights movement was at fever pitch with demonstrations throughout the South, prompting Johnson to propose and sign into law the Voting Rights Act, a monumental step towards civil and political equality. Coincidentally, the government was facing criticism for the escalation in Vietnam, with which a vocal segment of the population disagreed. It seemed as though a political and social revolution was capturing the American spirit.

Other revolutions were occurring as well, even in the medical community. By the time Ron Paul would finish his residency, the first human-to-human heart transplant had been performed and the birth control pill was experiencing widespread use.

It was during this age of change that Paul chose his career. Before volunteering for the Air Force, he received a year of basic medical training as a medical intern. Now he would continue his medical training as a resident physician. His grueling residency, filled with 80-hour work weeks, would allow him to learn and practice medicine under the watchful eye of experienced senior physicians.

Previously he was planning to complete his residency in internal medicine. However, after two-and-a-half years as an active duty officer, he began to favor obstetrics, the surgical specialty dealing with pregnancy. In July 1965, he transferred to the Pennsylvania Air National Guard in Oakland. There he would complete his residency in obstetrics and gynecology at Magee Women's Hospital. His progress would be monitored and administered through the University of Pittsburgh.

....

In Oakland, Ron and Carol were able to rent a house that was near both their parents' houses and directly adjacent to the house of Carol's aunt and uncle, Bob and Louis Clark. The two had a swimming pool in their backyard that the kids enjoyed. This came in handy as vacation time for Ron was scarce. The close proximity of their extended family was also important because Carol was three months pregnant at the time, and it always helped to have family nearby when someone was needed to look after their three young children.

The couple began attending St. Paul's Episcopal Church in Pittsburgh, as all of their children had been baptized in the Episcopal Church. Ron's family was Lutheran, and Carol's family was Presbyterian, so they were familiar with all three churches in the area.

By December of 1965, Carol was overdue in her pregnancy with the Pauls' fourth child. Because of the heavy snowfall at the time, Ron was worried that the couple might be snowed-in and unable to get to the hospital before natural birth, and so on December 21st, 1965, Robert Alan Paul was born by induction.

Ron continued to meet his monthly requirements with the Air National Guard, even while focusing on his residency. He was on night-call every other weeknight and every weekend, making family time his entertainment time. Ron's family life would be the cornerstone that would shape his views on the issue of life and abortion.

During his residency, Ron published several works, most notably "Evaluation of Renal Biopsy in Pregnancy Toxemia" which was published in the prominent medical journal Obstetrics and Gynecology in 1969.[1] Through this research, Ron and his colleagues explored the causes of toxemia in pregnant women, specifically pre-eclampsia, a medical condition where hypertension arises during pregnancy. Although the research was largely unable to determine a diagnosable cause of the toxemia, it found strong correlations which led to further breakthroughs.

All physicians until the 1970s were required to take the Hippocratic Oath before practicing medicine, in which they promise to do no deliberate harm. Paul took his oath seriously, and he included all life in that promise. As he would later write in his 1983 work Abortion and Liberty, "All of my medical training was directed towards saving life and preserving health." Before his residency, he had no familiarity with the process of disposing of the unborn. "The issue never came up. I never heard the word abortion," he later recalled.[2]

It would be late in his residency before he would experience the sight of an abortion, a day that would forever change his opinion on what he has called a "barbaric act", which made him an "unshakable foe of abortion" for the rest of his medical and political career.

As Ron was doing rounds at Pittsburgh Medical Center, he was called into an operating room where a hysterotomy abortion was being performed. The procedure is similar to a caesarian section, only requiring a smaller incision. At that time abortions were illegal in the State of Pennsylvania, but doctors performed them anyway, although medical residents like Ron were not required to participate if they objected. Ron was called in to observe the procedure, so he obliged.

Near the end of the procedure, Ron saw the doctors lift out of the mother a fetus that weighed approximately two-and-a-half pounds. He heard the baby gasp for air and it began to cry. What happened next shocked him even more. As the child was screaming and squirming, the doctors dropped the fragile infant into a bucket which was placed in the corner of the room. Ron stood dumbfounded as everyone in the room acted as though the screams of the baby didn't exist. After a few short minutes, the screaming ceased. Ron Paul walked out of the operating room a changed man.

To Ron, it seemed like the physicians were ignoring the Hippocratic Oath, which was still fresh in his mind. From that day forward, he vowed to fight for the sanctity of life, wherever that fight would lead him.

....

An experience of such magnitude would have an effect on anyone. For Ron Paul, it became a base for his political philosophy. As his philosophical beliefs developed, he came to realize that everything revolved around life and liberty, and "if you can't protect life, how can you protect liberty?"[3]

The reality of the abortion was too plain for him to ignore, and he began thinking about life. Specifically, what is human life and when does it begin? Eventually he came to believe that human life begins at the beginning. He concluded, "Medically and scientifically the argument is not whether a human life exists immediately after conception: it does."[4]

Conception is a common way to refer to the act of fertilization. The dictionary definition of fertilization means "the process of union of two gametes whereby the somatic chromosome number is restored and the development of a *new individual* is initiated."[5] Paul believed that at the point of conception, a new individual human being has been created, as the genetic material from the parents fuses to create a unique genetic code.

Being an individual person at this point, a fetus (or more appropriately at conception, a zygote) would be entitled to all the rights listed and not listed in the US Constitution and its respective state constitution. This includes the right to life, according to the Fifth and Fourteenth Amendments, which says, "No *person* ... shall be deprived of *life*, liberty, or property without due process," And "No State [shall] deprive any *person* of *life*, liberty, or property, without due process of law."

Although these amendments apply to the abilities and power of the government, Paul concluded from the document's wording that the taking of life from any person constitutes murder. By Paul's definition of human life, the fetus is human, therefore abortion is the taking of innocent life.

According to Paul, "Two persons conceiving new life are responsible for that life. If this responsibility is eliminated by causing the death of the innocent bystander, the concept of responsibility is destroyed. The unwritten commitment to the life conceived occurs at the time of conception."[6]

....

Although Paul considered himself a Republican, on many issues he believed that those in his Party had "lost their way." Although Republicans generally oppose abortions, Paul disagrees with the means to achieve its abolition.

As a Constitutionalist, Paul interprets the Ninth and Tenth Amendments to mean that the federal government does not have any authority to legalize *or* ban abortion; he states that "the federal government has no authority whatsoever to involve itself in the abortion issue." This was complicated even further with the Supreme Court decision *Roe v. Wade*, which took this jurisdiction away from the States.

Later in his career, Republicans introduced legislation to ban all partial birth abortions in the country. Ron Paul reluctantly voted for the legislation in order to "offset the effects of *Roe v. Wade*."[7] However, he did so with reservations, saying, "The best solution, of course, is not now available to us. That would be a Supreme Court that recognizes that for all criminal laws, the several states retain jurisdiction."[8]

Paul was weary of allowing politicians to decide every aspect of American culture. "When the State acts perversely and 'participates' in the destruction of the family and the destruction of life, the end of civilized society is at hand," he sadly observed.[9]

Ron valued innocent life due in no small part to his experiences as a father. In Pittsburgh, while his children were growing up in front of his eyes, he decided to pursue a career of obstetrics/gynecology as a practicing physician. And he would respect his Hippocratic Oath in the only way he knew. Paul vowed, "I will maintain the utmost respect for human life, from the time of its conception."[10]

CHAPTER 9

THE GOOD DOCTOR

1968-1974

Health Care

A little rebellion now and then... is a medicine necessary for the sound health of government.

THOMAS JEFFERSON

Near the end of Ron Paul's medical residency in Pittsburgh, Pennsylvania in 1968, he was performing surgery with a colleague and chatting, as doctors often do. The Soviets were gearing up to invade Czechoslovakia, which was in the midst of Democratic reforms. Eventually the topic of conversation turned to Ron's post-residency plans.

Ron and his wife, Carol, had both enjoyed living in Texas during Ron's service in the Air Force, when he was stationed as a flight surgeon at Kelly Air Force Base in San Antonio. They had planned to return to San Antonio; Ron had even been offered a position at the University of Texas Health Science Center, a new medical school which would open its doors in 1968.[1,2]

Ron's colleague had a different suggestion: the only practicing obstetrician/gynecologist (OB/GYN) in Brazoria County, Texas, was leaving his practice for personal reasons. The practice was in Lake Jackson, a small town approximately fifty miles south of Houston and ten miles upstream from the mouth of the Brazos River on the Texas gulf coast. The doctor there was looking for someone to take over his practice.[3]

Ron thought carefully about the costs and benefits of each career path, and later admitted that he was "torn between academic medicine and going into private practice."[4] He decided he should go to Lake Jackson to meet the doctor who was stepping down.

The Lake Jackson practice was a modern, one-story building.[5] The physician there had invested approximately five thousand dollars in a hydraulic table, a new technology at the time. He was eager to leave right away; as Ron remembers, "he essentially gave me the practice."[6] Ron agreed to pay off the balance of debt on the hydraulic table, and collect the remainder of the other doctor's receivables, which Ron then mailed to him at his new address. Ron would also inherit the practice's staff. After they made their agreement, the transition was rapid. As Ron put it, "I arrived July 4th, and he left the morning of July 5th."[7]

So, in July of 1968, Ron and Carol Paul arrived in Lake Jackson with their four young children and two collie dogs. They were, in Carol's words, "ready to start on a wonderful new life in a town that was full of churches and friendly people."[8]

Carol was initially a bit hesitant to leave their home in Pittsburgh. She was, however, persuaded by Ron's reassurance that if she were unhappy living in Lake Jackson after one year, they could go someplace else.[9] She quickly grew to love the small, rural town of Lake Jackson. In contrast to the cities of Detroit and Pittsburgh, where they had lived in the past, Lake Jackson was warm and sparsely populated. It was an excellent place to raise children, with many parks and sports fields where they could play.[10]

In the late 1960's, the corner of southeast Texas known as Brazoria County was an area dominated by agriculture, albeit not far from the major cities of Houston and San Antonio. More than two thirds of the county's land at that time was considered prime for production of such staples as rice, corn, and dairy – in fact, cattle outnumbered people.[11] The land was dotted with farms, businesses and, of course, the sprawling Dow Chemical plant.

The Dow site covered more than three thousand acres, and was the original impetus for Lake Jackson's existence.[12] The junction of the Brazos River with the Gulf of Mexico also provided a port and accompanying harbor about ten miles downstream from Lake Jackson, which were occupied by shrimp boats and larger ships.

With the population growth in Brazoria County during the late 1960's came an increasing demand for obstetrical care. As Ron had correctly predicted, his services were much needed. During his first day in practice, his office was filled with what he later estimated to be thirty women. He was soon delivering up to fifty babies each month.[13] "Within a few months," said Ron half-jokingly, "I was struggling to get a day off."[14]

Ron recalled that in the early days of his practice, there were no pagers or cell phones to let him know that he was needed at the hospital. Instead, if he was out on a weekend enjoying a little league game with his family, a police car would pull up to the baseball field and let him know that a call was coming in.[15] But despite the busy lifestyle that accompanied his practice, Ron was satisfied knowing that he was providing care to a medically underserved community. "They needed him so badly here," said Carol in a 1996 interview.[16]

At Dr. Paul's office, there were no frills or fancy decorations, but it was always kept neat and clean.[17] A small sign out front read: "Ronald E. Paul, MD."[18] The office reflected Ron's tendency to shy away from anything ostentatious. It was clear that the focus of his practice rested solely on his patients.

Ron's patients were as diverse as the population of Brazoria County itself. They ranged from the affluent to the indigent, and represented a wide variety of ages. Most patients had health insurance through private providers. Some who did not carry medical insurance paid for their care out-of-pocket; a few were eligible for Medicaid or Medicare. The majority of Brazoria County's inhabitants in the late 1960's and early 1970's were Caucasian. However, a significant portion of the women there were Black and Hispanic (predominantly Mexican).[19]

Some physicians in southeast Texas at the time were reluctant to care for poor women from racial and ethnic minorities. They could not pay for their care, and Medicaid reimbursements were too low or too cumbersome to obtain. By contrast, these women were welcomed at Dr. Paul's office. Ron quickly gained a reputation for helping those who had no money to speak of. Indeed, he believed in the moral responsibility of physicians to care for everyone, regardless of their ability to pay. He never worried about the financial impact of treating indigent women for free in his practice. In his words, when women came to him seeking his help, he "just took care of them."[20]

Most of his patients who were short on funds would one day pull themselves out of their situation and remain loyal patients. This business model was his belief in caring for the needy through voluntary means, as opposed to government intervention, taken to its logical conclusion.

From the outset, Dr. Paul never accepted payments from Medicare or Medicaid. He did deal with private insurers, and also accepted out-of-pocket payments. If he knew that a patient was stretched financially, he allowed flexibility on the price, even sometimes bartering with patients for goods rather than accepting cash.[21] According to Dr. Jack Pruett, Ron's long time practice partner, "He never even sent a bill" to poor patients who would have relied on Medicare or Medicaid at other physicians' offices. The practice was busy, successful, and lucrative – so much so, in fact, that Ron could easily afford to treat needy patients for free and still thrive.[22]

Many people are critical of the cost of health insurance, and there are real problems. Ron Paul believes health insurance attempts to insure too much. When you buy home or car insurance, you aren't covered for minor upkeep like replacing windows or painting walls. Car insurance doesn't pay for a tune-up or oil change, or even minor repairs. But for some reason, every doctor visit is expected to be paid for by health insurance. This is really a misinterpretation of insurance. Insurance is supposed to protect you from going broke, not from everyday costs like a checkup.

Ron Paul's practice not only afforded care to those in the lowest socioeconomic strata; his pricing scheme accommodated patients of a variety of incomes.

Dr. Pruett remembered the approximate costs of care during the mid-1970s at his and Ron's offices:[23] a Pap smear, a routine annual screening test for cervical cancer, cost $3.50. An office visit – which could include, for instance, the doctor taking a history, performing a pelvic exam, and answering the patient's questions and concerns – was $25. They charged $125 for a tubal ligation, which was performed at the nearby 127-bed Community Hospital of Brazosport, in Freeport.[24] Pregnant women could purchase a $350 package that included all prenatal care and office visits, prenatal vitamins, and the entire labor and delivery – no matter how long the labor took or when the baby was born.[25] Ron reserved samples of drugs such as birth control pills, which he received from pharmaceutical companies, for his needy patients. He would give them a few months' supply for free.[26]

These mid-1970s prices, compared with those in the earliest days of Ron's practice, reflected the inflationary economic conditions that troubled him so. In 1968, Ron recalls charging $5.00 for an office visit. A few years later, the price rose to about $7.50. The early 1970s were not only a time of inflation, but also government-imposed price controls.

Nixon naively attempted to freeze prices in August 1971 to keep products cheap, an unprecedented intervention in the free markets. Ron remembered when the Nixon administration attempted to freeze the price of his office visits at $7.50.[27] Initially it was promised to be a 90 day freeze, but it expanded to nearly 1,000 days as each measure failed one after another, until price controls were abandoned and the free markets were allowed to reestablish equilibrium.

Ron Paul frequently notes that in comparatively unregulated, unsubsidized markets such as computer hardware and mobile phone service, prices continue to decrease. And the technology continues to improve rapidly. Contrast that with medicine: it is a highly regulated, subsidized industry that keeps getting costlier. He wants to bring back these same market forces to bear on the medical industry. As Ron noted in an interview with the Kaiser Family Foundation, "If you want cell phones, you don't ask FEMA to set up a bureaucracy to deliver cell phones... No, the market does that, and those prices keep going down in spite of inflation."[28]

As a result of Ron's commitment to his patients and quality of care, he was popular and well-liked within the community. He believed that honesty was always the best policy. If a medical error occurred, which it rarely did, he would immediately explain to the patient what happened, and he would apologize. It was clear to his patients that Dr. Paul took his relationship with them seriously. As a result, no lawsuits were brought against him. In fact, Dr. Paul did not even carry malpractice insurance at this time.[29]

Ron was known for his integrity and honesty in all of his personal relationships. He and Dr. Pruett, for instance, practiced together for approximately 20 years, but never had a written contract of any kind.[30]

Dr. Paul and Dr. Pruett first met in 1974. Dr. Pruett had just finished his medical residency at Scott and White Memorial Hospital in Temple, Texas. The first several years of Ron's Lake Jackson practice had been, as he described it, a bit "overwhelming."[31] He had been considering adding a practice partner for some time.

Ron called the director of Dr. Pruett's OB/GYN residency program, and asked if there were anyone he could recommend. Dr. Pruett's name came up immediately.

As Dr. Pruett recalled, "When I walked into his office, the first thing he said to me was that there were two things that he and I had to agree upon or else there was no use for us to even talk. He said, 'Number one is, we do not do any abortions.'" Dr. Pruett expressed his agreement, and encouraged Ron to continue. "He said, 'Number two is, we also do not accept any federal funds. We are going to see Medicare and Medicaid patients for free, and we are going to treat them just like we treat everybody else regardless of what it costs us to do that.'"

Pruett was unsure about the idea of refusing federal funds at first, but the partnership worked well. Dr. Pruett immediately liked Dr. Paul. And for twenty years thereafter, they conducted their practice on nothing more than their word and a handshake, just as Ron's original guidelines had set forth.[32]

Their initial agreement was that Ron would pay Dr. Pruett a salary for six months. If both were satisfied after that time had elapsed, they would become full partners. Dr. Pruett was impressed by the trust that this agreement showed; it was unusual for a practicing doctor to add a full partner in such a short amount of time. But, after half a year had elapsed, both physicians were happy to enter into the partnership. Dr. Paul saw patients in the office on Mondays and Wednesdays; Dr. Pruett saw patients on Tuesdays and Thursdays. Whichever of them was not at the office would be at the hospital delivering babies and taking care of their patients. On Fridays, both did double duty, covering the hospital and the office as needed.

Because of that arrangement, the patients had access to at least one doctor who would be available twenty-four hours a day, seven days a week. Both physicians were seeing all of the patients, so they each took an equal share of any income that the practice generated.[33]

Ron worked tirelessly. He was often on call, delivering babies in the middle of the night. But he was as fastidious about caring for himself as he was for his patients. He ate a healthy diet, never smoked, and ran, swam, or rode his bike diligently every single day.[34]

In the 1970's in Texas, the legal concept of Joint and Several Liability allowed damages from any suit successfully brought against a doctor to be collected from an affiliated hospital, if the hospital were found to share any portion of the liability. Administrators at the Community Hospital of Brazosport were well aware of the risk this presented to them, especially from areas of medicine with intrinsically high complication rates such as obstetrics. The administrators announced that they would require all affiliated physicians to purchase malpractice insurance, and that anyone who refused to do so would be fired and replaced with someone who would purchase insurance. The high cost of malpractice insurance can be a significant factor in driving up costs for patients, and even deterring doctors from practicing in a certain field where premiums are high.

Drs. Paul and Pruett "saw the writing on the wall,"[35] and called a special meeting with the other area physicians who were also affiliated with the hospital. Nearly all of them pledged that they would not purchase malpractice insurance. The plan was to leverage the collective bargaining power of many physicians against the hospital in order to defeat the new requirement. However, a few weeks later, Drs. Paul and Pruett found out from hospital administrators that they were indeed the only ones who had not purchased insurance.[36]

This was an illustrative example of how most doctors around Ron Paul in the early 1970's behaved. They took their jobs seriously, and all they wanted was to practice medicine. But when it came to politics, or activism of any kind, few besides Ron deviated from the *status quo*.

In another example of his perpetual willingness to take a principled stance, Ron was an outspoken proponent of midwifery. He and Dr. Pruett worked with the Brazosport Birthing Center, a small area facility that employed approximately five nurse-midwives.[37]

Ron advocated the lessening of onerous licensure requirements for midwives, which he viewed as barriers erected by practicing physicians (with the help of government), to protect MDs from competition. He also advocated freer entry into the health care system for other types of providers, like naturopathic physicians and chiropractors.[38] "Physicians have always liked to protect their industry through licensure," Ron said in an interview with the Kaiser Family Foundation. "There are some things that a nurse can do every bit as well as I can do, but by law, they can't do it."[39]

Ron believed that fewer licensing requirements and restrictions lead to more competition, and in turn, lower prices for patients. Patients would be protected from harm because health care practitioners, no matter what their qualifications, would have to prove their merit to the toughest judge of all: the consumer. If they mistreated or harmed a patient, word would spread, and soon they would be out of business. Certifications from private organizations such as medical boards or nursing groups lend credibility to a health care provider, but they should not be mandatory requirements for that person to practice legally. Ron's embracing these principles was a testament to his faith in free-market economics – by advocating for the midwives, he stood up for his own competition.

Ron was also guided by his firm belief that abortions are morally wrong. He did not, however, advocate for federal abortion bans. Instead, he strove to promote a "pro-life culture." Dr. Paul would take the time in his practice to sit down and talk with an expectant mother whom he thought may be interested in ending her pregnancy. He was never preachy or overbearing, understanding the sensitive nature of the matter. But if asked for his opinion, he did try to persuade the mother-to-be to continue her pregnancy and perhaps offer the baby to another family for adoption.[40] One technique he used was to do an ultrasound for the woman, for free. He would show her the rudimentary image of the fetus and allow her to hear its heart beating.[41] Added to Dr. Paul's gentle reassurance was the fact that he or Dr. Pruett could arrange for an adoptive family to pay all of the expectant mother's medical costs. In this way, he was sometimes able to convince her to pursue adoption rather than terminate the pregnancy.[42]

Dr. Paul and Dr. Pruett arranged many adoptions during their partnership. The doctors maintained a list of families at their office who wanted to adopt a child. First, they vetted the families to make sure that their reasons for wanting to adopt a child were sound, and that they could provide a safe and loving home. When a woman wanted to give her baby up for adoption, they would allow her to meet the potential adoptive family, if she chose. Then they would arrange for the adoptive family to pay for 100% of her prenatal care and delivery.[43] Government regulation of adoption at the time was limited. All that was required for an adoption to take place were the two consenting parties, the doctor, and a lawyer.[44] True to their original covenant, under no circumstances did Dr. Paul or Dr. Pruett ever perform an abortion in their practice.[45]

Ron did not hesitate to publicize the fact that he did not accept government funds at his practice; he and Dr. Pruett spoke at county medical board meetings and other gatherings of physicians in the area, as well as individually with local doctors, explaining their business model.

In principle, most local physicians agreed with Dr. Paul in his consistent refusal to accept government money. However, in their own practices they faced pressures to accept government intervention in medicine in the form of Medicare, Medicaid, and all of the accompanying mandates and red tape. When faced with powerful institutions such as the American Medical Association and Texas Medical Board; all but Drs. Paul and Pruett quietly fell in line.[46]

Ron's opposition to Medicare and Medicaid stemmed from a few fundamental objections. First was his view that, as he later explained in a 2007 interview, "If I'm the government and I have to give you health care, I have to ultimately take it from someone else."[47] Whether it was through direct taxation or inflation of the money supply, the money had to come from somewhere. Ron pointed out that in contrast to the care he provided to needy patients on a voluntary basis, the taxpayers were not paying voluntarily. Their money was extracted from them by threat of force. Although proponents of Medicare and Medicaid characterized the programs as forms of charity given by the government, Ron emphatically disagreed – it could not be charity, because the money was not theirs to give.

Medicare and Medicaid were not the only objects of Ron's criticism. "Managed care" describes a common practice of health maintenance organizations (HMOs) refusing to pay doctors for procedures and treatments which fall outside of formulaic clinical algorithms.

The Health Maintenance Act passed in 1973, ushering in a new age of government managed healthcare. Ron later commented on this legislation and the climate it had created in health care:

> During the early seventies, Congress embraced HMOs in order to address concerns about rapidly escalating health care costs. However, it was Congress which had caused health care costs to spiral by removing control over the health care dollar from consumers and thus eliminating any incentive for consumers to pay attention to costs when selecting health care. Because the consumer had the incentive to control health care cost stripped away, and because politicians where unwilling to either give up power by giving individuals control over their health care or take responsibility for rationing care, a third way to control costs had to be created. Thus, the Nixon Administration, working with advocates of nationalized medicine, crafted legislation providing federal subsidies to HMOs, preempting state laws forbidding physicians to sign contracts to deny care to their patients, and mandating that health plans offer an HMO option in addition to traditional fee-for-service coverage. Federal subsidies, preemption of state law, and mandates on private business hardly sounds like the workings of the free market. Instead, HMOs are the result of the same Nixon-era corporatist, Big Government mindset that produced wage-and-price controls.[48]

What resulted from such legislation as the HMO Act of 1973 was the rise of managed care. Ron described managed care as "a general nuisance," noting that it dampened his efficiency as a physician.

Ron saw many examples of how managed care undermined his clinical judgment. For instance, HMOs placed time limits on office visits, refused to pay for procedures if the patient did not fit a specific profile, and refused to pay for the newest drugs, which were sometimes a better choice for the patient than older, less expensive ones. For Ron, this was the common thread between Medicare/Medicaid and HMOs: they undermined the doctor-patient relationship. Ron believed that it was the doctor's job to decide – with the patient – the best treatment on a case-by-case basis, synthesizing all kinds of information to make the best determination. HMOs, on the other hand, used "one size fits all" formulas, sometimes created by non-MDs.[49] Ron believed that these could never replace the personalized decision making of a physician who knew his patient.

One of Ron's objections to government intrusion into free market medicine is that a parasitic relationship can exist between the government and medical companies. This leads to a situation where the most successful corporations are those who know how to manipulate the government, rather than those who provide the best products and services to patients. Large corporations can also easily absorb the costs of new regulations and government requirements. By contrast, small companies are often bankrupted by additional legislative burdens, or they are simply deterred from entering the marketplace from the outset. In this way, a burdensome regulatory climate in the medical sector serves to insulate the largest HMOs and medical corporations from competition.

Paul sometimes refers to what he calls the "Medical-Industrial Complex," a parallel institution to the infamous Military-Industrial Complex. He says, "In the last 25 years we have developed a Medical-Industrial Complex because government runs medicine. We have corporate medicine; we don't have free market medicine."[50]

One of the biggest beneficiaries of this Medical-Industrial Complex is the pharmaceutical industry. Not only do they receive payment from expanded drug Medicare benefits, but the government also locks out smaller companies from entering the market via costly regulations.

Pharmaceutical regulations began in the 1960s after the drug Thalidomide, which was used to prevent morning sickness in pregnant women, was found to produce birth defects in some children of mothers who took it early in the first trimester of pregnancy. Between 8,000 and 12,000 children world-wide (mostly in Germany, where the drug was created) were born with defects. Political pressures on the government to "do something" resulted in intrusive regulations.

Although many people believed that a heavily regulated pharmaceutical industry made them safer, regulations made it difficult to introduce new drugs on the market. It could take ten years or more of clinical studies and billions of dollars just to pass a single drug through the Food and Drug Administration (FDA). The regulations also kept out competition, because newer, smaller research labs simply could not afford to comply with the costly regulations; nor could they operate for ten years without any income. The unseen consequence of burdensome regulations is the suffering of thousands of people each year who cannot be helped by newer drugs, because the drugs are either caught up in the regulatory pipeline or were never created in the first place.

Ron Paul believes such cumbersome regulations are unnecessary. To build a good reputation, a drug company must consistently produce safe and effective products with few side effects, and make them available at a reasonable price. Those companies who successfully do so are rewarded with sales. The natural inclination of drug companies to avoid lawsuits is enough to ensure that they test their drugs adequately.

Although some fear that large corporations have an advantage in the courtroom, it is worth noting that corporate law firms exist whose sole business model is to bring class-action lawsuits (where groups of people have been harmed) against wealthy businesses in order to extract billions of dollars from them. Although this system can be abused, it exerts pressure on companies to ensure the safety of their customers.

Delays in drug treatments result in death and suffering by those who otherwise would have benefited. A government managed healthcare system suffers from the same problems as other industries when the transactions are not controlled by consumers. The results are high prices and poor quality.

The cycle is predictable: government interventions cause problems that the government attempts to fix with more interventions. In 2003 the Federal Government was concerned about the rising cost of pharmaceuticals and enacted programs to pay for them. As Paul observed, "Congress claims the program will cost $400 billion over the next 10 years, but government cost projections cannot be trusted. Medicare today costs seven times more than originally estimated. Private economists estimate the true cost will be closer to $3 or $4 trillion over ten years, but even the government's figure of $400 billion represents the largest entitlement increase since the failed Great Society programs of the 1960s."[51]

Despite his disagreements with government and HMOs, Dr. Paul had become a well-respected member of his community almost immediately after he first began practicing in Lake Jackson. Anyone who knew a baby recently born in Brazoria County also knew Dr. Ron Paul. He was also well-respected by other area physicians, and had a reputation for keeping current with all of the latest medical journals.[52] However, it was his compassion that allowed him to win the hearts of those in the community.

Dr. Pruett recalls a time in the early days of his partnership with Ron Paul when they cared for a young Mexican woman. She and her husband had three small children; he worked in Galveston at an offshore oil refinery. She did not have health insurance, so she paid out-of-pocket for her prenatal care. Drs. Paul and Pruett had been caring for her all through her most recent pregnancy with triplets.

When she reached approximately 8 months gestation (an unusual occurrence, because women pregnant with triplets are at high risk for preterm labor and birth), they had instructed her to rest in bed until it was time for her to deliver her babies. In the past, she had always placed a lot of trust in the doctors, and had followed their medical instructions carefully. But one day, they received a call from this patient, saying that she had to go to Galveston. Her husband had suddenly become very ill. Dr. Pruett gave her the number of the nearest emergency room, and told her to go to that hospital if she started to have any contractions. She did make it back from Galveston before giving birth, but unfortunately, her husband did not survive his illness.[53]

When Drs. Paul and Pruett found out what had happened, they refunded 100% of the money that she had paid for her previous medical care, and delivered her triplets at no cost to her. After the babies were born, they arranged for local businesses and large companies to donate formula, diapers, and baby clothes. With six babies at home and her husband gone, she was unable to continue to support herself alone in the United States, and so she ultimately returned to Mexico. But for years, Drs. Paul and Pruett received her Christmas cards. She even sent them a handmade ashtray as a gift to express her gratitude for what they had done.[54]

The overwhelming feeling toward Dr. Paul during his initial years practicing medicine in Lake Jackson was affection. As Carol put it, "He just loved medicine; he loved delivering babies. Any other doctor can make you well, but the obstetrician actually gives you a present. And the present of new life is so special."[55]

But as Ron opined in a 1996 interview, "When your job is to bring new life into the world, it makes you really aware of what kind of a world these children are coming into, and what they have to face."[56] The adversity to which he was referring, of course, was political.

Although his medical practice had been deeply rewarding, his dissatisfaction with the nation's political climate had been steadily growing since the inception of his practice in 1968. Rampant inflation and mismanagement of the country's currency, price controls, and increasing government regulation of every aspect of Americans' lives were some of the issues that plagued him. When President Richard Nixon announced that he was severing all remaining ties between gold and the dollar in 1971, Ron felt he could no longer remain a spectator.[57]

Just as he had held fast to his principles in medicine, he felt that he could no longer keep quiet about what he saw as an out-of-control government in Washington, DC. It was time for Ron to begin a new chapter in his life. This reminds me, it would be worth doing a find and replace on D.C. and replacing with DC.

CHAPTER 10

RUNNING FOR CONGRESS

1974-1977

Taxes

It would be a hard government that should tax its people one-tenth part of their income.

- BENJAMIN FRANKLIN

Studying Ludwig von Mises as an intern had painted an unsettling picture of America for a young Ron Paul. Now that he was 39, he more fully understood that freedom was the only path to peace and prosperity. He was also disturbed to see the American government moving in the exact opposite direction needed to cure her ills.

Austrian economics in particular had taught Paul that Nixon's economic policies were decidedly against the free market. However, He wasn't hearing anyone debate those issues. Although many people didn't agree with the Nixon administration, what was missing was a principled critique of his government based on the ideal of a free society. Paul decided he must enter politics to start debating those issues.

As Paul later recalled, "I decided to run for Congress because of the disaster of wage and price controls imposed by the Nixon administration in 1971. When the stock market responded euphorically to the imposition of these controls and the closing of the gold window, and the US Chamber of Commerce and many other big business groups gave enthusiastic support,

I decided that someone in politics had to condemn the controls, and offer the alternative that could explain the past and give hope for the future: the Austrian economists' defense of the free market."[1]

Paul knew his election chances were slim, but he could use the opportunity to talk about his ideas. Even if he didn't win, his campaign could spread awareness of how a free society works.

But Carol Paul didn't quite see it that way, as Ron would later reveal. "I was looking for a forum to ventilate and politics has allowed me to do that. ... My goal was not to be in politics or be elected but to present a case for what I thought was important. My wife warned me that it was dangerous because I could end up getting elected. I told her that would never happen!"[2]

Paul knew his message would be unpopular when heard for the first time. Instead of promising handouts and benefits to interest groups, Paul's core proposal was to take the government off everyone's back. He knew this policy would make everyone better off, but it wouldn't sound that way to those hoping to get something for nothing. He believed that the influence of interest groups was much stronger than the force of educated pro-freedom citizens.

"At the time I was convinced, like Ludwig von Mises, that no one could succeed in politics without serving the special interests of some politically powerful pressure group,"[3] he recalled.

Limited-government politicians have an image problem because they won't give away free handouts. To defeat this perception, voters need to understand basic economics so they realize that they are the ones who will pay for dubious government plans. Thus, limited government candidates have a tough task: their campaigns must be educational in nature.

Lew Rockwell, who would later serve on Paul's staff, was well aware of this. "We never saw his office as a conventionally political one. It was a bully pulpit to get the message out. We sent out hundreds of thousands of tracts on freedom, inserted amazing articles in the *Congressional Record*, and drafted libertarian legislation as an educational effort," he said.[4]

Ron launched his political career as a Republican Party candidate for congress. As a Brazoria County resident, he ran to represent Texas's 22nd congressional district, which covers the constituency of the south-central portion of the Houston-Sugar Land-Baytown metropolitan area.

It was a difficult place and time to be a Republican. Not only had the Democrats historically held the district, but the Republicans were having a particularly difficult time with the Watergate scandal and President Nixon's resignation.

But none of that stopped Paul from trying. He made his first run for Congress in 1974 against a Democratic incumbent. Paul's campaign slogan was "Freedom, Honesty, and Sound Money", a declaration of the principles upon which he would base his entire career.[5]

Paul told voters that government was at the root of most economic failures. "Bureaucratic management can never compete with the free market in solving problems," observed Paul. "Central economic planning doesn't work. Just look at the failed systems of the 20th century. ... The big government nanny-state is based on the assumption that free markets can't provide the maximum good for the largest number of people. It assumes people are not smart or responsible enough to take care of themselves, and ... that politicians and bureaucrats have superior knowledge, and are endowed with certain talents that produce efficiency."[6]

He advocated voluntary solutions from the private sector. If someone was really destitute, they could always turn to private charities, foundations, or churches.

Journalist Henry Hazlitt, a student of Austrian economics, once wrote, "Everything we get, outside of the free gifts of nature, must in some way be paid for. ...all government expenditures must eventually be paid out of the proceeds of taxation; that inflation itself is merely a form, and a particularly vicious form, of taxation. ... For every dollar that is spent on the bridge a dollar will be taken away from taxpayers. If the bridge costs $10 million the taxpayers will lose $10 million."

Ron understood that confiscating wealth also decimated private industry jobs. Normally, citizens spend their money on goods and services. If they are deprived of that money, then they are unable to purchase certain products. Hazlitt concluded, "Therefore, for every public job created by the bridge project, a private job has been destroyed somewhere else."[7]

Fortunately, in the same way that the growth of government takes away money and jobs from the private sector, if government is scaled down, those jobs and investments return. For that reason, Paul made it his personal duty to fight for a limited government. Every dollar saved from government spending would go back to the hands of the people.

And Paul would not discriminate with his tax cuts. "Lower taxes benefit all Americans by increasing economic growth and encouraging wealth creation. I'm in favor of cutting everybody's taxes – rich, poor, and otherwise," he said. "Whether a tax cut reduces a single mother's payroll taxes by forty dollars a month, or allows a business owner to save thousands in capital gains and hire more employees, the net effect is beneficial. Both either spend, save, or invest the extra dollars, which helps all of us more than if those dollars were sent to the black hole known as the federal Treasury."[8]

He believed that, just because someone is wealthy, does not mean he is hurting others. To him, the path to prosperity is not to resent wealthy individuals, but rather to make more of them.

Of course, most politicians wouldn't agree with that, claiming that money raised through taxes could be used in important projects to provide for a better future for the country. Paul had a different position: if this money stayed in the hands of private citizens, they would use it more wisely than the government. After all, private investors are more prone to take good care of investments than a politician, since the former have their own money at stake, while the latter are handling other peoples' money.

"I reject the notion that tax cuts harm the economy," he said. "The economy suffers when government takes money from your paycheck that you otherwise would spend, save, or invest. Taxes never create prosperity. Private-sector innovation and productivity are the engines that drive our economy, regardless of what politicians tell us."[9]

....

Paul rejected the idea of using government taxation to correct so-called *economic injustice*. As he saw it, the equality that should be protected is the equality before the law, not equality of income. All people should be free to pursue their economics goals, and if they wish to earn more money then the average, they are entitled to do so.

By imposing larger taxes on business, government forces businessmen to adjust to a new reality – they must raise prices or cut back on expenses. Both workers and consumers will see prices go up and wages go down. The burden of government hurts everyone. Thus, Paul vehemently rejected all attempts of using the tax system to wage class warfare:

> The class war tactic highlights what the left does best: divide Americans into groups. Collectivists see all issues of wealth and taxation as a zero-sum game played between competing groups. If one group gets a tax break, other groups must be rallied against it – even if such a cut would ultimately benefit them. Yet the class warriors forget that American wealth is not static, but rather very dynamic. Poor people become rich, and rich people lose all of their money. Rich family dynasties are increasingly rare, and are quickly destroyed by unproductive spendthrift generations So when the left attacks the rich, they're attacking a fluid group that many poor Americans hope to join someday by moving up in life. Upward mobility is possible only in a free-market capitalist system, whereas collectivism dooms the poor to remain exactly where they are.[10]

Ron Paul understood the relationship between high taxation and failing businesses. Politicians naively expected US businesses taxed at over 35% to compete with Hong Kong and Japanese businesses taxed at 15% and 25% respectively. In reality, something had to give when money was sapped from operations; whether in research, production, marketing or employee pay.

....

Carol Paul's optimism regarding her husband's chances was correct, but her prophecy wouldn't be confirmed right away. Running for the first time on a new message, he faced Robert R. Casey, a senior congressman since 1958. It would be a tough battle to unseat such an established incumbent.

After the votes were counted, Casey came out on top, easily retaining his seat. Ron Paul, who never expected to win, went back to his medical practice and continued studying economics.

....

In April 1976, over a year after his defeat to Robert R. Casey, Paul had a second chance at politics, and he had President Gerald Ford to thank for it. Ford was Nixon's Vice President who stepped in after Nixon resigned. He appointed Democrat Casey to the Federal Maritime Commission. Casey accepted, which meant that his seat in congress would be vacant. In those situations, a special election is held specifically to fill that position until the next general election.

Paul saw his chance and put his name on the ballot once again. His new opponent was a relatively unknown Democrat named Robert Gammage, who had previously served in the local Texas State Senate. Gammage would attempt to move from local state politics to federal politics.

In the previous election, Paul was relatively unknown to voters in the 22nd district compared to the incumbent Casey. However, even though he was soundly defeated by a Democrat in the previous election, he had become a known commodity to voters due to his campaign. This time, he had the advantage while Gammage was the new face. Paul managed a narrow victory over Gammage.

The full term for an elected congressman is two years. Paul's first term, however, would be less than a year because his predecessor, Robert Casey, had already served out most of his term. The general election would be in same year, so he had little more than a semester to make an impact – and that's exactly what he did.

Traveling to Washington was an overwhelming experience for the farm boy who had once delivered newspapers to his rural neighbors. Although Paul knew he would be a lonely voice in Washington, he felt welcomed by the monuments dedicated to the founding fathers. To his dismay, however, the present politicians had allowed many of these monuments to fall into disrepair, with some suffering the indignity of graffiti.

Paul's first day in congress was even more overwhelming. His new workplace at The United States Congress, was housed in a single Romanesque building dating back to 1793, the massively domed Capitol Building. The front of the building had 365 steps (one for every day of the year) which Paul made his way up, despite his bad knee. The actual House Chamber, in the south wing of the building (the Senate Chamber is in the North wing), housed all of Paul's fellow congressmen.

Inside the square House Chamber was a semi-circle of seats for all 435 members of congress. The second level, which was open to the public, allowed the media and spectators to watch their congressmen in action. Around this second level were 23 stone relief portraits of famous lawmakers throughout history: everyone from Romans in the original Republic to Moses and Napoleon. Of these, two were American: George Mason, the father of the Bill of Rights, and Thomas Jefferson, one of Ron Paul's favorites.

All 435 seats converged on a large podium, where congressmen came forward to deliver their opinions on proposed laws. It was here, in April 1976, that an anxious 40 year old, political novice was sworn into office.

Paul's short first term would be a busy one. He quickly assembled a powerful staff, mostly composed of young intellectuals committed to the cause of freedom. Many of them, like Gary North and Bruce Bartlett, had written articles for The Freeman, a leading magazine for the freedom cause, read by conservative and libertarian alike.[11]

The young congressman practiced the same decentralized management strategy he advocated for the nation. His style of administration was congruent with his belief in the sheer effectiveness of freedom. Paul hired the best people he could find and left them alone to their work. He knew he could trust them, since he personally selected each one of them.

His office was also highly efficient. Instead of having a bulky staff and an all-controlling Administrative Assistant to make sure everyone was doing his job – a common practice for congressmen - Paul had a much less bureaucratic organization, in which Paul himself kept in personal contact with each of his employees.

Gary North, who served on Paul's staff during his first term, reminisced about their early days together. "When I joined his Congressional staff in June, 1976, he was the most junior Congressman, having been sworn in only two months earlier. ... In my three-person tiny office was John W. Robbins, a former student of Hans Sennholz in economics and of Gottfried Dietze in political science. In the main office was Bruce Bartlett, who later became one of the leading defenders in Washington of supply-side economics. This was a high-powered staff for a Congressman with two months' seniority."

As a member of the House of Representatives, Congressman Paul's primary duty was to debate and vote on the approval of all legislative bills. He was also required to take part on a Committee, which is an internal organization that deals with specific tasks. Congressmen may choose which House Committee they want to serve, such as the Agriculture Committee, the Committee on Education and Labor, and so forth.

Paul never forgot that his main reason for entering politics was due to Nixon's decision to close the gold window, so he wouldn't miss the chance of taking his case to Congress. Therefore, he joined the House Banking Committee, which dealt specifically with economic policy and all questions related to financial services.

In June, 1976, Paul had his chance to confront these policies, and in the process, stand out from his contemporaries. Each committee report is accompanied by a minority report, written by those who are in the minority on an issue. Since he was the only congressman to oppose re-financing the International Monetary Fund, he had the opportunity to present a minority report, stating his arguments to the Committee.

North was in charge of writing the report. He would later remark, "The House Banking Committee had been debating the re-financing of the International Monetary Fund (IMF). The ... committee was strongly in favor of putting more taxpayers' money into the relic of the Bretton Woods monetary conference of 1944. Congressman Paul was the only member of the committee who was opposed to the bill.

"It was my task to write the minority report on Saturday, so that he could hand it in on Monday. ... This minority report so completely amazed the bipartisan Establishment that Ron Paul was invited to testify to the Senate Banking Committee on his reasons for opposing the funding. I had never heard of this before: a freshman Congressman invited to share his views with a Senate committee. I have not heard of it since."[12]

....

Paul came to believe in a controversial solution to the taxation problem; he proposed destroying the IRS and, as he adds, "replacing it with nothing."

Eliminating the IRS had been proposed by other Libertarians such as Steve Forbes, who famously wrote, "We can't tinker with this tax code monstrosity or try to reform it around the edges. The only thing we can do with this hideous beast is kill it, drive a stake through its heart, bury it, and hope that it never rises again to terrorize the American people."[13] Bob Barr, a former Republican congressman, later added, "We should also burn the corpse and scatter the ashes to the four corners of the earth." In order to eliminate the IRS and prevent an unwelcome comeback, Congress would have to repeal the 16th amendment of 1913, which allows Congress to levy taxes on the states.

By destroying the IRS, most people wonder where government revenue would come from. As Paul later noted, "You may be surprised to know that the income tax accounts for only approximately one-third of federal revenue. Only 10 years ago, the federal budget was roughly one-third less than it is today. So perhaps the idea of an America without an income tax is not so radical after all."[14]

Paul's friend, economist Walter Williams, believed the United States would thrive without the IRS. "We have existed as a nation from 1776 up until 1913 without an income tax, and we became the most powerful and richest nation on the face of the earth during that period, so obviously it was not necessary," he observed.[15]

While Paul was a lonely voice in Congress fighting for tax cuts in the seventies, another school of economic thought was gaining a growing influence advocating a similar position. The *supply-side school*, which would influence the later Reagan administration, also advocated tax cuts with similar arguments. Like Ron Paul, they argued that less tax would stimulate economic growth, since private individuals would have more money to invest in their business and careers.

However, unlike Paul, supply-siders didn't believe that cutting government spending was equally necessary, because they believed that the economic growth would be enough to pay for the deficit that was being created. Democrats in the media often argued passionately against supply-siders because they believed it would cut down on government revenues. No one ever heard the other argument against supply-side economics by Ron Paul.

Ron's position was clearly different. "Tax relief is important, but members of Congress need to back up tax cuts with spending cuts," he observed. "True fiscal conservatism combines both low taxes and low spending."[16] This fundamental disagreement would eventually cause a rift between Paul and then Governor of California, Ronald Reagan.

Paul argued that cutting taxes without cutting spending would lead to a budget deficit that would increase the national debt. While supply-side policies might generate growth in the present, it would only postpone the problem of paying for government expenses. The only difference is that the cost would be deferred, but in every case, Americans would bear the cost.

Paul easily identified why the current generation of Americans was faring worse economically than the previous generation. "I disagree with the supply-side argument that government debt doesn't matter," he explained. "Debt does matter, especially to future generations that will be asked to pay for our extravagance. ... The bills always come due later ...responsible people restrain their borrowing because they will have to pay the money back. It's time for American taxpayers to understand that every dollar will have to be repaid. We should have the courage to face our grandchildren knowing that we have done all we can to end the government spending spree."[17]

Ron also knew that cutting taxes and spending would never be an easy task. To do so, it would be necessary to reduce both "the *size* and *scope* of government", a phrase he would often repeat throughout his career.

"The rotten system in Congress will change only when the American people change their beliefs about the proper role of government in our society," he said. "Too many members of Congress believe they can solve all economic problems, cure all social ills, and bring about worldwide peace and prosperity simply by creating new federal programs. We must reject unlimited government and reassert the constitutional rule of law if we hope to halt the spending orgy."[18]

Throughout his career, Paul opposed collecting taxes in an attempt to change the social fabric of a nation. "I do not support the idea of using tax policy for social engineering or supposed 'stimulus,' where certain activities are encouraged and others discouraged. This is not proper in a free society, and it instills the terrible notion that government should run the economy."[19] For Paul, much of what the government did was beyond its proper boundaries. Even though some of these tasks were important, private citizens could do a better job. He believed government should limit itself to duties that aren't suitable for individuals to take responsibility for.

According to Paul, "government has a proper role in guaranteeing free markets, protecting voluntary and religious choices and guaranteeing private property ownership, while punishing those who violate these rules – whether foreign or domestic. … In a free society, the government's job is simply to protect liberty – the people do the rest."[20]

Besides his activities in Congress, Paul also played an important role in the 1976 presidential election. Before the election, each party conducts a primary election; an internal election through which they select a nominee. Paul worked as a delegate of the Republican convention. These delegates are party leaders who are chosen during the primary process and who have the authority to choose the candidate who will represent the party in the general election.

Paul was not only one of those delegates, but he was the one who led the Texan delegation that supported Reagan for president in the National Convention. At the time, he was one of only four congressmen who supported Reagan over Ford. Although Reagan was unsuccessful in the primaries that year (Gerald Ford won), it was an important step for his nomination four years later – and thus, for Reagan's presidency.[21]

Congressman Paul also hadn't forgotten that his decision to enter politics was as much about educating people about liberty as it was about getting elected. In his first months in Congress, he founded the Foundation for Rational Economics Education (FREE), a non-profit, non-partisan, educational foundation dedicated to publishing books and a monthly newsletter. That newsletter, The Freedom Report, explained the principles of free-market economics, sound money and limited government.[22]

This unusually busy and active first term, however, would come to an end. Paul had to face Robert Gammage again in the end of 1976. This time Gammage had more time to prepare for the election, while Paul was understandably engrossed in his new activities in Washington. In a close contest, Paul lost by 268 votes out of 180,000 that were cast. In early 1977, he would go back to his district, family and medical practice.

The defeat was a devastating blow to Paul, but in a way, his short political career had been as successful as he could hope for. His campaign had never been about personality. It was about ideas, and his brief time in congress had done a great deal to advance them. Paul's campaigns and his first term in Washington had laid down the foundation for a network of citizens committed to the cause of freedom, which would prove to be the first step towards larger victories.

"My influence, such as it is, comes only by educating others about the rightness of the free market," said Paul. "The majority of the voters in my district have approved, as have those familiar with free-market economics. And voters in other districts, encouraged by my speaking out for freedom and sound money, influence their representatives in the direction of a free market. My influence comes through education, not the usual techniques of a politician. But the more usual politicians in Congress will hardly solve our problems. Americans need a better understanding of Austrian economics."[23] Privately, Paul vowed he would return to Washington. In the long run, this would also prove to be more than a political contest for a seat in Congress: it was the beginning of a much larger movement. Decades later, Ron Paul himself would remark, "The flowering of human society depends on two factors: the intellectual power of outstanding men to conceive sound social and economic theories, and the ability of these or other men to make these ideologies palatable to the majority."[24] This would become his life's work – and, in this regard, he was already a success.

Paul's defeat was offset by a happy announcement in 1977. Oldest daughter Lori Paul would soon marry Tom Pyeatt. Both Ron and Carol could soon look forward to an even larger family.

CHAPTER 11

IDEOLOGICAL LONER

1978-1980

Non-Governmental Organizations

The argument that the two parties should represent opposed ideals and policies, one, perhaps of the Right and the other of the Left, is a foolish idea acceptable only to the doctrinaire and academic thinkers. Instead the two parties should be almost identical, so the that American people can 'throw the rascals out' at any election without leading to any profound or extensive shifts in policy.

CARROLL QUIGLEY

R on Paul's heartrending photo-finish defeat in the election of 1976 led him back to his medical practice in Lake Jackson with Dr. Jack Pruett. In reality, he had never left the practice; taking only three months off to campaign for the special election earlier in 1976.

By January 1977 he was back at his lucrative practice full-time, and still not taking any federal dollars. The rejection of government money did not impair their financial success. According to Pruett, "we had a pretty busy practice, and a pretty lucrative practice."[1]

Due to the closeness of the previous electoral contest, Paul knew he must attempt to unseat Bob Gammage in the next election. The incumbent Democrat probably felt confident because Republican morale was still low following Nixon's resignation and he expected that the tradition of Democratic representatives in the district would continue.

In 1978, Paul was back on the campaign trail, working even harder than before. "He was a great politician," recalls Llewellyn Rockwell, Paul's Chief of Staff after the campaign. "He'd wear out three or four pairs of shoes walking neighborhoods."[2] And people were inclined to listen because "he has heavy content in everything he says. ... He's a great teacher. He's always seen his office as a bully pulpit."[3]

It didn't hurt that his medical practice had already won over most of the young families in the district. "I had real difficulty down in Brazoria County where he practiced," Gammage told National Public Radio, "because he delivered half the babies in the county. There were only two OB-GYNs in the county and the other one was his partner."[4]

The calm and polite doctor ran a tough and aggressive campaign, surprising his opponent. The campaign team knew it would be a close election. Two years earlier, he narrowly lost reelection to Gammage by 268 votes in the recount vote. This time, Paul's extra campaigning paid off. He won the 1978 rematch with Gammage by only a slightly wider margin – a mere 1,200 votes.[5]

....

Paul now had more time to assemble his congressional staff than his previous term. For his chief of staff, he hired 34 year old Lew Rockwell, a fellow student of Austrian Economics. Intensely rational, Rockwell had an uncanny ability to counter critics of the free market with a persuasive response backed up by a diverse set of historical examples. This ability won Rockwell the additional role of Paul's speechwriter.

Although he shared a similar belief system with Paul, the two men had contrasting personalities. Paul exhibited a gentlemanly grace when disagreeing with his opponents, whereas Rockwell could be harsh and dismissive. In Ron Paul's world there were no bad people, just sincere but misguided individuals. In Lew Rockwell's world, there were villains. He called those who benefit from the Federal Reserve "monsters" and labeled his opponents "fascists". The fire that kept his fight going had a different temperature from that of Ron Paul. His rhetoric clearly showed the outrage he felt towards the people who were, as he saw it, ruining a once great nation.

Despite a fierce demeanor, Rockwell occasionally revealed a poignant side, such as when discussing Fascism. He says, "It's militarism, it's belligerent nationalism, it's suppression of civil liberties, it's aggressive war, glorification of the nation state, demonization of the 'other' - that can be Jews or these days Muslims and Arabs. It's a very unfortunate tendency in the human heart."[6]

Congressman Paul's first full term focused primarily on three issues: his passionate opposition to the Monetary Control Act of 1980, a restoration of the gold standard and opposition to restoration of the military draft.

The life of a congressman is demanding, yet Paul continued to work part-time at his medical practice. "He was quite amazing in how much energy he had," Dr. Pruett recalls. "Out in Washington, they didn't believe in working on Fridays. Every Friday morning he'd hop on a plane and come home and see patients by Friday afternoon." If necessary he would work all day Saturday as well. "Bright and early Monday morning he'd get back on a plane to Washington." For Dr. Paul, medicine was his avocation as well as his vocation. "That was Ron's profession and I honestly believe that was what he wanted. He didn't want to be a politician."[7]

Paul lost no time after his election in aligning himself with like-minded men and women on both sides of the aisle in Congress. And perhaps it was no surprise that one of these friends was a fellow physician, the conservative Georgia Democrat Dr. Larry McDonald. The two physicians were outwardly much alike. Both were young, serving in Congress after a successful medical practice (McDonald was an urologist). They were also devotees of the Austrian School of economics whose policies included the preservation of national sovereignty and the dramatic reduction in the size and scope of the federal government.

McDonald was a top official in the militantly anti-communist John Birch Society, and eventually became the organization's president. Ron Paul frequented John Birch Society dinners as a speaker, and some of his congressional staff had been drawn from the ranks of professionals who had served at the Birch Society's headquarters in Belmont, Massachusetts. This included Llewellyn Rockwell, who had briefly worked in Belmont, as well as Legislative Assistant John W. Robbins.

"They were very good friends," recalled Rockwell of the two doctors. "They both had the same view of medicine and how government was an intrusion in it."[8] Paul and McDonald, along with two other Texas congressmen (Democrat Marvin Leath and Republican John M. Collins), voted against compensating Iranian embassy hostages on December 18, 1979. The two doctors stood virtually alone in the lopsided 369-4 vote, arguing that the mere fact that the hostages had gone through hardship did not earn them the right to pick the taxpayers' pocketbooks. Paul told the *Philadelphia Inquirer* that McDonald had been the most conservative congressman in the House and "he was the most principled, too."[9]

But Paul and McDonald had their differences as well, Rockwell stressed. "They were allied on domestic affairs, but, of course, not allies on military policy."[10]

McDonald was strongly anti-communist. Ironically, a journey later in his career to speak out against communism would result in a dramatic and untimely end to his congressional career.

But before that event would occur, the conservative Southern Democrat recoiled at the restrictions put upon the intelligence establishment in the wake of the Senate's Church Committee hearings in the mid-1970s. Ron Paul took a skeptical view toward intelligence bureaucracies and instead put a premium on personal privacy. And McDonald supported a restoration of the military draft along the lines of the Swiss model, arguing that "The all-volunteer military force is an alternative to a draft, but it is an expensive way to go … [T]here are serious questions as to whether a paycheck is an adequate substitute for patriotic fervor."[11]

In January 1979, at the time Paul returned to Congress, the military draft was no distant memory. It had been repealed less than six years earlier at the close of the Vietnam conflict, having been a political fixture for decades before that. Democratic leaders began campaigning to bring back the draft in order to avoid being painted as soft on communism.

Paul quickly took up the issue as many of his colleagues sought to force a return of conscription. Many – like McDonald – employed Cold War arguments that the quality or costs of the military in an all-volunteer force would endanger national security, or that youth owe their country some kind of service. "If a nation is free and morally and spiritually strong, the people will provide an adequate military for national defense," Paul countered in his

April 1979 testimony before the Committee on Armed Services. "A draft will not substitute for, nor create, a morally and spiritually strong nation. Force cannot overcome apathy."[12] Paul pointed out that a draft is only necessary for an aggressive military, adding that early in US history when the nation had been invaded, the Republic had more than enough volunteers to repel the invaders. Only in non-defensive wars was a draft necessary.

But Paul reserved his strongest criticisms for the argument that youth owed their government service, as conservatives sometimes argued. Paul pointed out that conservatives who made this argument morally disarmed themselves for liberal assaults on their wallet, saying, "The assumption is that the young, age 17 to 24, owe a segment of their lives to their country. This assumption is based upon the supposition that rights come from the state and are not natural. It also assumes that life itself is a privilege and not something that we are absolutely entitled to. ... Once this is granted, the conservatives have no defense against the liberal notion that the more productive have an obligation and therefore must be compelled to care for those who won't work or can't work."[13]

As always, at the bottom of Ron Paul's argument was the Constitution. "Our Constitution prohibits involuntary servitude and the Declaration of Independence has declared to all mankind that we are endowed by our Creator with the inalienable rights of life and liberty. With this heritage, the draft and compulsory national service are unacceptable."[14] Paul declared the draft "a form of slavery and "a waste of money" in a front page *Washington Post* story.[15]

"He worked closely with Pat Schroeder (D-Colo.) and David Stockman (R-Mich.)," to fight a restoration of the draft, Rockwell explained. "They were the three key people."[16] The alliance worked, despite the fact that Pat Schroeder was one of the most liberal members of the House and Stockman an old-style moderate Republican (though he had styled himself part of the *New Right*). Facing highly public, vocal opposition from this ideological mishmash of liberal Democrats, moderate Republicans and the "right-winger" Paul, the Democratic-controlled Congress dropped the measure.

Despite differences with McDonald on the draft and the intelligence establishment, the two doctors often co-sponsored many of each other's bills, thereby gaining instant bipartisanship for their respective legislation. Paul regularly co-sponsored McDonald's legislation to get the US out of the United Nations.

Both men had always been dogged opponents of international governmental banking institutions. Foremost among these institutions was the International Monetary Fund (IMF), established in 1944. The other was the World Bank, organized in 1945. Both institutions were UN backed creatures of the Breton Woods agreement. Although the descriptions of these institutions sound benign, they were planners that sought to intervene in free markets.

Paul argued in congress that "our sovereignty is being attacked in many ways; one by United States membership in the United Nations. Today we have, of course, the IMF and the World Bank that we have been involved in a long time, and just recently we had joined the World Trade Organization, which is another international government agency and government body that usurps our rights and our privileges and interferes in our legislative process, especially in the area of environmentalism and labor law."[17]

His arguments against globalist institutions included his sincere belief that they were contributing to economic misery. But his most essential objection was that Congress did not have the authority to delegate away national sovereignty through treaty provisions of the Constitution. "Our Constitution does not give us the authority to sell our sovereignty to an international government body, and even under the treaty provisions of the Constitution it is not permissible. The treaty provision does not allow us, for example, to undermine the Bill of Rights."[18]

Paul showed no fear of congressional leaders or powerful establishment figures during his first full term in Congress. Other politicians routinely traveled to congressional junkets abroad, which they called "fact-finding" missions. Asked by the *Washington Post* what he thought of these junkets, Paul didn't hesitate to call it a waste of money. "That's what we have ambassadors for," he told the *Post*.[19]

Likewise, Paul wasn't afraid to oppose the powerful role of private political and financial networks that lobbied to establish international military and economic interventionist policies. The most prominent private organization in place in 1979 was the Council on Foreign Relations (CFR), a 2,000 member US-based foreign policy organization founded in 1922.

At the time, David Rockefeller was the chairman of the CFR, serving in that role from 1970 until 1985. Not content with merely influencing US politics, he spun off the Trilateral Commission in 1973. This organization would attempt to influence politics in not only North America, but Europe and Asia. The Trilateral Commission at the time counted approximately 75 members each from the three regions.

Both organizations had open memberships and mostly open meetings, and styled themselves as study groups organized to form recommendations for government leaders. But the recommendations were inevitably for greater military interventionism, greater economic interventionism, and greater control by global organizations under the United Nations orbit.

The Council on Foreign Relations, despite its miniscule membership roster, had dominated the executive branch of the US government for more than a generation.

In 1979, CFR members were counted among:

- Seven of the nine most recent Secretaries of the Treasury
- Eight of the nine most recent Secretaries of Defense
- Eight of the nine most recent Secretaries of State
- All of the nine most recent National Security Directors
- Eight of the nine most recent CIA Directors

In addition, the Council on Foreign Relations claimed top officials of the Carter Administration as members: President Carter, Vice President Mondale, the Secretaries of State, Treasury, and Defense – and the overwhelming majority of the undersecretary and prominent ambassadorial positions at the State Department.[20]

Likewise, the Trilateral Commission membership roster was a mix of top business leaders and the elite of the Carter Administration: President Carter, Vice President Mondale, National Security Advisor Zbigniew Brzezinski, Secretary of State Cyrus Vance, Treasury Secretary W. Michael Blumenthal, Secretary of Defense Harold Brown and Federal Reserve Chairman Paul

Volker.

As congressman, Paul opposed almost every initiative out of the New York City headquarters of these two organizations. But he focused upon the impact of their policy recommendations, rather than engaging in name-calling and ad hominem-style arguments. "The power structure, basically, is made up of a lot of very powerful business and corporate leaders in the country," he later explained. "They have formed their own organizations. They've been around for a good while. They don't even hide it any more, the Trilateral Commission as well as the Council on Foreign Relations. No matter which party is in power, they will appoint to the major offices members of these two committees. And they always have control of the Federal Reserve System."[21]

In the latter remark, Paul was referring to the Federal Reserve Chairmen. Both Alan Greenspan and Paul Volker were founding members of the Trilateral Commission and later became heads of the Federal Reserve. Rather than broadening ideas, as think-tanks do, these groups effectively put more control into the hands of an elite group of establishment figures.

"He was always explicitly against the CFR and the Trilateral Commission," Rockwell explained.[22] Sticking to policy kept Ron Paul's legislative agenda grounded.

....

Government is often accused of "the left hand not knowing what the right hand is doing." No where was this more evident in 1980 than the Export-Import Bank of the United States. Known as the Ex-Im Bank, it was established in 1934 by an executive order from Franklin Roosevelt as part of his New Deal plan. The purpose of the Ex-Im bank was to finance and insure foreign purchases of US goods for customers unable or unwilling to accept credit risk, all in the name of increasing US exports.

Decades later, Paul noticed the Ex-Im bank was actually helping the United States' cold war opponent. He wrote to President Reagan, "Through the Ex-Im Bank, we are right now financing Yugoslavia's purchase and development of advanced telecommunications systems, computers, sophisticated aircraft, even nuclear power plants—all of which could conceivably be used for military purposes. This policy is suicidal and must be stopped."[23]

Paul accepted the argument of the followers of the Austrian School of economics that a regulated, centrally controlled economy was not sustainable. Without US taxpayer support, he argued, the Soviet bloc would collapse economically.

....

Ron Paul's consistent votes on principle and his refusal to be carried away with partisan bickering and name-calling led to a strange paradox. He was personally popular with the other congressmen, especially during congressional softball games where he was one of the stars. "He could have been a professional baseball player if he had not had a knee injury," Rockwell says. But Paul had few political allies in Washington. "He was friendly with everyone," Rockwell explained. "But he was ideologically a loner."[24]

He was an ideological loner because Paul criticized the actions of those in his own Republican Party as stiffly as those of the Democrats. He criticized President Nixon's wage and price controls as fervently as President Carter's profligate spending policies.

Opposition to global governing institutions and strict adherence to

American national sovereignty were key staples of Ron Paul's addresses. The only kinds of internationalism he favored were free trade and the actions of governments across the globe independently – and without coercion.

Ron Paul and Larry McDonald continued their friendship for most of two terms. They agreed with one another enough to help each other in congress, yet their disagreements provided for lively conversations. Unfortunately their friendship was cut tragically short.

Both McDonald and Senator Jesse Helms were invited to South Korea for the 30th anniversary of the *Mutual Defense Treaty*. McDonald missed one of his connecting flights due to poor weather and instead booked a flight aboard Korean Airlines Flight 007. During the flight, the Korean pilot went off course into Soviet Airspace and was subsequently shot down by a Soviet MIG, killing all 240 passengers and 29 crew, including McDonald.

Although many criticized the over-reaction by the Soviets, Paul pointed out the broader picture of the tragedy, observing that the United States Ex-Im Bank had provided funds that could have conceivably been used to build the MIG that shot down the airliner. He wrote to President Reagan, "The Soviet bloc already owes the West $100 billion; that has purchased many MIG-23s and SU-15s."[25]

Larry McDonald was well known for introducing bills that opposed the United Nations. After his death, Paul carried on his fight. He even introduced his own bill, The American Sovereignty Restoration Act (HR 1146) to withdraw the US from the United Nations.[26] Even in his later years in congress, Paul bi-annually introduced HR 1146, which would terminate the nation's UN membership and invalidate all UN diplomats' immunity.

And Paul later introduced HR 3090 in January of 1998, which would have ended US membership in the IMF. He also sponsored bills to withdraw from UNESCO (an agency of the UN) and to invalidate the International Criminal Court.[27] Through these actions, Paul carried on Larry McDonald's legacy by fighting for issues important to his Democratic colleague.

CHAPTER 12

GOLDEN YEARS

1980-1984

Gold Standard

I am an Enemy to all banks discounting bills or notes for anything but Coin.

Thomas Jefferson

The early 1980s were a golden age for Ron Paul; not in the conventional sense but instead a description of his devoted campaign to resurrect gold as a monetary form of exchange. The first steps towards this goal began with a close race for Ron's congressional seat.

Paul's congressional opponent was Democrat Mike Andrews, a former assistant District Attorney for Harris County. Beyond his public sector credentials, Andrews had experience working for a private law firm in the Houston area. His campaign came armed with an established reputation and a war chest dwarfing Paul's funds.

Congressman Paul's previous election had been tight and certain incumbency was far from established at this point. Many analysts still viewed Paul as a flash in the pan; a short respite from the Democratic Party's long held dominance of the 22nd district. This election would decide whether the Democrats could once again reign supreme in the region. The alternative was to acknowledge a deep-rooted shift in the district's politics.

Andrews's funding was easily $100,000 more than Ron Paul's.[1] His familiarity with the Houston area threatened Paul, who generally garnered the majority of his support from the southern parts of the district. Despite these electoral obstacles, Paul gave a strong challenge.

In third place was Vaudie Nance, an insignificant independent registering a thousand votes. Paul held 51.04% of the vote while his challenger clutched an impressive 48.31%. Separating Ron and defeat were only 5,704 votes.[2] He had maintained his Congressional seat by yet another slim margin.

This victory allowed him to make a strong defense for gold in Congress. His opponent too would eventually continue a fruitful political career in a neighboring district. Mike Andrews went on to win the 1982 House of Representatives seat for the 25th Texas district in the nearby Austin area. Here, Andrews would represent the district for a dozen years until 1995, finally ending his role in politics after a failed Senate seat attempt.

In 1981, sweetening Ron's victory was the birth of Matthew, his first grandchild from his oldest daughter Lori and husband, Tom Pyeatt. Little did Ron Paul know that Matt would be the first of seventeen grandchildren.

For Paul, it seemed like a good year to be a Republican when Ronald Reagan's election shook the political arena to its core. Reagan and Paul were political allies who helped each other early in their respective careers. Placing such an important friend in the White House opened a window of opportunity for bold new actions. Reagan would soon demonstrate that he had the political will to dramatically alter the course of America. His strength was exhibited early in his presidency when the PATCO union (Professional Air Traffic Controllers Organization) organized a nation-wide strike.

PATCO had uncharacteristically backed Reagan, the Republican candidate, for the 1980 election. Despite their support, the president used federal authority to break the strike and fire 11,000 workers unwilling to return to their government-monopoly jobs, which were unfortunately necessary for the national economy. Few men in history have had the political clout to turn against their own constituents, especially powerful unions. Reagan had demonstrated a strong determination to change how things were done in Washington.

....

With Reagan in office it seemed like change was possible, and returning to gold currency seemed within reach. Since Nixon's 1971 decision, the US dollar had been completely floated on the confidence in the United States government and economy. The last ties with gold and the dollar were severed. After abandoning all traces of gold, the US experienced a decade of stagflation; increasing inflation accompanied by rising unemployment. Unprecedented financial performance of precious commodities on the stock market reinforced the gold movement. On January 21st 1980, gold would hit a peak of $850 and would not reach the same nominal state until January 3rd, 2008. With these unusual and disconcerting market conditions, the climate was ripe for drastic change.

Ron Paul was one of the only politicians who understood the damage caused by inflationary policy. In a timely quote, Paul said, "Interventionist economists carelessly criticize the spreading of economic growth through a free-market society as the 'trickle-down theory.' But inflation, by trickling, then rushing through society, spreads economic misery among the poor, working, and middle classes, while enriching the special interests. It is this 'trickling-down' that deserves condemnation from everyone concerned about poverty."[3]

Even the Treasury held reservations about a free floating dollar unfettered by gold. Treasury Under-Secretary Solomon admitted to Congress, "Gold remains a significant part of the reserves of central banks available in times of need. This is unlikely to change in the foreseeable future."[4] This position seemed inherently contradictory; if paper money was truly an elite monetary medium, there should have been no need for the central banks to store gold reserves in "times of need".

Ron Paul, through the help of his non-profit organization, FREE (Foundation for Rational Economics and Education, Inc.), began organizing dinners in order to foster an educated and informed political body on the topic of gold. The dinners invited presidential aides and administrative officials in hopes of growing support for the gold movement.[5] Aiding this goal was Ron Paul's *Freedom Report* published and distributed by FREE.

With the intention of assisting gold legislation, FREE published Congressman Paul's book, <u>Gold, Peace, and Prosperity</u>. This short text summarized the history and problems associated with fiat money and offered as a solution a 100% gold-backed dollar.

Among the oft quoted economists in the book was Dr. Murray Rothbard, who wrote the introduction to the book. Renowned economic commentator and journalist, Henry Hazlitt, added the preface. Despite Paul only briefly discussing economic issues, Rothbard in his contributed introduction to the book describes Paul's knowledge with a single sentence: "His economics is as sound as a bell."[6]

The elevated price of gold, threatening inflation, and the building momentum of FREE's efforts facilitated the beginnings of serious debate in Congress regarding the future of the precious metal. The movement had recent legislative successes. In October 1977, Senator Jesse Helms of North Carolina managed to pass a bill permitting gold clauses in private contracts. During the push for the Gold Commission, Helms was an invaluable ally for Ron. Both men were strong believers in the free market. After all, the Council for a Competitive Economy identified Paul as having the highest percentage of votes for free economic competition in the House of Representatives at 91%. Helms similarly ranked in the top among Senators. Those against free market principles found themselves on the low end of the list, such as Chris Dodd with 16%. He would unfortunately become a fellow member of the Gold Commission, and a difficult obstacle for Paul to overcome.[7]

The pro-gold team defined itself in a hearing on October 2, 1980 called the *Subcommittee on Mines and Mining of the Committee of Interior and Insular Affairs of the House on Feasibility of a Return to the Gold Standard.* From the beginning, the division between Helms's version of the gold standard and Paul's would become apparent.

Helms believed gold should be linked to the dollar but not necessarily represent a certain weight of gold. Through this method, the Federal Reserve would attempt to fix the number of dollars to a certain ratio of gold subject to legislative change. This gold dollar version describes the pre-1971 era and most unfortunately the Great Depression gold standard. The central idea was to attach a small amount of gold to the dollar acting as a ball and chain, impeding rapid monetary expansion.

Helms' standard backed the dollar by an arbitrary amount of gold; say 10%. If the Federal Reserve decided to expand the money supply by printing additional money, it would have to acquire $1 of gold for every $10 of currency printed. This differed from Paul's view.

Paul felt the dollar should once again become a permanent word for a measurement of gold. For example, quoting a price at $15 dollars would be exactly identical to listing the price at 30 grams of gold. A dollar of gold in this fictitious example would be equivalent to 2 grams of the precious metal, unchangeable by any governmental authority. The government could not alter the definition of the dollar anymore than it could make citizens believe pounds and kilograms were the same.

The ratio in Helms's case could be subject to government adjustments, as was the case throughout the history of the gold standard. Debasement was all too possible. Murray Rothbard best sums Paul's position by stating, "The only genuine solution to the evil of inflation, then, is to separate money from the State, to make money once again a market commodity instead of a fiat ticket issued by the central government. ... The dollar must once again be simply a name for a unit of weight of gold coin."[8]

Lew Rockwell explains Ron's vision of a pure gold standard. "He thinks there were flaws with the previous gold standard, as indeed there were, but thanks to the work of Mises, Rothbard, Hazlitt and other great Austrian economists we know much more about the proper structure of a monetary system than we did in those days. He's mainly interested in something that can't be printed up at will by the government."[9]

One criticism of changing back to a gold standard is that it would disrupt the prior economy. However, Rockwell sees this as a good thing. "Well it would certainly be disruptive to the people who are ripping us off," he says. "All the big banks, the military industrial complex, and the government itself all do very well from the system. The rest of us don't do so well. It would be disruptive to some people but it would be the basis for a lasting prosperity and freedom for the rest of us."[10]

The same critics of returning to the gold standard were hardly as skeptical of disruptions that occurred upon leaving the standard in the early 1970s. Nixon's abandonment of the gold standard led to wild currency exchange variability on the world market accompanied by a decade of double digit inflation. The rollercoaster ride ended only after radically raising interest rates in the early 1980s, which caused a sudden and severe recession.

Paul's views were backed by the Austrian school of economics while Helms' were backed by mainstream neoclassical economists such as Arthur Laffer (who testified for the Gold Commission) and Robert Mundell, an accomplished academic. The problems of this disunity would become apparent as the commission rolled onward.

....

On October 7th 1980, an Act of Congress formed the Gold Commission in order to explore and study the role of gold in domestic and international monetary systems.[11] The Gold Commission was made possible by the efforts of Jesse Helms. Due to a delay caused by the Treasury Secretary, the Gold Commission appointees' names were not announced until nine months later on June 22nd, 1981.

In the intervening months, Ron Paul made his position clear by introducing some gold legislation of his own. "I think standardization of our monetary system – and perhaps the world monetary system, if the world were to emulate our practice – would remove any speculative premium that the Soviet Union and South Africa presently receive," he testified to the Committee on

Interior and Insular Affairs shortly before the 1980 election. "We would see a stabilization of the world price of gold and an end to inflation throughout the world."[12] To this end, Paul introduced HR 7874 in February, 1981, which would have returned the United States to a true gold standard.[13]

"Ron was on the Banking Committee, which was the key focus then," Rockwell stressed. A key part of that focus was stopping The Monetary Control Act of 1980, which would allow the government to print more dollars in order to pay for over-expenditures; a process known as 'monetizing debt.' This threatened to continue the inflation that had spiked during the Ford and Carter administrations.

"Ron Paul was the only man in public life battling the Monetary Control Act," Rockwell explains. "Ron was very prescient. He predicted that it would create massive inflation."[14] Predictably the bill failed to pass, and the value of the dollar did indeed continue to slide downward.

Other actions in congress also gained him attention. Although Paul would later earn an undeserved anti-Israel reputation for his opposition to foreign aid, in 1981 he was one of the few congressmen who stood up for Israel. When Israel bombed Iraq's Osirak nuclear plant, Paul defended their right to the action while Reagan and the UN opposed it.[15]

When June 22 finally arrived, the commission was mandated to finalize a report and make recommendations to Congress by March 1982. It was time to appoint members to the Gold Commission.[16]

During this time, Paul was a member of the House Committee on Banking and naturally assumed an available slot. Paul's excitement for the commission was based on the Banking Committee's resistance to discussing issues of monetary reform. Paul said at the time, "The House Banking Committee has been extremely reluctant to hold any hearings on this topic ... to repeal the privilege of banks to create money."[17]

The last four seats of the sixteen-person committee went to academics and private businessmen. Among the businessmen were gold dealer Herbert Coyne and former Rite-Aid corporation president Lewis Lehrman. The academics consisted of Arthur Costamangna, an economist and former chair of the CEA, and Anna Schwartz, an extremely knowledgeable economist best known for co-authoring A Monetary History of the United States with Nobel Prize winner Milton Friedman.

To many outside observers, the selection process appeared suspect. A pair of writers for The Washington Post wrote about the commission's biases in their article "Enemies of Gold." Quoting a high ranking administration official, the writers noticed "that this commission won't cause any trouble." The journalists clarified the situation by observing, "No chances were taken. Out of the 16 commission members, only two favor a gold standard-Rep. Paul and Lewis Lehrman."[18]

The first glimmers of hope for a balanced discussion fell apart early on. As The Washington Post noted, "The attention the Gold Commission is attracting, in the view of economist Alan Greenspan, 'has a lot to do with things other than gold.' Greenspan thinks that the commission will stimulate 'a dialogue showing general dissatisfaction on the way the whole financial system is working.'"[19] Unfortunately, a stimulating dialogue failed to materialize due to the heavily anti-gold appointees.

The chosen congressmen were hardly amicable to Paul's views, and the

Democratic members were particularly antagonistic towards a gold standard: Stephen Neal (North Carolina), Chris Dodd (Connecticut), and Henry Reuss (Wisconsin). Although Dodd was one of the most anti-competitive voting members in Congress, the real threat was Henry Reuss.

Congressman Paul called Reuss "the most anti-gold person in Washington."[20] Demonstrating his distaste for the glittering commodity, Reuss behaved childishly during Gold Commission meetings. The Wall Street Journal reported his behavior by printing, "The meeting began with Rep. Henry Reuss, a vocal opponent of the gold standard, crumpling a copy of Hard Money News, a pro-gold newsletter, and throwing it on the floor. The Wisconsin Democrat said he objected to the newsletter characterizing Federal Reserve Chairman Paul Volcker as 'a proven liar every time he opens his mouth.'"[21]

The decision to include three Federal Reserve governors was particularly troubling to Paul because it was effectively like allowing bank robbers to juror their own trial. Their preset animosity was displayed throughout the process, especially by Emmett Rice and Henry Wallich.

Emmett Rice revealed to the commission that he "believes issue of rules vs. discretion is subject for another commission. The commission should not make recommendations on monetary rule or how to run the current system."[22]

Anna Schwartz, recognizing Wallich's prejudices, notes, "Their primary concern was to limit discussion touching on the performance of the Federal Reserve. Governor Wallich argued at the first meeting that the subjects of inflation and monetary policy were not a proper concern of the Commission."[23]

According to the Federal Reserve governors, the Gold Commission created to study the role of gold in domestic and international monetary systems should not discuss inflation, Federal Reserve rules, or monetary policy. Although there were no official guidelines of narrow macroeconomic topics, the Federal Reserve participants desired to avoid all critical debate of the Reserve's performance.

Schwartz herself was not supportive of Paul's cause either. In her Reflections on the Gold Commission Report, Schwartz summarized Paul's views as purely a belief in the Constitution, brushing aside his other objections. Dr. Schwartz wrote, "They are obviously constructed from libertarian principles and a belief in the superiority of commodity money."[24] Contradicting her statement in the same article, she admitted Paul's "case for the gold standard is based on historical, theoretical, economic, and moral grounds."[25] Further, Schwartz compliments Paul's work by praising a "generally high level of scholarship, on US money and banking history in the nineteenth and twentieth centuries."[26] This was true praise from the economist who wrote A Monetary History of the United States, a near Biblical tome for professional economists.

The few gold standard supporters on the committee weren't particularly helpful to Ron's cause. Both, Lewis Lehrman and Arthur Costamagna believed in a gold standard melding the dollar to a fixed exchange ratio to gold, despite the fact that a similar fixed exchange rate managed by the Federal Reserve led to the deepening of the Great Depression.[27]

Paul's ultimate goal was the Gold Standard alone, without the Federal Reserve fixed exchange ratio. The Federal Reserve without gold is certainly a bad option. But Paul knew the Federal Reserve existing parallel to the Gold Standard was about the worst combination possible. This focus on an obviously flawed version of the Gold Standard allowed the opposition to concentrate on others' erroneous views instead of acknowledging Paul's separate version of gold money.

Although Paul, Lehrman, and Costamagna did not agree on their respective visions of the gold standard, they formed an alliance of sorts. This alliance was largely based on their agreement to a secondary aspect of the Gold Commission: introducing an American investment grade coin to compete with the extremely popular South African Krugerrand. The creation of an American gold coin was generally favored by the entire Commission but most feverishly promoted by the gold alliance.

During the commission, some members claimed not to understand the difference between Lehrman's gold standard views and Paul's,[28] which was surprising considering the high level of economic literacy on the panel. Noticing the disagreements, President Reagan revealed to reporters that, "they can't even agree on historical facts."[29]

Unfortunately, Reagan's support for gold was lukewarm. While campaigning earlier, Reagan had supported a gold standard, but since the presidential election, his rhetoric on gold died down to practical silence. He still supported the gold standard in private, but refused to speak out in public. During a 10-minute helicopter trip from the White House, Ron Paul managed to intercept Reagan to update him on the Gold Commission's situation. Reagan was surprised by Paul's revelation of hostility amongst the group. He told Ron that he still supported the Gold Standard and still hoped for a favorable outcome.[30]

Anna Schwartz speculated that if Reagan openly and boldly made a stance on gold, the votes in the commission could have gone quite differently. All four Republicans would submit to his backing as well as his economic advisors. Further, three of the four private citizens could have been convinced by such authority. Without the president's approval, no one wanted to align themselves with the underdog, Ron Paul.

After nine meetings, with 23 witnesses testifying before the panel, the Gold Commission finally voted 15 to 2 against the recommendation to allow dollars to be convertible into gold. Favorably, 12 to 3 voted recommending the minting of a new gold coin from the Treasury surplus. One of the three opposed to this move was Henry Reuss detesting every possible aspect of gold.[31]

On March 31, 1982, the Gold Commission issued two reports: the majority report and the minority report of Costamagna, Lehrman, and Paul. The minority report was surprisingly large, considering only three members endorsed the text. Endorsement does not necessarily mean direct support, however; the greater part was penned by Paul and represents his view on gold; not Lehrman's nor Costamagna's. Their acknowledgement was more a representation of solidarity in the greater struggle to promote gold than a true meeting of minds.

....

With the Gold Commission closed, Ron looked to reelection for his third term in 1982. His previous opponent had left for the 25th district, leaving the 22nd uncontested. Ron's District was the only Texas congressional seat without opposition, including independent, libertarian, or socialist candidates. The official election records show 943 opposing write-in votes and 66,536 votes supporting Ron.[32] It was clear Paul had finally solidified his position in congress.

By his third term, Ron had earned a reputation as a politician who could not be influenced. His perceived stubbornness was noticed as high as the presidency. "Some people hate Ron Paul because he can't be bought," begins Lew Rockwell. "I remember working for him in Washington one night late in the office when Reagan called him. ... This time he was putting unbelievable pressure on Ron to vote for some horrible new bomber. Ron wouldn't do it. They all eventually learned that his arm is un-twistable."[33]

The Gold Commission managed to create some beneficial results. Media attention to gold monetary issues prior to the commission was nonexistent, but the meetings reawakened serious academic debate. This wasn't merely a discussion amongst Austrian economists; it challenged politically diverse mainstream views of Robert Hall, Anna Schwartz, Robert Mundell, and Arthur Laffer.

The commission's recommendation for a gold coin resulted in bills HR 1662 and 1663, along with the Senate S 42, producing American Gold Eagles, one of the world's most respected investment grade coins. Ron Paul published The Case for Gold in 1982, with the assistance of John Robbins, Christopher Weber, and Murray Rothbard.

The book consists of the minority report with extra additions contributed by his three associates. The Case for Gold was first published by the Cato Institute in 1982. In 1983, Ron would publish Ten Myths About Paper Money, dealing with common misconceptions on the issue. The book demonstrates Ron's true determination to keep fighting, publishing, and staying hopeful for the future despite his recent failures with the Gold Commission.

Paul continued to actively follow developments concerning the Federal Reserve and the Treasury. He spoke at various organizational meetings, publicizing events such as the purchase of faster printing presses. Among these monetary topics, he discussed the addition of pink and blue colors to US bills as a security feature against counterfeiting.[34] The Congressional plan met the same fate as the gold standard, demonstrating the problem of inertia in Washington. Decades later, Americans had pink and blue currency. Maybe one day America will settle for a single color: gold.

CHAPTER 13

RUNNING FOR SENATE

1983-1985

The War on Drugs

Government exists to protect us from each other. Where government has gone beyond its limits is in deciding to protect us from ourselves.

RONALD REAGAN

After some initial disappointment with the Reagan administration, Ron Paul decided to raise his profile in politics. The next logical step was the Senate. If successful, instead of being one of 435 congressmen, he would be one of 100. Each state has two senators while Representatives are proportionally based on population. Senators hold their seats for six-year terms compared to two years for congressmen. It would be an ideal push for the message of freedom.

In 1984, senator John Tower, a 22 year veteran of the Senate, decided to retire due to being "fed up" with a "multi-layered bureaucracy"[1] in Washington. In his time, John Tower had achieved an extremely difficult feat by becoming the first Texan Republican Senator in the 20th century. The seat Tower acquired was none other than Lyndon B. Johnson's.

But once again, there seemed a strong chance that the Democrats might regain their dynasty controlling both Texas Senate seats. Tower's previous race was a close call, winning with only 12,000 votes; a 0.3% lead. The razor-thin victory made the challenge for his seat a free for all. Both Democrats and Republicans had equal opportunity to capture the position.

Ron Paul found himself in a similar predicament to Mr. Tower. He felt a great distaste towards legislative affairs at the time. As an elected House representative, Paul felt unable to alter the country's course of increasing debt and constant interventionism.

In a narrowly divided Senate, however, this new position could offer Paul the power to make a difference. The Senate split was 55 votes for the Republicans and 45 to the Democrats. Several Republican seats were viewed as uncertain in the 1984 election while the Democrats felt comfortable in holding their positions.[2]

Any vote that doesn't follow party lines in the Senate has the possibility of acting as a tie breaker in the process. An independent thinker in a 50/50 Senate split would almost have presidential veto power regarding any bill passing through. Few politicians are bold enough to vote against their party. Even fewer will do so when their vote will change the course of legislation. However, Ron Paul was a different breed of politician. His principled dedication to free market ideas instead of popular trends in party lines could reverse the direction in Washington.

With the chance to make a significant difference in politics, Paul jumped into the race ahead of his adversaries, who joined him soon after.

The Republican contenders facing Paul in the primary were Robert Mosbacher Jr., a Texas oil man with little political experience, Henry Grover, an uninspiring politician with absolute allegiance to Ronald Reagan, and Phil Gramm, a Texas representative and economist.

Gramm had recently caused a stir. Formerly a Democrat, he favored Reagan's economic policies and sided with the administration even to the point of divulging secrets from the Democrat Budget Committee. Using a rarely executed option, the Democrats removed Gramm from his position on the budget committee. Encountering hostility from his party, Gramm infamously switched sides. As a new Republican, he was re-elected to the House of Representatives with a special election and was now eyeing bigger prizes in the Senate.

Gramm's political stance could be seen as a harbinger of things to come in the Republican Party. As the neoconservative movement later grew, the lines between liberals and conservatives in the two-party sense became blurred (Gramm would later become one of John McCain's economic advisors during the 2008 presidential campaign). The list of characters in the neoconservative movement is a list of who's who on Gramm's 1984 campaign bandwagon. Among them were Karl Rove and Paul Weywich, CEO of the Free Congress Research Education Foundation.

On the Democratic side were far left wing Lloyd Doggett, former congressman Bob Krueger (who was said to have never stopped campaigning since his defeat in the previous election) and Kent Hance.

Hance was known as a *boll weevil*; a Texan breed of conservative Democrats who at times are remarkably similar to Republicans. The element of the boll weevil played a crucial part in Texas politics. Among this classification without a doubt were Kent Hance and Phil Gramm. In fact, some had labeled Gramm a super weevil considering that he was so Republican leaning as to actually defect. The weevils' views could be conservative covering issues from spending/taxation to immigration/social policy.

The Democratic race was evenly matched among the three. For this reason, it was difficult for Republican candidates to focus on any one opponent from the Democratic side. This led the Republican primaries to largely focus on their own candidates instead of comparing conservative candidates to liberal counterparts.

Paul's views differed vastly from his opponents. He was against practically all government intervention, especially with regard to foreign policy. Referring to South American interventionism, Paul openly made his stance during a debate with the other contenders by stating, "We don't interfere, we don't meddle, we don't send the CIA out to murder people."[3] During the race, the US still had troops in Lebanon and was actively retaliating against Hezbollah for the 1983 Beirut bombing of the international forces barracks leading to the deaths of 241 American servicemen.

In a climate favorable to broad interventionism, Paul's campaign attacked Gramm on foreign policy. He ran a television ad proclaiming, "Vote for Gramm and keeping the marines in Lebanon indefinitely or vote for Paul and bringing them home."[4] His opponent criticized Paul for not standing with President Reagan on this issue. With a bit of circumstantial irony, only eight days later on February 7th 1984, President Reagan announced that the US would begin to withdraw troops from Lebanon.

....

During the 1980s, Ron Paul had a different reputation compared to his later political career, when his credibility as a Republican fell into question. In the 1984 election, Paul was said to be "ultra-conservative"[5], "a Republican whose conservatism is so extreme"[6], and "a far-right wing politician who breathes fire against government regulation of anything."[7] The National Taxpayers Union acknowledged Ron as the "most ardent anti-spender in Congress."[8] In 1984, his opponent Gramm was the one whose conservative credentials were in question. The race was viewed as a struggle between competing branches of conservatism.

Only the *New York Times* didn't see it that way, writing, "Representative Paul" is "a gynecologist who is essentially a libertarian in Republican clothing."[9] These quotes show the different attitude of politics at the time. Old right Barry Goldwater principles were not some distant and strange political philosophy but instead a subset of conservatism as part of the greater whole. Perhaps it was not noticeable at the time, but a radical shift was occurring.

Texas electoral rules added even more pressure to the race. No candidate could be in two races on the same Texas ballot. In order to run for Senate, both Ron Paul and Phil Gramm had to abandon their chances of re-election in the House of Representatives. For Ron Paul, the decision could not be taken lightly.

This system caused tumult throughout the state's entire political structure. Representatives strive for the Senate, state legislators clamor to become representatives, councilman attempt to become elected legislators, and those on educational boards grab a tiny bit of power as councilman. The forfeiture of his position by John Tower created shock and unexpected upheaval all along the political ladder. Because of these rules, a candidate could not enter a race without weighing the consequences. Those with the most name recognition, such as Paul and Gramm, had the most to lose.

Ron Paul didn't hold back his views in the election. He expressed them unapologetically at debates, while Gramm even avoided attending the debates.[10] Reagan at the time was in full support of the Nicaraguan Contras, as well as giving military aide to countries in the region such as El Salvador and funding South American countries to combat drugs. It was politically dangerous to oppose these views for a Republican in 1984, but that's exactly what Ron Paul did.

First Lady Nancy Reagan took on illicit drug abuse with an awareness campaign under the slogan "Just say no". The slogan caught on and spread like wildfire, making her program one of the most publicized awareness campaigns ever. Ron Paul agreed with her philosophy, as he too recognized illicit drug use by young people as potentially harmful, but he disagreed about the means to achieving those ends.

Just Say No would have been fine with the majority of libertarians. After all, voluntary choice is the unifying idea of the freedom philosophy. The Reagan administration, however, thought differently. They used the heavy hand of government and the full force of criminal laws to coerce the public to say no, resulting in tens of thousands of arguably victimless offenders being thrown into prison.

By 1984, the drug war was in full swing, both at home and abroad. Yet Congressman Paul remained steadfast in his ideals.

The libertarian case for drug legalization, while extreme in appearance, is quite basic in the particulars. Drug use - that is, the temporary euphoria one experiences while under a drug's influence - does not cause the majority of drug-related crimes. Instead, the artificially inflated, black market price of illegal substances causes the problems. Prices are set by supply and demand. When the government bans drugs, arrests traffickers, and burns drug farms in Columbia, the supply is greatly reduced. With fewer drugs available on the market, users must pay higher prices.

Addicts struggling with drug addiction must find new ways to sate their habit while facing escalating prices. Few alcoholics are compelled to rob or trespass in order to acquire six dollars for a bottle of vodka. However, even a hard working drug addict will find it difficult to accumulate over a hundred dollars for a few grams of cocaine. The situation forces the drug addict to find other avenues to satisfy their financial requirements for drugs, often through crimes like robbery and prostitution.

By its inherently underground nature, the illicit drug business typically attracts those individuals with a penchant for criminal behavior. With no courts to settle disputes among rival dealers – or to settle disputes among the seller and the consumer – many of those involved in the illicit drug trade often turn to violence rather than diplomacy or the legal system.

Libertarians such as Ron Paul see a solution through legalization. A person could afford their drug habit without robbing others and simply hold a regular job instead. In the worst case scenario, a drug addict would become equivalent to a homeless alcoholic, able to beg for six dollars to get his fix. The libertarian alternative is not utopian but a real look at costs and tradeoffs. Most people would agree that non-violent addicts are preferable to murderers, robbers, and thieves.

Another side effect of high prices is the increased profits to organizations that produce and distribute illicit drugs. Without prohibition, profits would go to legitimate companies and businesses. When drugs or alcohol are prohibited, even more profits go to the Al Capones and Pablo Escobars of the world. In some cases, the money goes to terrorist organizations such as FARC (Revolutionary Armed Forces of Colombia) and al-Qaeda.

Ron voiced this problem long before other politicians when he noted, "Our laws drive up the price of drugs a thousand fold, to the delight of the dealers, the pushers, and terrorist nations around the world who all reap huge illegal profits."[11] Unfortunately, Paul's campaign was in an era without discussion and debate on the subject. Illicit drugs, particularly the cheap, potent form of cocaine popular in inner cities known as crack, were viewed as an absolute evil that must be eradicated at all costs.

The passive aggressive dislike of Paul's views became obvious when his campaign mailing list of 100,000 supporters were sent a letter urging them to support Gramm. Thanks to a safeguard by Ron's campaign, the security breach was quickly recognized. Paul's team had intentionally misspelled about a dozen names on the mailing list.[12] These dozen recipients received the anti-Paul/pro-Gramm letter with their names misspelled in the same manner.

Either someone had broken into Paul's offices or someone within the campaign had turned traitor. The letters were signed by Paul Weyrich, at the time an official of the Committee for the Survival of a Free Congress.[13] The campaign threatened to press charges and sue. This was later dismissed as no evidence was ever found to the identify the culprit.

....

In the Democratic race, the election results brought the three candidates remarkably close to one another. Each candidate had 31% of the vote with the differences measured in decimals. A run-off was held proclaiming Lloyd Doggett the winner.

The votes on the Republican side did not count favorably for Ron Paul. In last place was Henry Grover at 2.5% followed closely by Robert Mosbacher with 7.8%. Ron Paul managed to accumulate 55,431 votes giving him 16.5%. Gramm swept the primary with 73.3%. He went on to defeat Lloyd Doggett in the main election with 59%.

Ron Paul's calculated risk had failed and now he was a political outsider again. His last days truly added insult to injury by the theft of his mailing list and the lack of support from his own party in favor of a turncoat Democrat. Much of his disillusionment can be felt in his farewell address to Congress. In Paul's view, there was no allowable questioning of foreign policy on either side of the isle, "no dissent is permissible and all true debate is squelched."[14]

Further, there was no discussion into the fundamental philosophy of government's role in society. Congress became only a tool for forcibly transferring tax funds from one individual to the next. Paul explained to the congressmen present at his address. "Instead of asking which form of intervention and planning government should impose, perhaps someday Congress will debate intervention versus nonintervention, government versus voluntary planning, US sovereignty versus internationalism - the pros and cons of true liberty. Today the debate basically is only that of deciding who will be the victims and who the beneficiaries."[15]

Ron was also cynical of the contradictory nature of conservatives and liberals. One conservative would lambaste the subsidies of another as anti-market while protecting his own special interest subsidies. Logical consistency was absent in Washington decision-making. Congressman Paul pointed out, "Good conservatives explain why guns and teachers shouldn't be registered, and beg and plead and coerce the government into registering their own kids for the draft."[16]

He also noted the inconsistency of foreign policy. "South Africa, for their defective system of civil liberties, is banned from the Olympics, while we beg the murdering Communists to come."[17]

Paul specifically targeted liberals, who he believed "show greater concern for the lives of seals than for the life of a human baby."[18] The farewell address left no stone unturned and no hypocrisy unrevealed.

The virtues of liberty seemed all but lost in Congress with their lack of concern for run-away spending; indebting future generations. Paul remarked, "Those not willing to vote for the cuts either must believe they are not a threat or do not care if they are. I suspect the former to be the case."[19] and "the defender of liberty is seen as bizarre" on Capital Hill.[20]

He made special note of those who usurped the power granted to Americans through their representatives. "Sadly, I have found that individual Members [of Congress], even though we represent our half-million constituents, are much less important than most of us would like to believe. The elite few who control the strings of power are the only ones who really count in the legislative process."[21]

Disenfranchised and frustrated, Paul left Congress. His straight forward farewell address accurately summed up the problems facing 1984 America. However, one part was entirely wrong. Paul said in his introduction, "Thousands of men and women have come and gone here in our country's history, and except for the few, most go unnoticed and remain nameless in the pages of history, as I am sure I will."[22]

History does not remember the men who brought great subsidies to their districts, but instead remembers men such as Cato the Younger of Rome, whose principled stand forecast the fall of the Roman Republic, or Frederic Bastiat, who prophesized the rise of France's modern welfare state. The men who stood alone against the tide of empires in decay stand in our memories centuries later.

CHAPTER 14

MR. SMITH RETURNS FROM WASHINGTON

1984-1987

Constitution

I would rather be exposed to the inconveniences attending too much liberty than to those attending too small a degree of it.

- THOMAS JEFFERSON

In the decade since entering politics, Ron Paul's home town of Lake Jackson, Texas had grown considerably. From a population of about eight or ten thousand residents in the 1970s, it had more than doubled to about twenty thousand people by 1984. In accordance with Paul's personal philosophy, the town had grown out of the private sector.

The town was originally planned and built by the Dow Chemical Company, not far from the Brazos River, in the 1940s. Dow wanted to create a town for the many engineers, executives and other employees that would staff their petrochemical plant, the largest in the world, then being constructed in nearby Freeport. The greater metropolitan area, known as Brazos Port, had about 100,000 residents.

The original city planner, Alden B. Dow (son of the founder of Dow Chemical), designed the layout of Lake Jackson. Alden did not settle for a square grid-system typical of government planners. Instead he opted for scenic winding streets that coursed around the existing trees. Alden named the streets, always ending with the word *Way*, such as Center Way and Winding Way. Alden's whimsical nature is apparent by two streets that intersected: This Way and That Way.

The quaint roads provided an ideal route for Ron Paul's early morning bike rides. A street unofficially known as Church Road is home to places of worship for Methodists, Lutherans, Baptists and Catholics alike. The community was trusting and open.

Most residents in Lake Jackson have some connection to the nearby Dow Chemical plant. Ron Paul's oldest son, Ronny, a graduate from the University of Texas, was a chemical engineer at the Dow plant. In the summer of 1984 he married Peggy Jane Walker, a graduate of Texas A & M working as a chemical engineer for Dow when they met.

The people of Lake Jackson were stereotypically Texan: family-oriented, religious, warm and friendly. They enjoyed some of the highest per capita annual incomes in the country. Hard working and highly educated people, many were doctors, lawyers and other professionals.

Not surprising for an area where summertime temperatures typically exceeded 100 degrees – often with 100 percent humidity – mosquitoes were found in abundance. Clute, a neighboring city, celebrated the insect with an annual Mosquito Festival.

It was in this setting that Ron Paul would ponder his mixed experiences in Washington and plan his future. "If there was a theme for the years 1984 to 1987 for Ron Paul," said Matthew Pyeatt, Ron's oldest grandchild, "it was reflection. It was an opportunity for him to sit back and reflect on his own views, and to deepen his views."[1]

He was also returning to his chosen profession of medicine. Lifelong politics is certainly a goal for many who seek political office, but Paul welcomed his return to fulltime medicine. While serving in Congress, Dr. Paul kept his medical license current and occasionally practiced medicine when home.

His partner, Dr. Jack Pruitt, kept the practice operating full time while Dr. Paul was in Washington, using the same offices purchased by Paul when he first moved to Lake Jackson. During this interval, Pruitt abided by two inflexible conditions on their partnership: no abortions and no federal funds.

Often working *pro bono* or accepting discounted payments from needy patients, Dr. Paul spent 50 to 100 hours per week providing medical services to expectant women and delivering babies. In the 1980s the pager was state-of-the-art technology and Paul was among the first to own one, taking it everywhere so that his patients could always reach him.

Despite such commitment to his medical practice, he always found time for his growing family. Oldest daughter Lori Paul gave the family a second grandchild in 1985. His son Ronny married in the summer of 1984 and had a child, Laurie Jane Paul, in 1986. Dr. Paul was closely involved with both pregnancies, allowing Dr. Pruitt to oversee the births.

The Paul's third child, Rand, left Baylor University without a degree in 1984. He went onto medical school at his father's *alma mater*, Duke University, to study ophthalmology (the eye and visual pathways). Duke accepted him without a degree due to his phenomenal score on the Medical College Admission Test (MCAT).

Fourth child Robert graduated from high school in the spring of 1984 and continued his education at Hardin Simmons University in Abilene, Texas, joining the school baseball team and majoring in biology.

With so much going on in his life, Ron still found time to relax. He retained his love for swimming since his high school years, though curiously he never shed his claustrophobia, including his fear of going under water. In the early 1980s he had an Olympic-size swimming pool built in his yard. Partly it was for himself and partly it was for entertaining the younger members of the family. During this period he could often be found swimming laps or playing with his grandchildren in the pool.

The older members of the family had an on-going competition to see who would be the first into the pool at the beginning of each year and last to go in at the end of the year. The winner was invariably the one who could tolerate icy temperatures. Ron usually won.

An avid cyclist, he would frequently ride for ten, fifteen, or even twenty miles at a time. He was a popular man in the Lake Jackson area, and those who saw him on his rides would honk and wave at the friendly doctor and former congressman. As a keen gardener, he spent many hours raising organic tomatoes. All of these activities provided a contemplative environment to consider his future.

....

Ron Paul left the US House of Representatives with no intention of returning to politics, but he did not see an end to his role as a truth-seeker and truth-speaker for the American people. While in Congress he was forced to limit his association with the Foundation for Rational Economics and Education (FREE), due to its non-profit status, but without those constraints he could again speak through the foundation.

Over the next four years, Paul traveled frequently, talking to various groups about libertarian ideas. As founder and president of FREE, he routinely advised and warned Americans about the state of their government. During the early 1980s, at his home in Lake Jackson, Ron Paul created his own phone service. He began taping weekly announcements on a variety of issues – usually monetary concerns and the continued growth of the federal government – that were available to anyone calling a special phone number.

Ron also started a veritable publishing empire, albeit on a small scale, operated from offices in Nassau called Ron Paul & Associates. The new for-profit business produced the Ron Paul Investment Newsletter and his Survival Report to promote limited government and civil liberties. Both Carol Paul and daughter Lori sat on the board of directors of Ron Paul & Associates, making it a family affair. In 1984 the Ludwig von Mises Institute published his fifth book, Mises and Austrian Economics: A Personal View.

Paul's time in the House of Representatives demonstrated to him that the Republican Party had lost its way on the issue of civil liberties. He hoped Reagan would bring about meaningful change, but instead the Reagan Revolution became a useful catch phrase.

Ronald Reagan ran on platform to dismantle the disastrous Department of Education, yet he was unable to achieve even this minor victory during his two terms in office. Partly this was because the Democrats controlled the House of Representatives at the time, but it was also a lack of will on the part of the Republican Party, who became distracted by other battles. Reagan's rhetoric about freedom was sadly detached from the reality he was creating. His passion for the War on Drugs made government even more intrusive.

Paul used his free time to contemplate his own political philosophy and its implications. He began to see how expanding federal power was not only wrecking people's financial lives, but their personal lives as well. Paul knew there was one important tool available to combat the assault on citizens' personal affairs: the Constitution.

Ron never claimed that his conception of limited government was particularly original. Although relatively new in the scale of human history, it was several hundred years old by the 1980s. The idea of living in a free society, under a strictly limited government, was the original spirit which gave birth to America.

"We owe our Founding Fathers a tremendous debt of gratitude," he wrote. "They created a society based on the radical idea that the purpose of government was to protect the rights of the individual, preexisting rights granted by God rather than the state. For the first time in human history, a government was designed to serve the individual, rather than vice versa. This triumph of the individual over the claims of the state, the King, the collective, or society represents a great gift to humanity. The principle of a servant government is the ideal that made America the greatest nation on earth."[2]

Ron Paul has often been accused of being a radical. This is ironic because defending liberty is the exact opposite of proposing a radical new idea.

"Those who dismiss the Constitution ignore the link between the wisdom of our Founders and the freedom and prosperity we still enjoy today. America is not prosperous and relatively free merely by accident. It is prosperous and free because we still retain vestiges of our constitutional system of limited government, with its emphasis on property rights and the rule of law.

"Other nations are similarly filled with bright, hardworking people, and enjoy abundant natural resources. Yet why have they not prospered like America? The simple reason is they enjoy less liberty. Without liberty and property rights, the human spirit diminishes. More freedom always means more prosperity, which is why America enjoys a much higher level of material well-being than almost any other nation."[3]

The consistency demonstrated by Paul in his political career could be seen in his political ideas. His defense of free-market economics was in perfect accord with his philosophical view of a limited government – and both of them were directly related with the deep respect he had for the Constitution and the Declaration of Independence. Restoring the boundaries established by those documents is the core idea of Paul's politics.

"The principles enshrined in the Constitution and the Declaration of Independence define the American way of life," he wrote. "Without those principles we become just another country, governed by whim and expediency, with no guiding vision beyond the ambitions of the latest politicians in power. The purpose of the Constitution was to impose systematic limits on government power, limits that survive the political tides."[4]

Paul would take his time away from politics to put his thoughts to paper, in the form of a book that would eventually go by the name <u>Freedom Under Seige</u>. Paul's former chief of staff Lew Rockwell contributed the foreword to the book.[5]

Always a champion of the Constitution, Ron Paul made individual liberty *the* flagship issue of his book. He wrote in the introduction:

Two hundred years ago the United States Constitution was written as a guide for America's unique experiment in freedom. Today the free society that the Founders envisaged is barely identifiable. America is no longer a bastion of freedom. Prevailing ideology, grounded in economic ignorance and careless disregard for individual liberty, is nurtured by a multitude of self-serving, power-seeking politicians spouting platitudes of compassion for the poor who are created by their own philosophy. Reelection is paramount in the minds of most of those who represent us, while freedom and constitutional restraint of power are considered old-fashioned and unwise.[6]

Much like the authors of the Constitution, Paul believed that government remained the single greatest threat to freedom. "The feeling of frustration prevalent in the country today is certainly understandable," he wrote. "Something certainly has gone wrong. The role of government and the people's attitude toward government have changed dramatically since 1787, with most of the changes occurring in the twentieth century. It appears that we are in the waning days of the American Republic." [7]

Over the years, Ron Paul found he could trace most problems with government to the degree politicians ignored the Constitution. "We certainly are blessed with a unique and inspired Constitution, probably the best in the history of man, despite its shortcomings. Yet today, two hundred years since its ratification, the Constitution doesn't restrain the pernicious and steady growth of government at the expense of personal liberty."

The observation was not new. When the revolutionaries formed their constitution, they were curiously wary of allowing the government to hold too much power. Their fear was that their own government would exert too much influence on the lives of individuals within the country. They wanted a country where individuals would be free to do what they wanted, as long as they did not interfere with the liberty of others.

Thomas Jefferson once warned, "The natural progress of things is for liberty to yield and government to gain ground." Paul was sounding the call that a decrease in individual freedom was only to be expected when government force replaces private initiative and problem-solving.

Few in government were taking a principled stand for limited government and individual rights, and the choices that Americans could make regarding their own lives and property were dwindling. "Sadly, we rarely hear serious proposals for limiting the role of government to that of protecting liberty. Both liberals and conservatives give lip service to limited government ideas, but only to serve some special view of government that they might endorse, rather than to promote consistently the principles of freedom." [8]

Civil liberties are safe goals for government to pursue. Civil rights, on the other hand, quickly become a problem because people have an ever growing list of demands that can be disguised as rights: the right to a good standard of living; the right to own a house; the right to transportation; the right to nutritious food; the right to health. These rights, when demanded through the government, can end up devastating freedom because someone else loses their liberties when they are forced to supply rights for others.

The perversion of "rights" was a concern for Paul. "The concept of rights has been distorted to such a degree that the authors of the Constitution would not recognize what is today referred to as a 'right'," he wrote. [9]

Along with guaranteeing profits and solvency to some industries, the federal government was extending its role in providing health care, jobs, homes, and food. "Throughout the twentieth century, the trend has been away from limited government and toward big governments intervening in every aspect of our lives," Paul commented.[10]

Government regulations and attempts to force people to act morally were also troubling to Paul. Rights, according to the constitution, mean the freedom to peacefully pursue happiness for oneself – not the freedom of government to make others behave in a certain way or to stop others from making unwise decisions.[11]

....

In the years following his early political career, Ron Paul showed no concern with his legacy. He did not care what people in Washington thought of him, so long as he stayed true to his principles and continued fighting for a freer society. Happy and content, he worked hard at the job he loved and renewed his commitment to his community as well as his growing family.

During this period, the Holidays were especially important for the Paul family. With five children (youngest daughter Joy Paul was still at home) and several grandchildren, the entire family would converge on Paul's home to celebrate Christmas or Thanksgiving. Carol's parents, Bill and Carol Wells, and Ron's parents, Margaret and Howard, would often join them from Pennsylvania.

The huge gatherings necessitated an expansion of the Paul family home. Ron added a bedroom and kitchenette to allow out-of-town guests to stay closer to family. He also added an office in order to accommodate his expanding collection of Austrian economics books. His office served as a quiet retreat in his ongoing study of economics, constitutional government, and individual freedom.

"Family was such a huge part of his life," explains grandson Matthew. "He was the patriarch of the family, but he was the quiet, lead-by-example type of patriarch, not rule-with-a-fist. He was a disciplinarian, but if you ever asked one of his children or grandchildren if they'd ever received corporal punishment they would laugh. He demanded that the kids do well in school and behave, but that all seemed to fall into place, because he was very fair."[12]

Family was Ron Paul's primary motivation to continue fighting for freedom. His passionate support of freedom was grounded in the reality of his family life. When he was young, his family had the freedom to operate a dairy as they felt best. After his own family began, Ron wanted his children to grow up and live in a free society. Now, in his early fifties, with grandchildren on the way, he would fight even harder.

He continued his efforts to educate Americans about the looming shadow of oppressive government. As a congressman, he had fought for freedom, family and personal responsibility, and he would continue living for these ideals as a private citizen.

In spending more time with his family, Paul felt obligated to pass on to the next generation a truly free society. He soon realized his work in politics could not end until he had tried everything to bring freedom back to America. He had failed to enact change in the Republican Party, and now he would try a different party.

CHAPTER 15

THE LIBERTARIAN

1987-1989

Free Speech

There are more instances of the abridgement of the freedom of the people by the gradual and silent encroachment of those in power, than by violent and sudden usurpation.

JAMES MADISON

After three years away from Washington, enjoying his time with his family and working at his private medical practice, Ron Paul found himself drawn back into the arena of national politics. Although he said in his 1984 farewell speech, "It's difficult for one who loves true liberty and utterly detests the power of the state to come to Washington for a period of time and not leave a true cynic," few who knew Ron expected him to stay silent forever.

It came as no surprise when, on January 8, 1987, Paul sent a letter to Republican National Committee Chairman Frank Fahrenkopf announcing that he was leaving the party. He concluded the letter, "I therefore resign my membership in the Republican Party and enclose my membership card." This was followed by his registration as a member of the Libertarian Party. Shortly thereafter, he announced his intention to run for the Libertarian presidential nomination.

The Libertarian Party had found uneven success in the 1980s. Still a very young organization, in 1980 the party nominated Ed Clark. Clark tried to appeal to liberals disaffected with Carter and with the increasingly heated rhetoric over Cold War foreign policy, coupled with a moderate economic conservatism that played off widespread dissatisfaction with the economic disasters that plagued 1970s America. He represented a moderate libertarianism, attempting to appeal directly to the mainstream.

For his running mate, the Libertarian Party nominated billionaire industrialist David H. Koch, who pledged to largely finance the campaign with his personal fortune. This gave the duo a substantially larger operating budget than any Libertarian campaign before or since, and with it they were able to buy significant ad time on network television. The Clark campaign obtained ballot access in all 50 states, and ultimately pulled in just shy of a million votes; over 1% of the national electorate, still the high water mark for the Libertarian Party.

Four years later, after heated internal debates between supporters of ideological purity and those favoring mainstream acceptance, the Libertarian Party nominated attorney and longtime party insider David P. Bergland for the 1984 presidential campaign (along with Vice President nominee Jim Lewis). Bergland promised a return to core libertarian principles and an uncompromising ideological approach. His campaign, however, proved to be one of the least successful in the party's history, with just over 228,000 votes; less than one quarter of one percent of the electorate.

This left the Libertarian Party of 1987 pulled in two directions. There were many who were distrustful of compromising on core principles for the sake of mainstream political success, and there were others who argued that the Libertarian Party had to employ a big tent and reach out for Republican and Democratic votes.

Likewise, America at large found itself at a crossroads. Following the two terms of Ronald Reagan, conservatism remained on the ascent, although some questioned the Republican's ballooning deficits and substantial increase of the military-industrial complex. Foreign policy remained strictly confined to Cold War paradigms, but those were also the years when the Moral Majority had asserted itself within the GOP, to the continued chagrin of social liberals and moderate Republicans. The sitting Vice President, George H.W. Bush, was widely expected to run for Reagan's third term, but many openly questioned his commitment to conservative principles. The Democrats had no obvious successor to challenge him. Although they had retaken Congress in 1986, they were still smarting over their crushing defeat in the Presidential race of 1984, among the most lopsided in history.

With these considerations, the Libertarian Party deliberated over whether to make a concerted push into electoral significance, or whether to stay true to core values and homogenous principles even at the cost of mainstream acceptance. It was into this divide that Ron Paul stepped.

....

As a former Republican and early supporter of Ronald Reagan, many Libertarians had questions about Ron Paul's desire to challenge the establishment that year. Addressing the question in a speech on the campaign trail, Paul said, "I listened to Ronald Reagan in the '70s. He told me that he would balance the budget, cut back and get the government off my back. They are not off our backs, they are in our wallets and into our bedrooms and into our private lives more than ever before."[1]

The Libertarian Party, of course, had always believed in free speech. A large part of the attraction of the Libertarian Party, for many, was its openness to a variety of perspectives. However, among the major parties, many of the battles over free speech in the second half of the 20ᵗʰ century were focused on attempts by the establishment, be it political or cultural, to stamp out what it viewed as obscenity. Increasingly, this put Libertarians at odds with the conservative mainstream, which included the self-proclaimed Moral Majority.

Free speech enthusiasts also found themselves rowing against the current of mainstream liberalism, which had begun to emphasize political correctness and the negative repercussions of "hateful" speech. This led to a polarization of First Amendment advocates, who were forced to speak up for the most marginalized and often distasteful speech, and to push back against cultural conservatives and mainstream liberalism.

Being a former Republican congressman with socially conservative credentials, Ron Paul was not a typical free speech advocate. The path he took with his First Amendment appeals was often at an oblique angle to the sort of political atmosphere in which many libertarian free speech advocates operated. It was true that Paul was as tireless an advocate as anybody for getting the government "out of our bedrooms and out of our private lives", but he also widened the free speech argument to include more conservative values.

For instance, free speech in the realm of religious freedoms often emphasized protections for minority or counter religious perspectives. Paul took his message to the conservative mainstream by arguing that free speech helped protect *all* religious speech, including standard Christian-based expressions. On the floor of the House of Representatives, for instance, he argued that judicial decisions declaring prayer in school as unconstitutional misunderstood the nature and intent of the First Amendment:

> The Court ... has interpreted the establishment clause to preclude prayer and other religious speech in a public place, thereby violating the free exercise clause of the very same First Amendment. Therefore, it is incumbent upon Congress to correct this error, and to perform its duty to support and defend the Constitution. My legislation would restore First Amendment protections of religion and speech by removing all religious freedom-related cases from federal district court jurisdiction, as well as from federal claims court jurisdiction. The federal government has no constitutional authority to reach its hands in the religious affairs of its citizens or of the several states.[2]

He made similar appeals to Christian conservatives that adherence to the constitution would prevent government meddling in religious expression, home-schooling, and the right to public protest. Thus, there was no need to emphasize only unpopular speech, because the First Amendment protected *all* speech. Paul's case was presentable to both social liberals as well as cultural conservatives. No longer was the Libertarian Party's view of speech, unfairly or not, lumped in exclusively with the former.

Libertarianism has often been tainted by and confused with the philosophy of the Libertine (one who indulges in hedonism). As Paul reflected, "[The Libertarian Party] image has been tarnished, sometimes ... it was encouraged by themselves ... because when you believe in liberty you allow people to use their liberty in different ways and it becomes libertine, and they get this libertine image. While I was a very conservative individual who believed in liberty, I hope I compensated a little bit for that."[3]

Paul was equally at odds with an increasing tendency in mainstream liberalism to protect various groups from hateful or hurtful speech. Few politicians want to be seen as protecting racism or collectivism but, Paul argued, the First Amendment demands it:

> Disheartening as it may be, the political left, which was supposed to care more about the First Amendment than the right, has ventured in recent years to curtail so-called 'hate speech' by championing political correctness. In the last few decades we've seen the political-correctness crowd, in the name of improving personal behavior and language, cause individuals to lose their jobs, cause careers to be ruined, cause athletes to be trashed, and cause public speeches on liberal campuses to be disrupted and even banned. These tragedies have been caused by the so-called champions of free speech. Over the years, tolerance for the views of those with whom campus liberals disagree has nearly evaporated. The systematic and steady erosion of freedom of speech continues.[4]

Ron Paul's innovation was not only to set himself up as a libertarian defender of unpopular speech, but to make a direct appeal to the inherent inviolability of free speech on the grounds that it protected mainstream conservative values as well. This was not only a holistic approach to First Amendment advocacy, but a shrewd political gesture telegraphing his desire to make a direct appeal to mainstream Republicans and Democrats on the grounds that the Libertarian Party was advancing both a profoundly liberal *and* a profoundly conservative argument.

....

The Libertarian Party was often hostile to mainstream cultural conservatism—particularly following many years of "culture wars" in which the Moral Majority attempted to stamp out unpopular or minority views and social expressions.

In the fall of 1987, Ron Paul was certainly not the only candidate running for the Libertarian Party nomination. Among the other candidates were Jim Lewis, a bookbindery representative from Old Saybrook, Connecticut and the former Vice Presidential nominee; Harry Glenn, a retired welder from St. John, Indiana; and Paul's chief competition, Native American activist and longtime Libertarian ally Russell Means.

Means, of the Lakota, was one of the 20th century's most well known, tireless, and prolific leaders of the American Indian Movement. He had taken part in the Indian occupation of Wounded Knee, South Dakota, in 1973, and served a year in prison after being convicted of rioting and obstruction of justice. He was well known to the Libertarian Party as a committed freedom activist and instigator, and his political views were compatible with the mainstream Libertarian Party.

Paul's campaign was in stark contrast to Means' effort. As one Libertarian participant at the time noted, "There was concern, at least among what I respectfully call the lunatic fringe of the Libertarian Party, that Paul more closely resembled a mainstream candidate. Here was a successful doctor wearing a suit, a professional politician, running against this other guy in a leather jacket. We were worried that the Libertarian Party was beginning to resemble Republicans and Democrats."[5]

The conservative nature of both Ron Paul and his campaign troubled many in the Libertarian Party. One of the most visible points of divergence was Paul's pro-life stance, with a legislative record to match. Pro-choice Libertarians, a critical caucus in the party, vigorously objected to Paul's convictions and were only assuaged by assurances that Paul would not use his campaign to advance a pro-life agenda.[6]

Another caucus with significant disagreements with Paul was the Libertarian Republican Organizing Committee, or LROC. LROC began in 1985, inspired in part by the more ideologically purist campaign of David Bergland, and took as its mission a push to resist the dilution of libertarian principles for the sake of more mainstream acceptance. Thus, their skepticism of Paul's candidacy was perhaps to be expected.* Early in the race, LROC distributed pamphlets and newsletters outlining Paul's cultural conservatism and lack of adherence to an anti-state orthodoxy.[7]

Despite this turbulence, the Libertarian Party eventually embraced Paul, in part because of his perceived ability to reach out beyond the ranks of doctrinal libertarians. As the New York Times noted on the day of the Libertarian Party convention, "The voting for the Presidential nomination appeared to be influenced by delegate desires to broaden the party's base. Mr. Means was seen as potentially opening an avenue to ethnic minorities, while Dr. Paul was seen as offering the candidacy of a trained, articulate political campaigner skilled at fund-raising."

Ron Paul's run for the nomination proved unusually successful, and he won the majority on the first ballot. The final tally was 196 votes for Paul, 120 for Means, 49 for Jim Lewis, 3 for Mr. Glenn, and 14 abstentions. Andre Marrou, who had recently served a two-year term in the Alaska Legislature as a Libertarian, was nominated as the Vice Presidential candidate without opposition.

....

After securing the nomination, the ticket of Paul/Marrou began campaigning in earnest. The first task was to build a staff, and Paul pulled from a number of sources to accomplish this. He had several experienced campaigners from his congressional career to choose from as well as the Libertarian Party, so he used a mix of both. Paul chose Nadia Hayes from his own ranks as chief campaign strategist. Hayes had worked for Paul starting in 1974 with his congressional campaigns, and by now she was a trusted advisor. This trust would soon be tested.

Paul also picked a number of allies from the Mises Institute and a few other outside sources. Burton Blumert, owner of the successful Camino Coin Company and friend of economist Murray Rothbard, would act as the treasurer and advisor to the campaign. Rothbard himself, who had been active with the Libertarian Party since 1978, put his full support behind Paul. Lew Rockwell would take on the duties of speech writer.

The Paul campaign seemed well organized from the word go. Ron Paul himself soon proved to be exactly the "trained, articulate political campaigner" that the New York Times indicated the Libertarian Party hoped for.

---

* Justin Raimondo and Eric Garris, two organizers of LROC, became prominent Ron Paul supporters in later years.

One of their assurances to the Libertarian Party was that, given Paul's political experience, he would prove an adept fundraiser—which would be required not just to attempt a mainstream breakout, but even to successfully petition to get on ballots. To meet his obligation, Paul found support from his former congressional colleague, Jesse Helms.

Helms, a former Democrat, was very influential in Republican politics, although his fervent social conservatism made him a controversial figure. Helms was credited with rescuing Ronald Reagan's political career in 1976, resulting in a strong showing for Reagan that laid the groundwork for his successful 1980 presidential bid (Paul had also joined Helms as one of Reagan's four 1976 supporters in Congress).[8] However, it was unlikely Helms could openly endorse someone from another political party, even Ron Paul, without invoking hostility from Republicans and perhaps backlash from Libertarians.

Paul was able to arrange a meeting with the Helms organization. Eric Dondero, who was Ron Paul's travel secretary and advance man in 1988, describes the scene. "Ron and I went to meet Jessie Helms, but Helms was not able to attend. Instead we met with Carter Wren, a political operative in charge of Jessie Helms' fundraising operation. He hemmed and hawed. Helms didn't want to endorse Paul publicly. Wren let us know that Senator Helms supported Paul, but it could not be public."[9]

Although no public support was forthcoming, the private support offered by Helms was even more valuable. "Wren shied away from public support by the Senator, but did assist with campaign strategy behind the scenes for a short while, mostly with fundraising."[10]

The biggest boost to the campaign was done in secrecy. "We met in a dark back room straight out of a movie," Dondero recalls. "Wren said 'We'll give you our top fundraiser,' and jotted a name on a pad with an address and phone number. Then we went back to Houston to give this gentleman a call."

The gentleman in question turned out to be a political fundraising powerhouse, David James. After an initial conversation, James flew to Houston to meet with the Paul campaign. In their very first meeting together, "Ron hired him on the spot," says Dondero. James would remain with Paul's organization for decades after the meeting.

The gift from Jesse Helms paid dividends as, under the stewardship of James, fundraising began to accelerate markedly. Estimates vary, but by October the campaign had raised over two million dollars, a healthy sum at the time for a third party challenger.[11]

Ballot access was another early hurdle. Getting a candidate's name on the national ballot is nearly prohibitive for third party candidates. As Paul noted, "The laws are very biased, whether it's the Libertarian Party, or the Constitution Party, or the Green Party. It's very tough to compete. You don't gain credibility. You don't get into the debates. Even getting on ballots is tough."[12] Ultimately, Paul was able to get on the ballot in 46 states, excepting North Carolina, West Virginia, Indiana and Missouri. Missouri in particular proved a contentious battle, and the fight between Libertarians and the Secretary of State's office spurred lawsuits that went all the way to federal appeals court.[13]

....

After overcoming these hurdles, Paul was able to go about the business of taking his case to the American people. He found two strong early bases, which made for strange bedfellows.

The first was a contingent of economic and cultural conservatives who had previously supported Pat Robertson for the Republican nomination. Robertson had mounted a significant grassroots challenge to Vice President Bush for the party's nomination and proved to be Bush's toughest opponent in key states like Iowa and Michigan. Robertson was the last of the Republican challengers to concede the race. After Robertson suspended his race, a number of prominent Robertson supporters began circulating on his behalf, enticed by Paul's conservative twist on libertarianism. "If we expect George Bush to carry the standard of our vision, we are wrong," one letter by Robertson's supporters stated. "[Ron Paul] will carry the standard."[14]

A second base of mainstream appeal formed as a result of Paul's many college appearances. Paul carried to those events a message of social liberalism, with a heavy emphasis on free speech and the value of liberty in protecting diversity. As one collegiate publication put it at the time, quoting Ron's son, Rand Paul:

> Paul said the Libertarian party's major strength is its diversity - it attracts fundamentalist Christians who supported Rev. Pat Robertson in favor of home schooling as well as gay and lesbian rights activists in San Francisco who fear government interference in their personal lives.

> "You have to believe to a deeper degree than a Republican or a Democrat in the philosophy of individual rights," [Rand] Paul said.

> "People shouldn't be treated as gay, white, black or yellow; they want to be treated as individuals."[15]

The irony was that the Paul campaign was appealing to both Christian fundamentalists and liberal co-eds for exactly the same reason: to protect individual expression and raise the alarm when the majority, be they liberal secularists or majority fundamentalists, began stamping out the free expression of counter views. Paul identified that all parties had a stake in free speech, because it could at any point turn against their own interests. As he put it, "The temptation has always been great to legislatively restrict rudeness, prejudice, and minority views, and it's easiest to start by attacking the clearly obnoxious expressions that most deem offensive. The real harm comes later. But 'later' is now approaching."[16] This was a message that had resonance with voters in wildly divergent blocs.

....

There was, however, the mater of getting that message to larger audiences. Access to mainstream media channels was always a challenge for third party candidates, and though the Libertarian Party had been more successful than most in that regard (by virtue of their status as America's largest third party), it was still challenging to find avenues for getting the message out. At the time, cable television was not as popular as it would become and the Internet was in its infancy. Although CNN was founded years earlier, the 24-hour news format was not yet ubiquitous. Thus, despite the fact that the former congressman had credibility as a viable political figure, national media appearances were hard to come by. "There was a major network blackout in the 1988 campaign," recalls Dondero.

However, Ron Paul and his campaign had committed themselves to the philosophy that any opportunity to get the message out was valuable, so what little television time he was able to garner often came through appearances that more mainstream political candidates avoided. One notable appearance found him on the Morton Downey Jr. Show.[17]

Morton Downey Jr. had become infamous as a loudmouthed, bullying host of radio and daytime television. His controversial television show, which ran for two years at the end of the 1980s, is often credited with popularizing trash TV. The discourse would often descend into shouting matches between Downey, his guests, and his audience. Downey styled himself as a right wing populist, and appeared to take great relish in ambushing his guests and attempting to expose them as frauds or phonies (or, better still, instigating fights). Chain-smoking and aggressive, he took as his show's emblem a big mouth.

Ron Paul appeared on the Morton Downey Jr. Show on the Fourth of July. Downey introduced the candidate as "a man who could be snorting cocaine in the Oval Office." Appearing with a handful of other political activists, including New York Congressman Charles Rangel, it soon became apparent that Paul was the focus of the show, which was a barely concealed attempt at exposing him as a loon.

If Downey and his audience expected an easy target, they had underestimated Paul, who refused to be shouted down. What followed was a riotous discussion of libertarian ideals, mainly regarding the war on drugs.

Turning the show's right-wing populist sensibility on its ear, Paul countered charges that he was in favor of drug dealers by demanding that people take individual responsibility and not ask the government to do it for them. During the course of the program he had co-opted one of Downey's favorite rhetorical weapons, accusing guests of pansy liberalism, and had turned it back on Downey and his fans, once again making the case that not only was libertarianism consistent with conservative principles, but that it was the only philosophy that was.

The half hour program would crop up years later as a popular set of YouTube videos, which dispelled reservations that the mild-mannered country doctor could endure the abuse and scorn of audiences over political sacred-cows, like Reagan's drug policy. The program proved a vindication of not only Paul's idealism and political skill, but libertarianism's ability to compete in the free market of ideas.

....

Despite these inroads, Paul's difficulties breaking into the mainstream only worsened as the general election continued into the late fall. One staffer at the time noted that national media coverage of the Paul campaign entirely dried up in the final leg of the race.[18] If Paul wanted to garner more than one million votes, he would need more exposure.

The campaign adopted a new strategy to court national media coverage, and responsibility fell to Nadia Hayes. The top of their wish list included network television and a front page article. According to Dondero, a large New York newspaper "promised Ron that if they bought a full page ad, the Libertarian Party would get a front page article. It was common practice back then to make these arrangements. The ad department called us about ten times per day, and they absolutely promised a front page article."

After a week of designing the ad and obtaining verbal assurances, the campaign placed the ad. "They took the bait and it cost something like $48,000, then they stopped returning her calls," says Dondero. "A week passed and there was no article."

The Paul campaign had made assurances to Libertarian supporters that, like the 1980 Clark/Koch ticket, they would be hitting the airwaves in October. But by the time October came, the promised media blitz had "largely failed to materialize."[19]

There had been some promising signs. It seemed like media coverage was about to take off in October when PBS allotted Ron Paul a half-hour segment on the popular MacNeil/Lehrer NewsHour. It was a big break for a third party candidate; the appearance garnered more exposure for Paul than he had received the entire campaign. "That was the highlight," says Dondero. "The MacNeil/Lehrer show was really popular at the time."

The campaign hoped other network news broadcasts would soon follow. But instead of taking off, an event at UCLA two weeks before election day proved emblematic. Paul was scheduled to speak with one of the largest crowds the campaign had seen so far, with hundreds of college students eager to listen to his message. Before the event, Ron received word that he would finally have the televised news coverage the campaign had promised to donors. Campaign staff had received assurances, related by Hayes, that CBS and ABC news would be covering the rally. Before the event, a section in front of the stage was cleared to make room for TV cameras.

Paul waited backstage for the television vans to arrive as the throngs of students gathered. "We waited for one hour, but there were no TV stations. It was so devastating," recalls Dondero. "It was a wonderful event. I'm standing in the front, hearing all these students applauding." Paul delivered his message to the students, but the empty press section had turned an exuberant rally into a disappointment. "After the speech, he was looking at me and shaking head. He wasn't blaming me. He spoke to a huge crowd! But that didn't matter to him. The only thing that mattered to him was the television coverage…It was a huge disappointment for the donors. We were very upset that there was no coverage. So much money went into it." As the Presidential race moved into the home stretch, Paul was largely passed over by the media.

Unfortunately for Paul, things would only get worse. One week before the election, Burt Blumert discovered that over $100,000 was missing from Ron Paul's investment newsletter account. Blumert and Lew Rockwell questioned the treasurer of the account, Nadia Hayes, and soon realized something was amiss.[20] They went to Ron Paul, asking him to level formal charges against Hayes.

Paul was understandably reluctant to file charges against his trusted advisor and wanted to give her a chance to explain the situation. Hayes' husband was in financial trouble due to a failing boat business, and despite Paul's confidence in her, it soon became clear that Hayes had been using campaign donations for her own personal use. Regrettably, Paul's efforts to obtain restitution did not work, and attempts at resolving the situation internally proved unsuccessful. It became clear that Paul had been betrayed by one of his most trusted supporters.

On November 7th, 1988, one day before the election, the dam burst. As The

American Libertarian explained it, in "a bizarre twist, tough-talking campaign manager Nadia Hayes was sacked the day before the election. ... Paul campaign chair Burt Blumert and Paul campaign ghostwriter and direct mail fundraiser Lew Rockwell showed up ... unannounced and unexpected [at HQ]. Staff were told that they should leave ... locksmiths turned up late in the day to change the locks on the office doors."

As the puzzled volunteers departed, Nadia Hayes' staff was escorted to a back room in the rented office space by local police detectives from the Nassau Bay Police Department. As one staff member present at the time stated, "It was the most bizarre experience of my life. Here we were all set for an election party, busy trying to set up with state coordinators and state chairs, then they came in ... and shuffled us into the back storeroom."

The campaign team remained in the backroom for almost six uncomfortable hours while lawyers, accountants, and police detectives searched through files in the main office. No one was allowed to leave the room, other than supervised breaks to the washroom until all the evidence was collected. At the end of the ordeal, instead of the traditional last minute electoral push, the campaign office was closed and staff and volunteers were sent home. It was a crushing end to the campaign, made worse by the fact that it was one of their own at the center of it.

At the conclusion of the investigation, campaign manager Nadia Hayes was arrested by the Nassau Bay, Texas Police Department. Paul later brought charges against Nadia on March 23, 1989. His trusted lieutenant was convicted by the Harris County Grand Jury of embezzlement of roughly $140,000, sentenced to six months in jail and ordered to pay restitution.[21]

....

Ron Paul ended his 1988 campaign in 3rd place. The Paul/Marrou ticket received 431,499 votes, or almost half of 1 percent. Despite the harrowing final days, he received more votes than all other third party candidates combined. His final showing was greater than the 1984 Libertarian Party result, though significantly worse than 1980.

It was no secret that the Paul campaign had hoped to exceed Ed Clark's one million votes, and by that standard they had failed. But despite a last minute scandal, media blackout, and an untraditional campaign by mainstream (or Libertarian Party) standards, he was still able to pull in half a million votes and receive support from significant contingents of both conservatives and liberals, showing that libertarianism was by no means a niche ideology.

However, his campaign also illustrated that organizational difficulties and the deeply ingrained hurdles that any third party campaign must face were nearly insurmountable. Reflecting on these years, Paul would in part attribute the institutional challenges inherent to any third party run as reasons why he went back to the Republican Party, and would not in the future consider further third party runs.[22] In that sense, he had failed to square the third party circle, or solve the riddle of breaking out into the mainstream, as much as he and his supporters had hoped.

Paul himself remained unbowed throughout the election. "We live in a society where the only measurement is power and money," Paul said the week of the election, dismissing questions about his electoral relevance. "I happen to believe truth wins out in the end."[23]

....

The legacy from the 1988 race is mixed, both in the course of Ron Paul's history, and the Libertarian Party's. Following the embezzlement scandal, the Libertarian Party was rife with rumors, innuendo, and bad blood. This gave ammunition to many dissenters who were already unhappy with the ideological marriage between themselves and what they perceived as mainstream conservatism. In 1989, differences between the more libertine aspects of the party and the conservative wing flared, with heated words exchanged between the promethean Lew Rockwell and Libertarian Party leadership. While Ron Paul himself remained on good terms with the Libertarians (accepting an invitation to address the 1991 Libertarian Convention), in the end, Blumert, Rockwell, and economist Murray Rothbard departed bitterly,[24] and Paul's critics from his nomination gained credibility and prominence.

The Libertarians nominated Ron Paul's 1988 running mate, Andre Marrou, in 1992, and running a more traditional Libertarian campaign, he only managed to pull in about half of Paul's total (291,627 votes, or 0.28% of the electorate). The tensions and internal debate inherent in Paul's fight for the Libertarian Party nomination in 1988 would arise again within the Libertarian Party, particularly in 2008, in which another former Republican congressman would get the nomination on the promise of expanding mainstream appeal.

Dondero is even more direct. "In 1985 the Libertarian party was near death, it was on life support," he states flatly. "[The Paul campaign] brought the Libertarian Party back from the brink of death, and gave it the kind of credibility it lacked."[25]

And for Paul, it proved a seminal experience. It gave him valuable experience in dissenting against the establishment. The campaign represented his first foray into national politics, and the network he created that year, both in terms of donors and credibility as an instigating force for freedom, would prove valuable in the coming decade. Despite the tensions and dramas of the 1988 campaign, Paul's run for the Presidency that year marked him forever as a champion for liberty.

As judge Learned Hand once noted, speaking about the freedom of speech, "In the end it is worse to suppress dissent than to run the risk of heresy." The Libertarian campaign gave Ron Paul his first formal taste of running the risk of heresy, and it was that impulse that would one day guide him back to the Republican Party, back to Congress, and back to national politics.

CHAPTER 16

BACK TO MEDICINE

1989-1995

Free Trade

Free trade is not based on utility but on justice

EDMUND BURKE

With Republican George H. W. Bush declared the winner, the smoke of the 1988 presidential race was beginning to clear. Ron Paul had some thinking and reassessing to do in regard to the direction of his career – and his life.

Ron had learned an important lesson in the 1988 race: the political deck was stacked against third parties.[1] "I probably invested close to a year," he told Texas Monthly Magazine in a later interview. "It was a lot of time and effort. Sometimes I had some ambivalence about how productive it was."[2] In his typically polite and optimistic manner, Ron had understated the frustration he felt after the 1988 general election.

One thing that Ron never doubted, however, was his passion for medicine. After the 1988 election ended, he naturally returned to his obstetrical practice in Lake Jackson, Texas. Ron's practice partner, Dr. Jack Pruett, had been diligently caring for their patients during the times when Ron was away. But even during his first stint in congress, Ron maintained a strong presence at the office. "Every Friday morning," Dr. Pruett recalled, "he would come back to Lake Jackson. He would often times see patients, he would take call late at night, he would deliver babies on Saturday and see patients, and then return to Washington at the crack of dawn on Monday morning. It was just amazing what he was able to do."[3] Ron himself remembered assisting with surgeries and maintaining an open appointment slot on Saturday mornings for his patients, while simultaneously serving in the House of Representatives[4] – a testament to his boundless energy. It was easy for Ron to transition back into full-time practice, because he had never truly left in the first place.

Some elements of obstetrical practice in the early 1990s, however, stood in contrast to the way things were at the inception of Ron's practice in 1968. Malpractice insurance premiums were rising. Health Maintenance Organizations (HMOs) were becoming more and more involved in managing various aspects of patient care.

Ron noticed a big change when he returned to medicine after his political career, mostly due to the Health Maintenance Act of 1973. "You had to call, and wait, and argue. They'd say, 'no, you've got to do this first. You've got to do the laparoscopy before you do the hysterectomy. You have to try this medication before you try that.' You'd do what they told you, and it doubled and tripled the costs. It just inflated them. It annoys the patients. It annoys the doctors. It's terrible. Managed care is just third party interference – another creation of government."[5]

As he was apt to do, Ron also found a way to make a living by embracing his beliefs. Ron believed in hard money – precious metal-based or precious metal-backed currency, as opposed to un-backed paper currency, which, he believed, had historically been vulnerable to debasement by governments and central banks.

Ron had served on the House Banking Committee as a member of Congress, and was known as an advocate for a return to the gold standard. He spoke passionately about hard money not only in Congressional buildings, but also at other venues around the country. Unbeknownst to Ron, one of these speeches would lead him to enter into a successful business venture and lifelong friendship with Burton Blumert, dealer in precious metals and sole proprietor of Camino Coin Company.

Blumert has been a coin dealer since 1959, and had developed an excellent reputation within the trade. As such, he regularly attended events related to coins and precious metals. Naturally, he and Ron Paul crossed paths in the early 1970s. "I met him at a coin convention," Blumert said. "He was speaking about gold and the [Vietnam] War. We had coffee together." That meeting was the beginning of, in Blumert's words, "a long and abiding friendship."[6]

Blumert remained close to Ron in the years that followed. He was affiliated with the Ludwig von Mises Institute, a scholarly organization founded in 1982 that promoted libertarian principles and the ideas of Austrian economics.[7] Ron was on the Mises Institute's Board of Directors. "He was loyal throughout," said Blumert. "He was there at every meeting that we had."[8] Blumert also chaired Ron's 1988 presidential bid, sharing in the excitement of promoting the ideas of liberty while simultaneously sharing in the frustration of attaining ballot access and major media coverage. A number of other prominent libertarians also surrounded Ron as friends, fellow board members of the Mises Institute, and organizers of his 1988 campaign, including Lew Rockwell, an editor of several publications and Austrian economic scholar who had worked on several of Ron's previous campaigns, and Murray Rothbard, a radical libertarian writer, philosopher, and economist.

When Ron returned to medical practice after leaving Congress and contending for the Texas Senate and the United States Presidency, Blumert saw an opportunity for both of them to combine their individual talents. Blumert proposed a joint business venture, and the Ron Paul Coin Company was formed. Camino Coin was the parent company, with Blumert as the sole proprietor. Ron brought his good name and reputation to the business, along with a diverse group of supporters he had amassed during his presidential campaign.

"You couldn't ask for a better name for the coin business," Blumert said. "Ron had always been friendly to gold, historically and otherwise, so he was perfect for heading up the company." As always, Blumert's top concerns for the business were reputation and customer service. "Anyone who is a principled libertarian cannot be anything but above board, and always thinking of the client's welfare. That's what builds a business, of course. It wasn't an accident that Ron accepted my offer to manage his coin company. We had become friends by that time. He knew and respected what we were doing, and to this day I'm very proud of that."[9]

During the decade-long business venture, Ron Paul Coin Company sold thousands of "Ron Paul Survival Kits." The kits were, as Blumert described them, "a big hit."[10] The kits consisted of surplus ammunition cans from World War II, filled with a mixture of coins. According to Blumert, there was "a silver kit for the fellow on a modest budget, and there was one with gold and silver for those who could afford it."[11]

Most of the coins in the Ron Paul Survival Kits were American coins. According to Blumert, the last minting of a pure silver coin in the US was in 1953. Approximately fifty years later, a silver dime was worth about $1.30. These sold in the Ron Paul Survival Kits at thirty or forty cents each. The US twenty dollar gold coins, last minted in 1907, which contain about an ounce of gold each, were worth approximately $1200 a century later. The kits also contained US silver dollars. "Everyone who bought one of these survival kits," Blumert joked, "survived."[12]

At that time, the late 1980s and early 1990s, Ron and his colleagues published several newsletters – *The Ron Paul Investment Report, The Ron Paul Political Report*, and *The Ron Paul Survival Report* – which were mailed out to a list of subscribers. At the suggestion of Lew Rockwell, newsletter editor, the Ron Paul Coin Company included special offerings with some of the newsletters.

"Imagine having a city the size of Utica, New York as your client base," said Blumert. "They were very good clients, and very loyal." Blumert reportedly received offers from other coin dealers to buy the mailing list for hundreds of thousands of dollars. But, he said, "of course, we would never sell it. That's the way Ron is." The Ron Paul Coin Company was even said to have had congressional customers.[13]

Although Ron enjoyed his association with the company, he was not in it for the money. He explained, "You only make five or ten dollars a coin so you've got to sell a lot of coins to get rich. I was just promoting something I believe in."[14] Ron was later forced to divest himself of the company in 1996 when he returned to the House of Representatives, due to strict congressional rules that prohibited outside sources of income.[15] Still, up until that time it was an additional source of income for the doctor, who prohibited his children from taking federal college loans, instead paying for their education himself. This, combined with the income from his obstetrical practice, allowed Ron and his wife, Carol, to build a second home in the nearby town of Surfside Beach in 1990.

Ron's self-prescribed remedy for his frustration with big government came in the form of his involvement with freedom-oriented institutions. He founded his Foundation for Rational Economics and Education (FREE), described in its mission statement as "a non-profit, non-partisan, educational foundation dedicated to public education on the principles of free-market economics, sound money and limited government,"[16] in 1976 while serving in the House of Representatives. In 1989, he established The National Endowment for Liberty (NEFL), an offshoot of FREE. NEFL was created for the purpose of producing electronic media programs to advance the mission of FREE.[17]

After the dismissal of Nadia Hayes, Jessie Helm's former campaign fundraiser David James took over her position within Ron Paul's organization. The Houston-Clear Lake office on Nasa Road One was used for the publication of Ron Paul's several newsletters. With the arrival of David James, their activities took on a larger scope.[18]

Due to their relative lack of media coverage during the 1988 Libertarian presidential run, Paul and his associates were eager to bypass the establishment media. The natural outlet for airing his views was through cable television, which was blossoming in the 1980s.

"David James' big project was a Ron Paul cable television series," explained Dondero. "He had a dream of a libertarian television show nationwide that would air every Wednesday."[19]

David James worked on the television series from 1989 to 1991, acting as Executive Producer. They modeled their production on Public Broadcasting Service (PBS) series – unlike PBS, however, they did not use public funds. Instead they used funds from NEFL to produce the series, with Ron Paul as the chairman of the endowment fund.[20]

James titled the show At Issue, and set out to create a weekly half-hour program with news items, interviews and panel discussions, hosted by Paul and moderator Mike Hayes. The show had multiple studio cameras, a quality news set, and professional editing.

The half-hour show contained several segments, reminiscent of The McNeil-Lehrer Report on PBS. The first segment featured a documentary report with on-site interviews with politicians and businessmen, background music, and even reenactments. The longer second segment featured an in-depth discussion of the issues at hand with a featured expert. Interspersed between segments were spots touting the National Endowment for Liberty as the show's sponsor, and explaining that the show was funded entirely by voluntary contributions from individual donors. Supporters could sponsor the show by sending donations to the endowment.[21]

James was diligent in producing the show, even going so far as to offer a preview of each episode to a focus group of Americans to gauge their reactions. Paul himself not only appeared on the show,[22] but was also involved in the production.[23]

At Issue was successful at attracting an interested audience. As the show became more popular, Dondero recalled that it even aired on some widely-viewed news networks. "They were good shows," he said. "Walter Williams was a guest, and Milton Friedman. They were well produced."[24]

In 1991, after Paul hit on many important libertarian issues, the series ended. The shows did not disappear altogether after the series ended its run, however. Many At Issue shows later appeared on the popular video website YouTube for the next generation of viewers curious about the ideas of liberty.[25]

With the 1992 presidential election fast approaching and the lessons of 1988 still on their minds, Ron's closest friends and political strategists considered a second bid for the United States Presidency. They had been just as frustrated as Ron by the barriers to ballot access and media coverage for third parties. As Blumert said, "We felt that the experience we had in 1987 and 1988 indicated that a third party was not the way to run." They, and Ron, decided that should he ever run for president again, he would do so as a Republican.[26]

Ron had opposed the Persian Gulf War from the outset, and felt strongly enough that he wanted to raise the issue publicly in the 1992 election. So, in 1991, his supporters formed an exploratory committee to challenge then-President George H. W. Bush in the Republican primary.

Burt Blumert was the chair of the committee. In October 1991, they began fundraising, raising ten to twenty thousand dollars in the first few weeks.[27]

However, during this time Patrick Buchanan, a senior Republican advisor to the Nixon, Ford, and Reagan administrations and political commentator, entered the race as a challenger to Bush. Many of Buchanan's positions were similar to Ron's. A private phone conversation between Ron and Pat Buchanan followed. Because of Buchanan's anti-war stance, Ron was amenable to his ideas, so Ron stepped back from the race and let Buchanan take the reigns as the anti-war candidate.

Ron was not altogether disappointed to drop out of the race. Blumert speculates that privately, Ron was not ready to make that run, having been burned in the 1988 race.[28]

They quickly found a home for the unused money that the exploratory committee had raised. As Blumert recalled, the funds they had at the time were "turned over to a PAC – America First Political Action Committee."[29]

Another important event ongoing at this time was the adoption of the North American Free Trade Agreement (NAFTA), signed by the United States, Canada, and Mexico in 1992 and ratified by the United States Congress in 1993. As a student of economics, Ron strongly opposed NAFTA. It was abundantly clear to him that despite its name, NAFTA was not about free trade at all.

"We don't need government agreements to have free trade," Ron wrote. "We merely need to lower or eliminate taxes on the American people, without regard to what other nations do."

With regard to tariffs, he stated his belief that they are, "simply taxes on consumers... As economist Henry Hazlitt explained, tariffs simply protect politically-favored special interests at the expense of consumers, while lowering wages across the economy as a whole. Hazlitt, Ludwig von Mises, Friedrich Hayek, Murray Rothbard, and countless other economists have demolished every fallacy concerning tariffs, proving conclusively that unilateral elimination of tariffs benefits the American people."[30]

In contrast to those who favored politically mediated "protection" of certain industries, Ron was never one to support political favors for any group. He voted against subsidies, tariffs, and government intervention in a myriad of industries, including subsidies for the many farmers in his district.

"Free trade occurs in the absence of government interference in the flow of goods," he wrote, while "free trade agreements" such as NAFTA represent "more government in the form of an international body. It is incompatible with our Constitution and national sovereignty, and we don't need it to benefit from international trade."[31]

By 1995, Ron Paul was once again ready to run for the United States House of Representatives. As he geared up for what would be one of the toughest and most exciting elections of his career, Ron juggled campaigning and caring for his patients with his typical brand of finesse. "All through '95, getting ready for the '96 election, I probably campaigned for seven months," he said. But Ron was able to maintain an appropriate level of flexibility in his schedule. He kept seeing his patients, and even made his last delivery after he was sworn in.[32]

It was grace, persistence, good company, and commitment to his deeply held principles that sustained Ron Paul in the years between his Libertarian presidential campaign and his re-election to the House of Representatives. The 1990's were both a productive and an introspective time for Ron. However, he could never stay silent on the issues he saw plaguing America, at the root of which was an ever-expanding federal government. By the time the 1996 campaigns began to take shape, it was clear: Dr. No was back.

CHAPTER 17

DR. NO RETURNS

1995-1996

Freedom to Bear Arms

Both oligarch and tyrant mistrust the people, and therefore deprive them of arms.

ARISTOTLE

In 1995, the Republican Party promised a revolution that included tax cuts, spending cuts, reigning in regulations, repealing unneeded laws, and dismantling entire unconstitutional federal agencies. Americans believed their sincerity and the Republican Party decisively captured both houses of Congress, winning a majority in the House of Representatives for the first time since 1952, when a teenaged Ron Paul was running track at his Green Tree, Pennsylvania high school.

To Ron Paul, it seemed as if the GOP was finally to embody his most deeply-held ideals of liberty. "I thought they might be serious about shrinking the size of government, which has always been my goal," he later recalled.[1]

Paul had been out of Congress since 1984, but never far from politics in the intervening years. He had a following of over ten thousand enthusiastic libertarian supporters whom he had attracted from across the country during his earlier political career and through his work with FREE. This network of anti-tax, pro-Constitution, pro-free market activists would play an important role in what The New York Times Magazine many years later referred to as "one of the stranger Congressional elections of modern times."[2]

Adding to Paul's reawakened interest in congressional politics was the fact that his home state of Texas seemed to be at the forefront of this new Republican Revolution.

Fiscal conservative Rep. Dick Armey of Texas's 26th District was elected House Majority Leader, while Paul's successor in the 22nd District, Rep. Tom DeLay, was named Majority Whip (Armey's second-in-command).

Tax-cutting champion Rep. Bill Archer of the 7th District assumed the chairmanship of the powerful House Ways and Means Committee, which is responsible for writing federal tax legislation.

Sen. Kay Bailey Hutchison decisively won her first full term by a 30-point margin in a seat previously occupied by a Democrat.

And future president George W. Bush upended Democratic Gov. Ann Richards, thanks in part to his support of "concealed carry" legislation to allow licensed Texans to keep pistols hidden on their persons in public establishments for the purpose of self-defense, which Richards vetoed.[3]

Nationally, many other Democrats, including Speaker of the House Tom Foley, lost their seats to Republicans over their support for an ill-conceived "assault weapons" ban. President Clinton, who signed the ban into law, angrily blamed the NRA's efforts for the defeat of as many as 20 congressional Democrats.[4] They had underestimated the importance Americans attached to their right to keep and bear arms.

The political winds had unmistakably shifted toward a desire for less government and more freedom. For 59 year-old Ron Paul, the time to re-enter politics seemed right. His partner in obstetrics, Jack Pruitt, felt ready to dissolve their busy practice, needing more time to look after his ill wife. And as ever, Ron's family, all true believers in the cause of liberty, were supportive of his decision to seek office.[5]

Again he set his sights on the House of Representatives. Having moved with Carol and the family from their home in Lake Jackson to their beach house in Surfside, he faced the prospect of winning over a soon-to-be-redrawn district, different from the one he had represented in the 1970s and 1980s.

Ron thought it would be an unwise political move to run against DeLay, a powerful Republican member of the House. However, the Pauls' new beach house, just twenty minutes away from Lake Jackson, was situated in the 14th congressional district. Ron recalled, "It was so close, and we were spending half our time down there anyway, so we just used that as the political address. That became my voting address. I ran from Surfside Beach in the 1990s."[6]

His new 14th District was a sprawling, mostly rural area comprising 22 counties in the coastal region of Texas, lying just outside the large metropolitan areas of Houston, San Antonio, Austin, and Corpus Christi. Historically, it was a Democratic district, and the incumbent Democrat Paul would have to beat was Greg Laughlin. However, a strange political twist would soon change everything.

Paul reached out to DeLay to help him get in touch with Armey and the rest of the Republican delegation from Texas.[7] Before announcing his candidacy, he hopped a jet to Washington, DC, with high hopes for a productive meeting. He assumed the Republicans would be interested in the possibility of using his candidacy to increase their number, perhaps offering him financial support and endorsements in his bid to defeat the Democrat.

"A court-ordered redistricting was coming up in Texas, and I told them, 'If you guys help protect my interests in this, I can gain his seat for you,'" he recalled.[8]

The Texas Republicans were interested in increasing their number, but not in the way Ron Paul assumed when he announced his candidacy to them. "I didn't think they were going to do what they did," he later noted.[9]

What they did was follow newly installed Speaker of the House Newt Gingrich's strategy of boosting the Republican majority by convincing Democrats to switch parties. In this case, that meant courting the politically moderate Laughlin to join the Republican Party.

Laughlin would prove to be a willing convert. Before the Republican takeover of Congress, he was in line for a seat on the House Ways and Means Committee, a prized position that attracted large campaign donations from political action committees (PACs) and the Texas oil industry.[10] If he switched parties, the Republican leadership, which now controlled committee assignments, would make sure he got his Ways and Means spot. Laughlin became a Republican in June of 1995.[11]

Ron Paul was stunned. Now instead of running against a Democrat—one who had been bitterly attacked by the GOP leadership as a liberal in previous elections—he suddenly faced a primary battle with an incumbent Republican.

Another wrinkle was that rancher Jim Deats, who ran against Democrat Laughlin in 1994, had also entered the Republican primary fray. It would be a difficult campaign for Ron Paul, who was less well known in the district than either of his two rivals.

That was only the beginning. One by one, over the next few months, the leaders of the GOP establishment shunned Ron Paul (and Deats), instead lining up behind Laughlin, who they thought was a safe bet. Their indifference, and even outright hostility, toward Paul stemmed from their belief that he was not a team player. They believed his history with the Libertarian Party and anti-drug-war stance would not appeal to mainstream Republican voters, particularly religious and socially conservative ones.

"My image was completely different in 1996 than in 1976," he later said of the campaign. "You can't just get passed off as an average Republican having done what I did. We got hit hard."[12]

"Hard" proved to be an understatement. All told, Laughlin raised more than $1 million through the Texas and national Republican leadership, as well as from the PACs of 72 Republican members of Congress.[13] By January 1996, Gingrich himself was campaigning in the 14th District for the newly minted Republican Laughlin. "I believe it's very important that Greg wins the primary," he said on a campaign stop. Other congressional Republicans, including Sen. Hutchison and Texas's senior senator, Phil Gramm, followed suit.[14]

As a result, Paul found himself polling far behind, at 6 percent to Laughlin's 44 percent, but he remained determined. First, he reached out to friend and strategist Tom Lizardo, whom he had met in the 1980s, for campaign advice. Despite the long odds, Lizardo moved to Texas to join the campaign.

"He was the type of person who struck me very clearly as capable of taking an uphill battle and doing something with it," Lizardo recalled.[15]

Paul also hired Eric Dondero, the former Young Republican who previously supported him in his 1988 Libertarian bid. Dondero moved from Florida to Texas in order to act as his campaign coordinator.

Daughter Lori Pyeatt and Carol Paul, both longtime board members of Paul & Associates, would campaign almost as hard as Paul himself.

And of course, he had David James, the chief officer of Ron Paul &

Associates. James was a skilled fundraiser and Paul would need his abilities more than any other time in his political career.

James tapped into his national network of limited-government, pro-freedom supporters to out-fundraise Laughlin (*The Dallas Morning News* estimated more than 60 percent of his campaign contributions came from outside Texas).[16] Paul fought back by taking out newspaper ads reminding voters that just 15 months earlier, when Laughlin was a Democrat, Gingrich had been slamming him as a "Clinton clone." The Paul campaign also sent out mailings reprinting a Republican attack from the same period that suggested Laughlin had taken illegal campaign contributions from a convicted criminal.[17]

Paul's television spots also struck at Laughlin's reputation for taking trips abroad at the taxpayer's expense.

"We just had one little ad that we put on," Carol Paul recalled. "And it had one little man in an airplane, and it said, 'He went here,' and the airplane flies to one side of the screen, and then, 'he went here,' and then, 'he went here...'"[18]

While the Republican establishment opposed Ron Paul, he did enjoy one key endorsement: that of his friend and baseball Hall of Famer Nolan Ryan, a Lone Star State native who pitched for the Houston Astros and Texas Rangers, among other teams. Ryan served as his honorary campaign chair throughout the primary.[19]

Perhaps most importantly, Ron Paul remembered the value of personal contact with the people he hoped to represent in Washington. With the help of his family, he spent countless hours canvassing the district. His granddaughters wore red, white, and blue dresses, hand-sewn by Carol, and got the attention of potential voters.

"We would all fan out," Carol later explained. "Two of our granddaughters might go to a door, with one of their moms. And they'd say, 'I'm Laura and I'm Valori, and our Granddad's walking in the neighborhood. Would you like to meet him? He's running for Congress.'"

When they met "Granddad", many of the people recognized Ron Paul as the man who had delivered their babies. Strategist Tom Lizardo, now Paul's chief of staff, ultimately attributed the campaign's success to this personal connection.[20]

The Laughlin campaign struck back by portraying Paul's Constitutional positions against federal involvement in drug prohibition as crazy, irresponsible, and un-Republican.

"They tried to paint me as a drug pusher," Paul later recalled. "But the voters weren't buying it.* I had never advocated legalization and they knew it. I had condemned the federal war on drugs."[21]

March 12, Primary Day, dawned bright and warm. Turnout was much higher than expected, with more people voting as Republicans than as Democrats for the first time in Texas history. When the polls closed, the Pauls watched, patiently but a little tensely, as the returns came in. Late into the evening, the final tally showed Laughlin with 42 percent of the record 34,000 ballots cast; Paul, 32 percent; and Deats, 24 percent.[22]

Laughlin and his establishment backers were disappointed he did not receive more than 50 percent needed for an outright victory. A runoff election

---

* The federal government's 1993 paramilitary action against the Branch Davidian sect in Waco, based in part on false allegations the Davidians were operating a drug lab, was still relatively fresh on the minds of many Texans.

was scheduled in April between he and Ron Paul to determine who would win the nomination. Deats dropped out, earning the distinction of being one of the few Republicans to endorse Paul as he did so.[23]

The GOP establishment pulled out all the stops to ensure a Laughlin win in the runoff. The National Republican Congressional Committee provided Laughlin's campaign with support in the form of phone calls and mailings.[24] Newly elected Gov. George W. Bush got involved, producing pro-Laughlin radio ads and declaring before an audience of hundreds in Laughlin's hometown, "The definition of welcome for this Governor is not only to say behind closed doors 'you are welcome,' but to say 'I have helped you win our party's nomination in any way I can.'" The governor's father, former president George H.W. Bush, also weighed in, endorsing Laughlin.

In response to a video the Paul campaign produced featuring past praise from Ronald Reagan, former Reagan attorney general Ed Meese flew to Texas to campaign against Paul, who, Meese reminded Republican voters, had been sharply critical of Reagan during his 1988 Libertarian presidential campaign.[25] And despite Ron Paul's support of the rights guaranteed under the Second Amendment, even the NRA contributed to the campaign against him.[26]

With the entire might of the Republican establishment aligned against him, it appeared unlikely Ron Paul would prevail. However, Texans have an independent streak. On the night of the election, Paul convincingly beat Laughlin in the low-turnout runoff.[27] The Republican efforts were in vain.

Now the stage was set for the general election in November against the Democratic nominee, Charles "Lefty" Morris. As bruising as the primary was, Paul knew he faced another serious challenge in the form of Morris, a 56-year-old personal injury lawyer from Bee Cave who had the backing of the AFL-CIO, a major labor organization. Little did he know just how bitter the race against Morris—later labeled a "months-long hate campaign" by The Austin Chronicle—would become.[28]

The national Republican leadership, so opposed to him in the primary, offered Paul no help in the general election.

"We thought we would qualify for a nice sum from the Republican National Party—I think it's like $65,000 or $70,000— because they always reserve that amount of money for the nominee of the party," he said after the election. "But in this case, an exception was made and they spent it in the primary. ... So we then had to do our own fundraising."[29]

The Texas Republican Party, however, became more accommodating. "After Ron won the GOP nomination, mainline Republicans were unsure as to how to treat him," recalled Eric Dondero. "We reached out to the Bush people. After my conversations with [Bush advisor Karl] Rove, he put out the word to key Houston-area, Austin, and Victoria Republicans to back Ron Paul. All of a sudden like a tidal wave all the GOPers came on board our campaign."[30]

....

For his part, Democrat Charles "Lefty" Morris picked up where Laughlin left off. He immediately worked to publicize Ron Paul's anti-drug-war views, characterizing them as absurd and out of touch. Then in May, Morris campaign staffers discovered a Canadian neo-Nazi website that linked to old issues of The Ron Paul Survival Report, under the heading of "Racialists and Freedom Fighters."

Despite the fact that Ron Paul had no control over who linked to his newsletters, the media reaction was explosive. Newspapers across the state reprinted provocative passages from the newsletters, including a suggestion that former black Congresswoman Barbara Jordan was a "half-educated victimologist" and a supposition that "95 percent of the black males in [Washington, DC] are semi-criminal or entirely criminal." The Morris campaign heavily implied Paul was a racist and demanded that he release the entire contents of all his old newsletters for public examination.[31] The Dallas Morning News picked up the story and the president of the Texas NAACP (National Association for the Advancement of Colored People) denounced the newsletters and demanded an apology from Paul.[32]

Publicly, Paul held his ground. Campaign coordinator Eric Dondero Rittberg traded on his Jewish background, going so far as to wear a yarmulke to a press conference, and accused the Morris camp of ludicrously trying to paint Ron Paul as a Nazi. Paul himself denied the charge of racism, saying, "I'm for freedom of speech, even for ugly things, but calling me a Nazi is the most aggravating, insulting thing that an opponent has ever done." (For his part, Morris asserted he never called Paul a Nazi.) Of the inflammatory content in some of his old newsletters, Paul said the "academic, tongue-in-cheek" writings were being taken out of context, even as he refused to release all his back issues.[33] If people had questions about his character, he said, they could "come and talk to my neighbors."[34]

Privately, Paul regretted the controversial content in his old newsletters. In an interview years later, he admitted, "I could never say this in the campaign, but those words weren't really written by me. It wasn't my language at all. Other people help me with my newsletter as I travel around. ... They were never my words, but I had some moral responsibility for them."[35]

All through the long, sweltering Texas summer, the heated battle continued. Paul lost ground in the polls following the newsletter controversy, but thanks again to his large nationwide contributor base, he outraised Morris nearly three-to-one, garnering $1.2 million to Morris's roughly $472,000. To help Morris, the AFL-CIO underwrote numerous anti-Paul ads, while the Paul campaign used their war chest to generate television and radio spots and mass mailings that portrayed Morris as a tool of shady lawyers' organizations and labor unions.[36]

Cooler weather arrived with the November 1996 election day. Nationwide, voters received their first chance to express, via the ballot, their opinion so far of the Republican Revolution. They would also choose whether to give US Sen. Bob Dole of Kansas, who beat back an early primary challenge from conservative populist Pat Buchanan, the presidency and with it, Republican control of all three branches of the federal government, executive, legislative, and judicial.

The issues were much the same as they were in 1994: the need to lower or eliminate taxes, balance the federal budget, abolish wasteful and useless agencies, and restore respect for federalism. The question of the Second Amendment and what it meant regarding citizen gun ownership also became a major topic nationally after April 19, 1995, when ex-military man Timothy McVeigh used a homemade bomb to destroy the Alfred P. Murrah federal building in Oklahoma City, killing 168 people. President Clinton seized on the tragedy to blame Republicans for stirring up hatred toward government and retroactively justify his "assault weapons" ban, even as the House of Representatives, led by the Republican majority, voted to repeal that ban as an unwise and unjustified infringement on Americans' Second Amendment rights. As ever, candidate Ron Paul came down on the side of the Constitution, agreeing in an issues survey to "Repeal all bans and measures that restrict law-abiding citizens from owning legally-obtained firearms."[37] His reasoning went far beyond the expediency of supporting a position popular in a state where gun ownership is widespread to encompass the Founders' intent in including the Second Amendment in the Bill of Rights in the first place.

But what was that intent? In his 1987 book Freedom Under Siege, Ron Paul agreed with the 19th-century political philosopher Lysander Spooner that "when all else fails, the gun owned by the individual is to be used to protect against tyranny of the state."[38] Paul would elaborate on the idea of the Second Amendment as a bulwark against oppressive government in numerous other speeches and writings throughout his career, noting "It is practical, rather than alarmist, to understand that unarmed citizens cannot be secure in their freedoms. … By banning certain weapons today, we may plant the seeds for tyranny to flourish ten, thirty, or fifty years from now."[39]

Meanwhile, in the race for the 14th District, the last polls predicted a dead heat between Paul and Morris. Again the Paul family waited through the day to learn if the past year's hard work would result in victory. When all the votes were tallied, it was clear Ron was the winner by the razor-thin margin of 51 percent of, in the words of The Austin Chronicle, "a race that both sides admit has been unusually brutal."[40] Morris was shocked and refused to concede defeat even well past midnight, when all the morning editions were going to press naming Paul the winner.[41]

Nationally, the weak candidacy of Republican Bob Dole—who only half-heartedly embraced the limited-government goals of the Republican freshmen of 1994—lost in a landslide to the incumbent President Clinton, winning only 40.7 percent of the popular vote, with independent Ross Perot trailing far behind with 8.4 percent.[42] Congressional Republicans, thought to be vulnerable following the tragic Oklahoma City bombing, maintained convincing control of both houses.

The results in Texas's 14th District were just as undeniable. Ron Paul and his message of strictly limited, Constitutional government would return to Washington after a 12-year absence. And this time, despite a continuing Democratic presence in the White House, he believed real progress would finally be made to halt and even reverse the uncontrolled growth of the state at the expense of Americans' freedom.

With his political career reestablished, Ron felt it was time to close the medical practice. Dr. Pruitt required more time to spend with his ill wife, and Paul would have little time away from Washington. After he was sworn in, the sixty-year old Congressman made his last delivery and then retired from the medical profession.[43] He would now dedicate the remainder of his career to politics and soon become a strong force for freedom in Washington.

Unfortunately, he was soon to discover that the Republicans were more interested in maintaining and consolidating their political power than in fulfilling their pledges to shrink the size and scope of the federal government.

CHAPTER 18

THE PROPHET OF CAPITOL HILL

1997-1998

Global Government

In the next century, nations as we know it will be obsolete; all states will recognize a single, global authority. National sovereignty wasn't such a great idea after all.

STROBE TALBOT, BILL CLINTON'S DEPUTY SECRETARY OF STATE

After a twelve year absence from Congress, Paul was eager to renew his attack against big government. As with his previous terms, his role would be largely educational, both to the American public, and hopefully to his fellow politicians. Although none of his colleagues suspected it at the time, his speeches to congress would prove prophetic.

Paul set about to assemble a new congressional staff, choosing mainly from his campaign staff. Eric Dondero was hired as a Senior Aide and District Representative, remaining in Brazoria County while Paul worked in Washington. It was up to him to represent Congressman Paul to constituents; speaking for him, handling questions from his constituents, scheduling his appearances, and dealing with local government representatives.

On January 3, the 105th session of Congress began. Paul wasted little time making his return known. One of his first official acts was to urge every member to follow his lead in opting out of the lucrative pension plan. Having refused to participate in what he considered an immoral system since his first term in 1976, he reaffirmed his decision as he began his 5th term in 1997, at the age of 61.

Eligibility requirements for Congress' taxpayer funded pension plan are more relaxed than what is available to tax paying citizens in the private sector. After only *five years* of service, a Member of Congress becomes vested and can begin receiving payouts after the age of 62, or at any point after 25 years of service.

"The situation is even worse today than it was before," Paul noted. "When I served in the late '70s and early '80s, the congressman had to actually write a letter to enter the program. I simply chose not to sign up. Today, however, everyone is automatically placed in the system and house members are required to write a letter requesting that they not be included in the program."

Paul felt that, rather than simply discussing ways to cut spending and taxes, this was an immediate and practical measure. Every member of Congress could take part and it would benefit taxpayers. Paul told congress that he felt enriching himself for life was an "arrogant insult" to his constituents.[1]

This wasn't the only measure Paul would take in an apparent crusade against his own financial security. In February of 1997, Paul voted for HJ Resolution 2, which proposed a Constitutional amendment to limit the number of terms for both House members and Senators. Like the pension plan, the absence of term limits creates an incentive for elected officials to remain in office for life. He believed that as long as a behavior is subsidized, it will continue to perpetuate itself.

The existing system in Washington provided little incentive for Congressional members to ever return to the private sector. "Only when we limit the size of the federal government," he explained, "when we end the programs which allow for federal handouts, will we see our Congress returned to the citizen-legislature intended by the Founders of this nation."

Many of Paul's colleagues voted in line with him on HJ Resolution 2, but it failed to receive the required two-thirds majority, with a vote of 217-211.[2]

Although Paul favored term limits, he did not voluntarily limit his own congressional career because that would force him to desert the battle in Washington. To others, it seemed logical that if he supported term limits he would limit his own terms, just as he refused Medicare at his private medical practice. The apparent contradiction would one day come back to haunt him.

Before the end of his 5th term in Congress, Paul would also cast another vote which helped to solidify his reputation as "The Taxpayer's Best Friend," this time against a Congressional pay-raise. Aside from lucrative perks, Congressmen received a hefty salary of $165,000.[3] "I have never and will never vote to increase Congress' pay," Ron said "It's shameful that Congress seems to think that they should be raising their own pay at the same time the American people see their taxes increasing, federal spending going up, and the national debt getting larger."

Ironically, Congressional members were simultaneously contemplating ways to cut benefits to veterans and the elderly. Although Paul generally opposed government handouts, he saw this as an indication of how out of touch the average representative was with his constituents.[4]

....

The intervening years did not soften Ron Paul's stance on the issues of gold and sound money. He continued his vocal opposition to any legislation that threatened what he considered pillars of freedom. Paul joined two influential banking subcommittees: the Domestic and International Monetary Policy committee, and the Financial Institutions and Consumer Credit committee.[5] The Financial Institutions and Consumer Credit committee exercised jurisdiction over the actions of the Federal Reserve, while the International Monetary Policy committee monitored the results of the policies the Fed implemented. Always an outspoken critic, Ron now had an additional pulpit from which to hold the Federal Reserve accountable.

Ron also continued to defend the constitutionally protected rights of personal liberty and privacy. In April 1998, he introduced what would have become the 28th Amendment to the US Constitution; HJ 116, known as the Liberty Amendment. The amendment, originally proposed in 1952, would prohibit the federal government from engaging in any activities not specifically authorized in the Constitution. The amendment would not only reinforce the ninth and tenth amendments, but also repeal the sixteenth amendment, which introduced the federal income tax.

While discussing the proposed 28th Amendment, Ron noted, "Over the years this amendment has enjoyed widespread support and has been introduced several times in the past by various Members of Congress, but finally this measure has a chance of success, given the conservative Congress and mood of the country in favor of a more limited, constitutional government which respects individual liberty."

Unfortunately for Paul, his hopes were rebuffed. The Republican Congress was not interested in legislation that they felt might hinder law enforcement and the Liberty Amendment was not ratified into the Constitution.[6]

....

Later, Paul introduced a key piece of legislation, HR 4217, known as the Freedom and Privacy Restoration Act. It was drafted in response to the Department of Transportation's move to establish a national identification system. "Under the current state of the law, the citizens of states which have drivers' licenses that do not conform to the federal standards by October 1, 2000, will find themselves essentially stripped of their ability to participate in life as we know it," said Paul. "On that date, Americans will not be able to get a job, open a bank account, apply for Social Security or Medicare, exercise their Second Amendment rights, or even take an airplane flight, unless they can produce a state-issued ID that conforms to the federal specifications."[7]

Congressman Paul's specialty, as usual, was to identify potential threats to the rights of American citizens. He believed that the national ID was just another move toward cradle-to-grave oversight.

Ron questioned the motives of the national ID. "Our first question should always be, 'Why does the federal government want to know every detail of our lives, and have so much control over our every move?' The answer is often very simple: more money for the politicians to spend and more power for them to wield," he said.

Over time, many American's would come to see the Federal Government's desire for a national ID as an unavoidable consequence of 9/11, when in fact plans were in motion far before any such national emergency.

....

Throughout the first part of his term, Ron Paul was distracted by matters at home. His father, Howard, was not well. At 93 years of age his heart was growing weaker and he was frequently in the hospital. Paul gave his father the best medical advice he could as a physician, but he could not halt the injustices of aging. On May 23, 1997, Howard Caspar Paul passed away.

It was hard to be sad about a man who had lived such a full life, and who had witnessed so much of his family's successes, including Ron's. The family flew to Pennsylvania for the funeral to console Ron's mother, Margaret.

After the funeral, he returned to Washington with a fresh perspective and a resolved determination to fight for what really mattered to him: life and liberty. Ron was understandably low-key for the first few weeks after his return, but he could not afford to remain so for long.

The defining issue of Ron's 5th term in Congress was his stand on national sovereignty. Ron began to seriously question the interventionist policy that the US had been involved in for decades. On the House floor, Ron frequently voiced his opposition toward US policy, and specifically the role unelected, international organizations like NATO and the United Nations played in embroiling the United States in foreign conflicts.

Ron reminded Congress that, "George Washington, in his farewell address, told America to be weary of 'entangling alliances'. He understood very clearly what has since been either ignored or forgotten: foreign leaders will not do, nor can they be expected to do, what is best for American citizens. If we want what is best for this nation, Americans should be running America, not ceding rights and authority to international organizations."

With this in mind, in April of 1997, Congressman Paul sponsored HR 1146, the American Sovereignty Restoration Act. The legislation would end US participation in the United Nations. This included all UN military operations, an end to diplomatic immunity for UN envoys operating in the United States, and preventing UN access to federally-owned properties.[8]

Ron knew that the United Nations was no friend of US sovereignty, but he laid the blame where it belonged: at the feet of Congress and the President. Throughout his five terms in Congress, Ron witnessed a breakdown in the Constitutional separation of powers, with an increasingly disproportionate amount shifting to the executive branch. He often addressed Congress' failure to restrain the President from overstepping his constitutionally established boundaries.

At the time, the United States was intruding in the Bosnian conflict. Known as the Wars of Yugoslav Succession, it began just prior to Bill Clinton's first term in office, when the southeastern European nation declared independence from Yugoslavia. This resulted in war between Bosnian Serbs, who wanted to remain part of Yugoslavia, and the Croats, who supported Bosnian independence.

Using the justification of UN support, President Clinton deployed US troops to the region in January 1996 with plans to get out within a year. Eighteen months passed, and Clinton now maintained that the troops would remain until June of 1998. Congressman Paul felt that this "peace mission" was beginning to resemble Korea, Vietnam, Somalia, and even the Persian Gulf War.

In a speech given to Congress on July 15, 1997, Ron argued that "not only has Congress failed in its responsibilities to restrain our adventurous presidents in pursuing war, spying, and imposing our will on other nations by installing leaders, and at times eliminating others, throughout the world these past 50 years, we now, by default, have allowed our foreign policy to be commandeered by international bodies like NATO and the United Nations."

He went on to address the complicity of Congress in continuing to fund an operation with no end in sight. "The recent two billion dollar additional funds in the supplemental appropriation bill were the cue to the president that the Congress will not act to stop the operation when under pressure to support the troops." In Paul's view, the best way for Congress to support the troops was to bring them home, rather than continuing to fund and escalate a conflict once the troops are engaged.[9] Paul felt the cost of participation in the UN was too great, and the benefits too few for the American people.

Paul even had some personal battles against the UN. In a press release, Paul addressed what he called the "logical outgrowth" of our meddling abroad under the banner of the United Nations.[10] This time the UN was starting to intervene in the affairs of Paul's 14th District in Texas.

The Brazoria County Detention Center was under investigation regarding a 1996 incident where law enforcement officers allegedly beat several prisoners. It seemed obvious to Paul that this was a state-level incident, yet somehow the civil rights issue had piqued the interest of the United Nations, and they wanted to hear testimony and weigh in on the matter.

Ron was livid. "According to our Constitution," he explained, "it is exclusively the responsibility and duty of state and local governments to make criminal laws, investigate crimes, and punish instances of official abuses of power. To say the UN has some right even to comment, let alone investigate and 'admonish' the United States, in reference to this or anything we do, is completely contrary to the very basic concept of national sovereignty."

Congressman Paul noted that the US was currently operating as a police-force in Bosnia, under the leadership of a UN taskforce. "If we were not so quick to violate the sovereignty of other nations and get ourselves involved in their internal problems," he said, "we would not have to worry about them wanting to meddle in ours. Given how often we've arbitrarily sent US troops in to 'monitor' situations in other countries, I wouldn't be surprised if the UN decided someday to put blue berets on our deputies and run the sheriff's department from the UN Security Council. It would be completely consistent with how we have intervened in other countries."[11]

In September 1997, Paul announced his support for an amendment to HR 2267, the Commerce, Justice, State Appropriations Act, which would deny $100 million in US funds designated for the UN. The organization claimed it was owed $1.3 billion in back dues by the United States. However, the Government Accounting Office, an investigative arm of Congress, showed that the US had in reality over-paid the UN approximately $3.5 billion:

> First and foremost, Congressmen take an oath to uphold the Constitution, and there is nothing in the Constitution which authorizes Congress to tax the hard-earned money of Americans to ship off to power-hungry international bureaucrats. Second, Congressmen are morally obligated to do what is in the best interest of the taxpayers. Not only does the US not owe the UN money, the UN owes our nation a significant sum. We owe it to the small farmers and the auto mechanics and the secretaries and the entrepreneurs to be responsible with their money; if we waste more US tax dollars with the UN, this

Congress is as empty morally as the savings accounts Congress raids each year to fund these ridiculous programs.[12]

Even with the Constitution on his side, Congressman Paul was often a lone voice in the House of Representatives on many issues. As 1997 came to a close, it became apparent that the United States was headed for another foreign entanglement, this time over concerns that Iraq was not following the terms of their ceasefire agreement.

In November, Ron expressed his concerns. "We have been told by the Ambassador to the United Nations that the reason we must threaten force in this area is that Iraq is a direct threat to the United Nations." He added, "Here all along, I thought I was here in Congress to protect the security of the United States."[13]

In a personal letter, he urged President Clinton to avoid using military force in Iraq, since it would only worsen a situation brought on by decades of interventionist foreign policy. "The real problem for the United States is not Saddam Hussein, but rather our foreign policy," Paul wrote. "I hope your administration will mark a radical departure from others of this century, by following the advice of our Founding Fathers."[14] Clinton was unmoved.

Congressman Paul continued to speak out against what seemed to be the inevitable: military force in the Middle East. He was critical not only of the ease with which the Clinton administration, and his fellow House members, seemed ready to go to war with Iraq, but the hypocrisy of the policy itself. Why Iraq? Why not China, or North Korea, or Russia? What were the underlying motives that lead to singling out Iraq for their alleged possession of weapons of mass destruction, when the same could be said for any one of these other nations?

More importantly, why now? At the time, Clinton was embroiled in the embarrassing Monica Lewinsky scandal. News of an inappropriate relationship with the 22 year-old intern, and subsequent impeachment hearings, dominated the newspapers and television media in 1998. The coincidental timing did not escape the attention of Paul.

On January 27th, 1998, he addressed the House:

> Mr. Speaker, it appears the administration is about to bomb Iraq. The stated reason is to force UN inspections of every inch of Iraq territory to rule out the existence of any weapons of mass destruction. The president's personal problems may influence the decision, but a flawed foreign policy is behind the effort. ... There was a time in our history that bombing foreign countries was considered an act of war, done only with the declaration by this Congress. Today, tragically, it is done at the whim of presidents and at the urging of congressional leaders without a vote, except maybe by the UN Security Council.[15]

Paul went on to explain that the United States' role as the enforcer of UN policies would only serve to strengthen Hussein, unify the radical Islamic fundamentalists and increase the likelihood of terrorist attacks on American citizens.

Two days later, Paul gave what he called a "State of the Republic" address on the House floor in response to President Clinton's State of the Union address. Again, he pointed out the influence of the United Nations on foreign policy, and the resulting erosion of US sovereignty.

"These days," he said, "not even the United States moves without permission from the UN Security Council. In checking with the US Air Force about the history of U-2 flights in Iraq, over Iraq, and in their current schedules, I was firmly told the Air Force was not in charge of these flights, the UN was."[16]

On February 12, 1998, Congressman Paul introduced HR 3208 as a piece of emergency legislation. The bill was drafted to protect the troops and prevent President Clinton from initiating the use of force in the Persian Gulf. The legislation prohibited Defense Department funds from being used for offensive actions against Iraq without Congress declaring war.

Paul commented, "It's horrible that our nation has reached a point where it takes legislation like this to force the President and the Congress to follow the Constitution, which is the supreme law of the land. I am disgusted by and opposed to any leader who uses lethal force and horrendous weapons against his own people; but until Hussein takes steps against the United States, it is up to the Iraqis to determine what to do with him." Paul refused to have any part in activity that would put American soldiers in harm's way to enforce UN resolutions.[17]

In the twelve years between his fourth and fifth terms in Congress, Paul had become increasingly concerned with the threat of global government on US sovereignty. As he saw it, the representatives of the American people had a decision to make: either continue funding and maintaining a world Empire, or restore the Republic at home. In the latter half of his fifth term, he became more vocal in his opposition to the goals of what George H. W. Bush called a "New World Order," the military-industrial complex, and the Clinton administration's obsession with promoting a policy of worldwide military occupation.

After years in congress, the pattern was clear. Every time a tyrant was vanquished in one part of the world, another one rose up in another, requiring US military involvement.

In March of 1998, Paul addressed the issue in the context of the continuing conflict in southeastern Europe, this time in Kosovo:

> Mr. Speaker, last week it was Saddam Hussein and the Iraqis. This week's Hitler is Slobodon Milosevic and the Serbs. Next week, who knows? Kim Jong Il and the North Koreans? Next year, who will it be, the Ayatollah and the Iranians? Every week we must find a foreign infidel to slay, and of course, keep the military industrial complex humming. … Planning and military involvement in Kosovo is senseless. Our security is not threatened, and no one has the foggiest notion whether [UN Secretary General] Kofi Annan or Bill Clinton is in charge of our foreign policy. But we cannot maintain two loyalties, one to a world government under the United Nations and the other to US sovereignty protected by an American Congress. … Concern for American security is a proper and necessary function of the US Congress. The current policy, and one pursued for decades, threatens our security, drains our wallets and - worst of all - threatens the lives of young Americans who stand tall for American defense, but not for Kofi Annan and the United Nations.[18]

In the fall of 1998, the attention of Congress shifted again to the Middle East and former-ally-turned-enemy, Saddam Hussein. The Iraq Liberation Act passed 360-38 in the House. The Act was a Congressional statement of policy calling for regime change in Iraq. The stated reason for the Iraq Liberation Act was to "establish a program to support Democracy in Iraq." Primarily, this legislation moved forward based upon findings that Saddam Hussein had committed various violations of international law, failed to comply with its obligations following the previous Gulf War, and had ignored UN resolutions.

Congressman Paul certainly did not see any of these reasons as a justification to declare "virtual war" on Iraq and give the President "tremendous powers to pursue war efforts against a sovereign nation."[19]

On October 5th, one legislative day after the House passed the bill to the Senate, Ron addressed the House. He highlighted the unintended consequences of entangling alliances overseas, and pointed out that one of the reasons cited for supporting "regime change" was Iraq's invasion of Iran and use of chemical weapons between 1980 and 1988. Paul agreed that the actions were worthy of condemnation, but highlighted that "the whole problem is we were Iraq's ally at the time, giving [Hussein] military assistance, giving him funds, and giving him technology for chemical weapons."

He continued, "Not too long ago, a few years back in the 1980s, in our effort to bring peace and democracy to the world, we assisted the freedom fighters of Afghanistan. In our infinite wisdom, we gave money, technology and training to Bin Laden."[20] Ron Paul was wary of a coming tragedy if the United States continued on their path of foreign intervention.

Despite his opposition, the act went on to pass unanimously in the Senate, and President Clinton signed the bill into law on October 31, 1998. This set the stage for Operation Desert Fox, a four-day bombing campaign that ensued sixteen days later. Coincidentally, the campaign occurred at the same time the House of Representatives were conducting impeachment hearings against President Clinton.

When Clinton eventually sent troops into Iraq on December 16th, 1998, Paul boldly called on President Clinton to resign for the good of the country:

> Once again President Clinton is using American troops to deflect attention from his record of lies, distortions, obstruction of justice and abuse of power. Even if one can look past the constitutional prohibition against the US policing the world, the timing of this new attack against Iraq screams of hypocrisy by a president who has shown a complete disregard for our military, our Constitution and our national defense. Iraq has been 'disobeying' the United Nations for years now, but suddenly, on the verge of his impeachment, this president decides to launch an attack, in essence an unconstitutional declaration of war. … How many American soldiers and innocent Iraqi children will die so that this president can hide from justice? How many American citizens are now at increased risk from terrorist attack because of this president? How much innocent blood will have to flow to cover this president's sins? This attack has no basis in protecting our national security and only increases the danger to our people.[21]

As one of his last duties in his 5th Congressional term, Congressman Paul voted for all four articles of impeachment against President Clinton. He observed, "There is a major irony in this impeachment proceeding. A lot has been said the last two months by members of the Judiciary Committee on both sides of the aisle regarding the Constitution and how it must be upheld. But if we are witnessing ... a serious move toward obeying the constitutional restraints, I will anxiously look forward to the next session when 80 percent of our routine legislation will be voted down."

Ultimately, Ron felt that there were more serious crimes that should have been thoroughly investigated. "The fact that President Clinton will most likely escape removal from office I find less offensive than the Congress' and media's lack of interest in dealing with the serious charges of flagrant abuse of power, threatening political revenge, issuing unconstitutional Executive Orders, sacrificing US sovereignty to world government, bribery, and illegal acts of war, along with the routine flaunting of the constitutional restraints that were placed there to keep our federal government small and limited in scope."[22] It was a pattern that Ron feared would continue for the remainder of Clinton's term.

CHAPTER 19

TAKING ON
ALAN GREENSPAN

1998-2000

Inflation

> *If the American people ever allow private banks to control the issuance*
> *of their currency, first by inflation and then by deflation, the banks and*
> *corporations that will grow up around them will deprive the people of all*
> *their property until their children will wake up homeless on the continent*
> *their fathers conquered.*

THOMAS JEFFERSON

Few people consider Ron Paul to be a typical politician, but his campaigns historically have been more conventional than his politics. Paul always tried to surround himself with staffers who knew how to run an effective campaign and he was never afraid to go on the offensive when necessary.

Like his hard-won but narrow victory in 1996, Ron Paul's 1998 campaign did not prove to be easy. He had no Republican primary opponent this time, but the Democrats nominated a seemingly formidable opponent in Loy Sneary, a rice farmer from Bay City and a former Matagorda County judge.[1]

Ron Paul's campaign team began by accusing Sneary of engineering a pay raise for himself and using increased taxes to fund a new wasteful government bureaucracy.[2] One memorable campaign ad told voters to be "leery of Sneary."[3]

This approach worked with voters. Ultimately, Ron Paul raised $2.1 million for his campaign, compared with $734,000 raised by Sneary, a major factor in Paul's comfortable victory of 55% to 44%.[4]

Paul's sixth term started in January 1999, which included the last two years of Bill Clinton's presidency. Clinton had been impeached (but not removed from office) and was considered a lame-duck president.

Despite being in the majority party in the House, Ron Paul continued to live up to his nickname, Dr. No. He would often vote contrary to the Republican leadership, as they, like the Democrats before them, repeatedly brought up legislation attempting to allow the federal government to do things not authorized by the Constitution.

Although Paul opposed the Social Security system from both a moral and Constitutional standpoint, on January 6, 1999, almost immediately after being sworn in to his new term, he sponsored legislation to protect Social Security funds.[5] As long as the federal government had a retirement program and payroll taxes were being collected for it, he reasoned that the funds ought to be set aside for the promises made to retirees, not spent on other unconstitutional boondoggles that benefited unrelated special interests.

Meanwhile, the Clinton administration trumpeted how fiscally responsible the president was, taking credit for a balanced budget and even federal "surpluses." While the budget deficit was certainly less than in previous and subsequent years, Ron Paul understood that the administration and Congress were using accounting tricks to make their claims of responsibility. On January 11, 1999, Paul wrote, "In recent years, President Clinton and Congress have claimed to produce a balanced budget. This balancing act has only come as a result of numerous accounting shenanigans, including taking money out of the Social Security Trust Fund. The trust fund has little actual money in it; it instead holds IOUs from the federal government, promising to eventually—someday, maybe—pay back the fund."[6]

In order to build a coalition in support of the Constitution, Ron Paul helped form the Republican Liberty Caucus, a group of representatives interested in the American ideals of limited government and freedom. The group consisted of about 20 congressmen who met every Thursday for lunch to listen to guest speakers, such as former CIA analyst Michael Scheuer.

Members of the caucus included Rep. Walter Jones of North Carolina, who, in 2003, was an enthusiastic supporter of the Iraq war, but later became an outspoken critic of it. Although Liberty Caucus members did not always vote in unison, they generally attempted to vote along constitutional lines.

Throughout 1999, Paul continued to sponsor and co-sponsor bills, including but not limited to, restoring Second Amendment rights, withdrawing from the United Nations, and enacting across-the-board tax cuts. By the end of the year, he had cosponsored a total of 200 bills in Congress.[7] Although he favored ending the federal income tax, he still worked to get tax relief in anyway, which included supporting legislation to offer tax credits for seniors, educators, parents, and many other groups.

In February 2000, Paul continued to support seniors by offering the Pharmaceutical Freedom Act, which was to assist seniors with prescription drug costs through tax credits.[8] In April, he introduced the Cancer and Terminal Illness Patient Health Care Act, which would have waived Social Security taxes for individuals with a terminal illness.[9] Although neither of these bills received additional support (as was the case with many of his bills), Congressman Paul would often propose legislation in an attempt to draw awareness to important issues.

In October 2000, Paul opposed the so-called "privatization" of Social Security, warning of the dangers of allowing the government to invest people's retirement funds in the stock market. He instead favored setting aside Social Security funds and allowing people to opt out of the system.

Throughout the year, he also continued to question the wisdom of military intervention abroad. He doubted many of the government and media's claims about genocide in Kosovo, which eventually were shown to be unfounded. And on October 12, when the USS Cole was bombed while harbored in Yemen, he connected the dots between an interventionist foreign policy and the primary motive for the attack, which claimed the lives of 17 sailors.

It was, however, in Paul's continuing role on the House Committee on Financial Services (previously known as the House Committee on Banking and Currency) where he made his largest impression in his second term back in Congress. The committee does not hold much power, but serving on this committee gave Paul a fitting role as the often lone critic of fiat currency, the unstable Federal Reserve System, and Fed chairman Alan Greenspan.

Greenspan had assumed his chairmanship over a decade earlier, when Ronald Reagan appointed him to the post in 1987. Greenspan was influenced in his early career by Ayn Rand, the novelist who wrote Atlas Shrugged, a highly influential novel, especially in libertarian circles. Greenspan met Rand through his first wife, Joan Mitchell, who was friends with the wife of Nathaniel Branden, another noteworthy Rand associate. Greenspan remained friends with Rand until her death in 1982.[10]

In many ways, Greenspan's chairmanship of an institution legally enabled to print money was at odds with his early career and his relationship with Rand. In 1966, for example, he wrote an essay entitled "Gold and Economic Freedom", published in Rand's book Capitalism: The Unknown Ideal, in which he unequivocally stated the moral case against fiat currency and for a monetary gold standard. He wrote: "In the absence of the gold standard, there is no way to protect savings from confiscation through inflation... This is the shabby secret of the welfare statists' tirades against gold. Deficit spending is simply a scheme for the 'hidden' confiscation of wealth. Gold stands in the way of this insidious process. It stands as a protector of property rights. If one grasps this, one has no difficulty in understanding the statists' antagonism toward the gold standard."[11]

Since Greenspan's early writings were libertarian in nature, his career in politics in general, and his time as chairman of the Fed in particular, are viewed by many libertarians as a betrayal. Ron Paul has a signed copy of Greenspan's original essay on gold. When he requested the signature, Greenspan told Paul that he "wouldn't change a single word."[12] However, in practice, Greenspan deviated widely from what he originally wrote.

Ron Paul later noted Greenspan's about-face on gold vs. fiat currency:

> I had an opportunity to ask him about his change of heart when he appeared before the House Financial Services committee last week. Although Mr. Greenspan is a master of evasion, he was surprisingly forthright in his responses to me. In short, he claimed he was wrong about his predictions of calamity for the fiat US dollar, that the Federal

Reserve does a good job of essentially mimicking a gold standard, and that inflation is well under control. He even made the preposterous assertion that the Fed does not facilitate government expansion and deficit spending. In other words, he utterly repudiated the arguments he made 40 years ago. Yet this begs the question: If he was so wrong in the past, why should we listen to him now?[13]

Starting in 1997, Paul had the opportunity to question Greenspan twice a year until Greenspan retired in 2006. Paul believed that a currency, like any other good in a free market, could not and should not be centrally managed, planned, and controlled by a group of individuals. His questions reflected this belief.

Paul's approach to monetary policy reflected his study of the Austrian school of economics, which, contrary to much of the mainstream, points out that what many call inflation – i.e., rising prices – is only a symptom of inflation, which is an increase in the money supply. He noted: "Austrian-school economists demonstrate that true inflation is monetary inflation. True inflation therefore can be measured by an increase in the money supply… While Treasury printing presses can print unlimited dollars, there are natural limits to economic growth. This flood of newly minted US currency can only increase consumer prices in the long term, as more and more dollars chase available goods and services."[14]

Austrian school economists oppose all fiat currencies from a moral standpoint because such currencies are the equivalent of government counterfeiting, which in turn is the equivalent of theft. Today's fiat currencies are the modern form of coin clipping, a practice of kings who would clip the edges of gold and other precious metal coins, thereby decreasing their intrinsic value, while they, the kings, re-melted the clipped metal into their own personal stash of bullion. Today, this same kind of wealth transfer from "commoners" to the privileged and politically connected is accomplished via a fiat currency and a central bank. Of course, the modern system has a more sophisticated and hidden way of controlling the money supply by buying and selling US treasury bonds and manipulating interest rates.

Another problem with the inflation of a fiat currency is that it causes boom and bust cycles. Ron Paul relied on his knowledge of Austrian economic theory when he warned of excesses in the market in 1999. On July 22, he suggested to Greenspan that he resign so as not to take the blame for economic problems to come: "My suggestion is, it is not so much that we should anticipate a problem, but the problem is already created by all of the inflation in the past twelve years and that we have generated this financial bubble worldwide and we have to anticipate that. When this comes back, we are going to have a big problem. We will have to deal with it. My big question is, why would you want to stay around for this? It seems like I would get out while the getting is good."[15]

Paul's prediction could not have been more accurate. On March 10, 2000, the NASDAQ stock exchange reached its peak and collapsed through the next few years, losing over 70% of its value. The S&P 500 and the Dow Jones Industrial Average would also decline significantly, but not nearly as much as the tech-heavy NASDAQ. This marked the popping of the "dot-com bubble."

Paul would again warn of the housing bubble caused by low interest rates and easy money (courtesy of the Fed) years later in his career in 2004 and

2005. On October 27, 2005, Paul opposed legislation dealing with Government Sponsored Enterprises (GSEs), warning of further government involvement. Ron stated, "Perhaps the Federal Reserve can stave off the day of reckoning by purchasing the GSEs' debt and pumping liquidity into the housing market, but this cannot hold off the inevitable drop in the housing market forever. In fact, postponing the necessary and painful market corrections will only deepen the inevitable fall. The more people are invested in the market, the greater the effects across the economy when the bubble bursts."[16] Paul would again be proven correct with his Austro-libertarian knowledge, as this was right around the peak of the housing bubble.

In his sixth term, Congressman Paul sponsored legislation that called for the abolition of the Federal Reserve.[17] This has been his primary stance, but he has also proposed other legislation through the years that would not directly call for the abolition of the Fed, but instead would potentially lead to it. For example, Ron Paul has sponsored legislation that would repeal all legal tender laws.

Legal tender laws give a monopoly to the federal government and the central bank over the money supply. Since it is illegal to refuse acceptance of Federal Reserve Notes, US citizens are forced into using fiat currency no matter how much the Fed increases the money supply. With the power to create money out of thin air, there is no limit to the amount of bonds issued, which means the federal government can run up deficits with virtually no limit. By contrast, state governments cannot print money and are therefore more prone to balanced budgets.

Congressman Paul later sponsored the Honest Money Act to allow for competing currencies. He reasoned: "Repeal of legal tender laws will help restore constitutional government and protect the people's right to a medium of exchange chosen by the market, thereby protecting their current purchasing power as well as their pensions, savings, and other promises of future payment. Because honest money serves the needs of ordinary people, instead of fiat irredeemable paper-ticket electronic money that improperly transfers the wealth of society to a small specially privileged financial elite along with other special interests, I urge my colleagues to cosponsor the Honest Money Act."[18]

Although many proponents of monetary reform suggest a return to the gold standard, the libertarian position is to let the free market decide society's preferred medium of exchange. The reason that a gold standard is brought up is because the market decided that gold was the best medium of exchange for thousands of years. Gold has all of the good qualities of money. As Alan Greenspan himself originally said, "Gold, having both artistic and functional uses and being relatively scarce, has always been considered a luxury good. It is durable, portable, homogeneous, divisible, and, therefore, has significant advantages over all other media of exchange."[19] Of course, a gold standard does not mean that gold has to be carried everywhere. Paper money that is backed by gold could be used as well as electronic technology like bank cards.

The need for reform has gradually become more and more apparent. The US dollar, in 2000, was worth less than 6% of what it had been worth in 1913 when the Federal Reserve was formed.[20] Ron Paul was also later vindicated when Congress, in 2006, was compelled to make it illegal to melt pennies and nickels.[21] The currency had depreciated so much that the metal content of the coins were worth more than the value assigned to the coins. In other words, it actually cost more than one cent to make a penny and more than five cents to make a nickel. The government currency was demonstrably inefficient.

Ron Paul's questioning of Greenspan was always interesting in that it did not follow the typical Washington script. In fact, Congressman Paul often seemed to be the only person not awed by Greenspan's reputation as the "Maestro" of money manipulation.

For example, Paul asked how much gold the US government had, as Fort Knox was not open for audits. He also inquired about the actions of the President's Working Group on Financial Markets (also known as the Plunge Protection Team). These issues are not public knowledge and Ron asked these questions, not because he expected a good answer, but because it drew attention to the government's secrecy. He asked questions that often seemed to be more for educational purposes for the general public.

On July 25, 2000, Paul asked Greenspan, "Where do the Austrian economists go wrong? And where do you criticize them and say that we can't accept anything that they say?"[22] Greenspan seemed to give an evasive answer, saying that many of the Austrians' theories are still right. His vague responses were typical of those holding the chairman position and he gained a reputation through the years of using "Fed-speak," or not being forthright in his answers and discussions. It was always a challenge for Congressman Paul to come up with questions that were hard for Greenspan to dodge.

On another occasion, Paul asked Greenspan if he thought that policymakers at the Fed wielded too much influence over the economy. Greenspan admitted that "It is inevitable that the authority which is the producer of the money supply will have inordinate power."[23] Although Congressman Paul seemed to be a thorn in Greenspan's side, there was perhaps a certain level of respect for each other as Paul always hoped that he was casting doubt in Greenspan's mind.

Aside from taking on the Fed, Congressman Paul's 6th term in Congress was full of political activity. Of course, the biggest political event in the year 2000 was the presidential election, the closest in history with Vice President Al Gore against Texas Governor George W. Bush.*

George W. Bush campaigned in 2000 for a more humble US foreign policy. Paul later said of Bush, "As a gentleman and as an individual, he's fine. I've talked to him quite a few times. I just think that his speeches were great in 2000 but he was misled by neoconservative advisors and he was overtaken."[24]

As Bush lost the popular vote total to Gore, but won the presidency with electoral votes, Congressman Paul affirmed his support for the Electoral College and dismissed calls to change the system designed by the Founders. He affirmed the fact that the US is supposed to be a constitutionally limited republic and not a democracy.[25]

....

Congressman Paul's sixth term in the 106th Congress marked the end of the Clinton presidency. The Bush presidency would bring a whole new set of challenges. Now the Republicans would no longer take on the role of opposition party to the executive branch. Ron Paul, of course, would be the exception.

---

* Harry Browne also ran for president that year as the Libertarian Party's nominee for the second time in a row. Ron Paul knew Harry Browne and respected his work. When Browne died over five years later in early 2006, Paul paid tribute to his life on the House floor.

CHAPTER 20

BLOWBACK

2000-2002

Terrorism

Peace, commerce and honest friendship with all nations - entangling alliances with none.

THOMAS JEFFERSON

It was a cold day on January 28, 2000 as Ron Paul headed into his Congressional office in Washington, DC. In a few short days, he would celebrate his 47th anniversary with Carol. It was the Friday of the first week of the 106th Congress' return to Washington after their holiday break. The National Oceanic and Atmospheric Administration were alerting DC residents of a major snowstorm which had already dumped nearly a foot of snow in parts of Oklahoma and was rapidly heading northeast.[1] It was expected to arrive by the following Sunday, bringing snow and ice to the already bleak Federal city.

Later that afternoon, the 64 year old grandfather would be speaking on the floor of the House of Representatives. He would try to derail a proposed expansion of OSHA powers to regulate home offices.

The same week, the Pentagon released the details of a failed ballistic missile defense system test. Seven years and $33 billion was all it cost American taxpayers for the Defense Department to produce the non-working system.[2]

In addition, the Clinton administration announced its intent to send $1.3 billion in foreign aid to Colombia bringing the total to $1.6 billion over two years.[3] Under the auspices of the War on Drugs, the expenditures would make Colombia the third largest recipient of foreign aid behind Israel and Egypt.

This was an election year. In addition to his Congressional duties and his plans to write <u>A Case for Defending America</u>, his tenth book, Paul would have to plan and execute a re-election campaign. His Democratic opponent was Loy Sneary, whom Paul had defeated in 1998.

Paul's fourteenth district was enormous by any standard.* It stretched from the coastal town of Surfside on its eastern edge, an outskirt of Houston, all the way to Johnson City, roughly 50 miles west of Austin, a span of almost 250 miles. From the south, the district began just north of Corpus Christi and reached to Georgetown, 20 miles north of downtown Austin, again almost 250 miles. The district swallowed up 22 Texas counties and contained three media markets.

In spite of this, Paul insisted on shaking hands and speaking in almost every corner of the district. Dragging family members and staffers along, Paul would routinely cover 300 miles in a single day.

There were no Republican challengers this year. According to senior aide Eric Dondero, ever since he reached out to the National Republican Party in 1995 they had left Paul alone and even helped his campaign financially. Thus, he had the luxury of planning for the general election rather than running two campaigns.

Having run against Sneary once before provided Paul with a clear advantage. But the Democratic National Committee was again, as it had in 1998, willing to spend as much money as necessary to unseat Paul. Fortunately Paul had fundraising powerhouse David James on his side.

Sneary's campaign strategists decided to attack Paul by painting him as "some sort of right wing monster." Dan Cobb, editor of the *Victoria Advocate* (a paper which routinely endorses Paul's opponent), would later say, "It should be obvious by now that you can't attack him. All you can do is run a positive campaign. People in the Fourteenth [District] feel they know exactly where Paul stands. He is consistent and adheres to his principles. He has great personal integrity."[4]

Sneary, the rice farmer from Bay City and a former Matagorda County judge, had high political designs. On June 9, 1999, Sneary testified in front of the House Committee on Agriculture, representing the US Rice Producers Association, to argue against economic sanctions on Iran.[5] Ironically, this was a position shared by Paul. However, on most other issues, they were polar opposites.

As Cobb had noted, attacking Ron Paul was a poor decision. Paul had a loyal following within his district, but he had also gained a reputation as a maverick outside his district and possessed a healthy mailing list. By this time, though most Internet connectivity was still via dial-up modem, Paul's speeches and fundraising letters were regularly reposted to various Internet websites and news groups. His strict Constitutional stance on gun control was greatly received and his name became synonymous amongst members of the burgeoning patriot movement. The donations started pouring in from all over the country.

Sneary styled himself as a man of the people and drove around his district in a black Ford Bronco plastered with campaign signs. In spite of heavy

---

* The infamous gerrymandering plan by Tom Delay in 2003 reduced the area of this district.

Democratic National Committee backing, Sneary raised just over $1.1 million, half of that from political action committees and party officials, to Paul's $2.4 million. A whopping 93% percent of Paul's total came from individual donors, giving an average of forty dollars each.[6] He was proving himself to be a true "man of the people."

When the returns finally came in, Paul garnered sixty percent of the vote. The results perplexed many observers who couldn't understand how a man who refused to bring home the "pork" could still endear himself to voters.

To his constituents, there was nothing perplexing about it. Paul had won their trust and loyalty because his actions reflected his words. A month after the election, Congressman Paul's office announced, as it had done every year, it would be returning $50,000 to the US Treasury rather than spending it.

Paul was returning to Congress in a year in which the GOP had finally achieved the holy grail in American politics: a majority in both houses (though only by Vice President Dick Cheney's tie-breaker vote in the Senate) and a Republican President.

On January 3, 2001, Ron Paul was sworn in for his seventh term as a Congressman. On the same day, he introduced a bill that would protect the identity of all Americans by changing the very nature of the Social Security number. It was obvious to Paul that requiring the number for identification purposes while also sharing it with private organizations was itself the root cause of identity theft.

Paul's belief that the true purpose of government was to protect the rights of its citizens was made clear in his speech introducing the bill. Of this singular responsibility, he said, "I would remind my colleagues that in a constitutional republic the people are never asked to sacrifice their liberties to make the job of government officials a little bit easier. We are here to protect the freedom of the American people, not to make privacy invasion more efficient."[7]

Gentle and not-so-gentle reminders of this sort were a constant during Paul's tenure. Paul had not forgotten or ignored their true purpose as representatives of the people, and he would, to the chagrin of many of his colleagues on both sides of the aisle, remind them of this fact on every available occasion.

Though the Republican platform contained many planks to limit government power, the newly-elected President was seeking to expand government. Specifically, he sought to expand welfare programs with a proposal for "faith-based initiatives"–earmarking billions of dollars for use by religious organizations to provide welfare and education for those considered disadvantaged.

The Contract with America of 1994 had propelled Republicans into a majority for the first time in forty years, yet by 2001 they had completely abandoned it. President Bush, even prior to any Congressional approval, had created the *Office of Faith Based and Community Initiatives* via executive order,[8] ostensibly to improve delivery of government services and remove barriers which typically prevented religious organizations from receiving federal funds for such purposes.

Of Bush's plan, Congressman Paul remarked during a June speech on the House floor, "Those who claim that the faith-based initiative merely saves charitable programs of religious organizations from discrimination miss the most basic point. The main reason faith-based programs are successful is the fact that free people choose to fund them and that free people choose to participate in them."[9]

According to Paul, the true danger of such a scheme was that it would corrupt the very institutions which did so well without federal money. The organizations which received taxpayer funds to augment their work "may even change the religious character of their programs in order to avoid displeasing their new federal paymaster."

On July 10, 2001, Ron's mother Margaret passed away at the age of 93, the same age as her late husband had. She was an able woman who raised five successful children through often difficult times. Although both Ron's parents witnessed his success in politics, neither would see the full effect their son would have on the American public.

Paul suffered from the loss of his mother, but an even greater loss was about to befall the American public. Back in January 2000, Paul laid out his statement of beliefs in a speech titled "A Republic, If You Can Keep It," based on the famous words of Benjamin Franklin. In it he made some startling predictions. Among them, he noted that Americans "are placed in greater danger because of our arrogant policy of bombing nations that do not submit to our wishes. This generates the hatred directed toward America, even if at times it seems suppressed, and exposes us to a greater threat of terrorism, since this is the only vehicle our victims can use to retaliate against a powerful military state. … The cost in terms of liberties lost and the unnecessary exposure to terrorism are difficult to determine, but in time it will become apparent to all of us that foreign interventionism is of no benefit to American citizens, but instead is a threat to our liberties."

At the time, most of his colleagues thought he was exaggerating the dangers of US policy.

Paul consistently sought the guidance of the US Constitution and the traditional GOP platform planks. He wasn't entirely alone; some Republican pundits still touted the limited government mantra, though Paul's colleagues in the House and Senate were for the most part abandoning the GOP's platform. As Michelle Malkin asked in January 2001, "Where have all the fiscal conservatives gone?"[10]

In a few short months, politics would change dramatically and even pundits like Malkin would embrace an unprecedented growth in government power and spending.

September 11, 2001 started out like any other day in Washington, but by the day's close, the mantra that America was now at war would be repeated by every media pundit, news anchor, and politician, save a select few.

Political sentiment immediately after the attacks on the World Trade Center complex in New York City was focused on revenge and military response. As early as September 13, the House had introduced a bill which would authorize the President to mobilize troops against the attackers, though there was not, as of yet, a clear enemy.

Paul was of the belief that such a response warranted more debate and consideration. Panic could lead to unnecessary killing and the loss of domestic liberties. There was a historical tendency for governments to ask citizens to give up their liberties under the guise of promised peace and security.

On September 12, 2001, Paul tried to diffuse a rush to judgment. He urged his colleagues to seek counsel from the Constitution:

In our grief, we must remember our responsibilities. The Congress' foremost obligation in a constitutional republic is to preserve freedom and provide for national security. Yesterday our efforts to protect our homeland came up short. Our policies that led to that shortcoming must be re-evaluated and changed if found to be deficient. ... When we retaliate for this horror we have suffered, we must be certain that only the guilty be punished. More killing of innocent civilians will only serve to flame the fires of war and further jeopardize our security. Congress should consider its constitutional authority to grant letters of *marque and reprisal* to meet our responsibility.[11]

Paul's suggestion of using letters of marque and reprisal demonstrated both his knowledge of law and his ability to devise clever but appropriate solutions. While Paul did vote to authorize the President to use military force in Afghanistan, he wanted to provide what he believed to be a more effective tool against terrorists.

One lingering question in Washington was how to respond to the attacks. The enemy consisted of just nineteen men with box cutters - a very different enemy. Once bin Laden and his terrorist group al-Qaeda were identified, it was clear that it was not a nation that attacked the United States, but rather a group of individuals with no state sponsorship. Therefore, a direct invasion of a country was unwarranted. But how could the United States retaliate if they could not send their army against a foe?

Authorized in Article I, Section 8 of the US Constitution, the remedy against enemies which did not directly represent a state or nation was the letter of marque and reprisal. In atrophy since the late 19th century, it was intended for use on such occasions where mobilization of armed forces would be ineffective or inappropriate.

Letters of marque and reprisal allowed the government to empower private citizens to target criminals, such as pirates, who operated outside the boundaries of any provable national directive or did not reside in any given legal jurisdiction. Privateers, required to put up bonds as insurance against unlawful acts, could operate in secrecy and without the same public scrutiny to which armed forces would be subject. There was one wrinkle to using privateers in the modern age: piracy was generally defined in legal terms as an act committed upon the high seas.

Paul dealt with this problem by drafting a bill which would broaden the legal definition of piracy to include hijacked aircraft. Dubbed the "Air Piracy Reprisal and Capture Act of 2001", it defined acts such as those which occurred on September 11, 2001 as air piracy. Perpetrators of such atrocities could now be, upon passage of the bills, targeted by privateers.

The privateers referred to in the Constitution were essentially private warships, when the US Navy was virtually non-existent, and hired mercenaries in the late 1700s. Although the term mercenaries conjures up images of Hessian soldiers or the infamous Blackwater Worldwide (formerly Blackwater USA), they are sometimes ideal for small scale military operations because they cost less than staging a full scale operation. Most importantly to Paul, their operations result in less human death. They are also not restricted to hiring only US citizens, so they can hire international personal such as former Iraqi Republican Guard and even former al-Qaeda members to help track down targets.

Even before the bill was drafted, spectators on the Internet had already started dissecting Paul's September 12 statement. Free Republic, a conservative discussion site, saw several forum posts debating the merits of letters of marque as a viable alternative to full scale military conflict.[12] The Liberty Committee - headed by Kent Snyder, who would years later become Ron Paul's campaign manager in his bid for the Presidency - was also working behind the scenes to bring the non-military solution to the forefront of public debate.

On October 11, 2001, Paul introduced both the air piracy bill and the "September 11 Marque and Reprisal Act of 2001."[13] One of Paul's concerns with a pure military solution was that those in the Middle East would perceive a US retaliation to be unfocused and directed at Muslims in general rather than on those who had specifically planned and executed the attacks of September 11. Paul explained the bill to his colleagues:

> Letters of marque and reprisal resolve one of the most vexing problems facing the country: how do we obtain retribution against the perpetrators of the attacks without inflicting massive damage on the Middle East which could drive moderate Arabs into an allegiance with bin Laden and other terrorists. This is because using letters of marque and reprisal shows the people of the region that we are serious when we say our quarrel is not with them but with Osama bin Laden and all others who would dare commit terrorist acts against the United States.[14]

While there were a relatively small number of Americans enthusiastically supporting the Constitutional approach, the media, Congress and the President himself were dismissive, if they even mentioned it, perhaps because a small mercenary army set against the actual culprits would not allow a major reshaping of the Middle East or massive military expenditures that the neoconservatives desired.

Congress had, in the weeks following the attacks, introduced several bills which undermined the liberties of American citizens under the guise of protecting them from terrorists. The most infamous of these was the *PATRIOT Act*.

Paul was suspicious of the process by which the bill was handed to representatives. He noted, "My concerns are exacerbated by the fact that HR 3108 lacks many of the protections of civil liberties which the House Judiciary Committee worked to put into the version of the bill they considered. In fact, the process under which we are asked to consider this bill makes it nearly impossible to fulfill our constitutional responsibility to carefully consider measures which dramatically increase government's power."[15]

Over his objections, the PATRIOT Act was passed and signed by President Bush.[16] Paul was one of only three Republican House members who had voted against it.[17]

On the eve of its signing, Paul spoke of the "sad state of affairs" in which the country had landed in the aftermath of the 9/11 attacks.[18] It was clear that the current climate in Washington was enough to bring down even the spirits of a man so well known for his virtually limitless optimism. People who even remotely shared his views were being vilified in the press. Paul found it disturbing that people who were debating in good faith were being marginalized for political gain.

Paul told his House colleagues, "Throughout our early history, a policy of minding our own business and avoiding entangling alliances, as George Washington admonished, was more representative of American ideals than those we have pursued for the past fifty years. Some sincere Americans have suggested that our modern interventionist policy set the stage for the attacks of 9/11, and for this, they are condemned as being unpatriotic."

Paul was heartbroken. The rush to provide remedies to government-caused problems was further growing government and expanding the powers of agencies he had been seeking to abolish since his first term in Congress. The Remnant - as he called those who still understood freedom, a term initially coined by Albert J. Nock - appeared to be dwindling. The number of his Republican colleagues who were still dedicated to the ideals of the original American Revolution was close to zero. President Bush quickly jettisoned the "humble foreign policy" he had proposed during his campaign in favor of something Norman Podhoretz would later dub "World War Four."

By December, the Bush administration had already begun a press campaign linking Saddam Hussein to al-Qaeda. Congress was already considering a joint resolution – House Joint Resolution 75 on December 19, 2001 - to expand the war on terror into Iraq even before the first bombs had fallen in Afghanistan. Paul wondered aloud, "Is military action now the foreign policy of first resort for the United States?"[19]

....

In late 2002, Paul and his friends were stunned to learn of the untimely death of Tony Payton, a political strategist who had helped Paul achieve his stunning 1996 victory. He also worked closely with Nadia Hayes in 1988, before her conviction for embezzlement. "Ron was close to Tony," explained Eric Dondero, one of Paul's senior aides at the time. "And Tony and Nadia were real tight political partners. Tony defended Nadia throughout the ordeal."[20] After Hayes' betrayal, Paul didn't want to hear her name mentioned by any of his staff, but the death of their mutual friend changed him.

Dondero recalled, "In one weak moment I asked him, 'Ron should I try to contact Nadia and let her know Tony died?' He thought about it and said, 'Yeah, you should.' He really took an interest in it, too." It was finally time for forgiveness.

CHAPTER 21

AMERICA REGRETS

2002-2004

Military Industrial Complex

In the councils of government, we must guard against the acquisition of unwarranted influence, whether sought or unsought, by the military-industrial complex.

DWIGHT D. EISENHOWER

In late 2002, Ron Paul faced re-election. After winning an uncontested Republican primary, Paul faced off against Democratic challenger Corby Windham, a 33-year old bilingual lawyer, former soldier, and former teacher from San Marcos. Windham's impressive credentials made him a serious contender.

Paul's platform contrasted with his rival's on many issues, but crucially Corby appeared lax on immigration. It was an unpopular position in the southern district and ultimately only helped secure votes from the 15% Latino population in Brazoria. On November 22, Paul held his congressional seat convincingly with 102,661 votes to 48,192.[1]

Immediately after securing his spot in the 108th Congress, Paul began speaking out against Washington's drive to war with Iraq. In the months preceding the election, the Bush administration had taken an increasingly aggressive stance towards Saddam Hussein. The previous August, the Senate Foreign Services Committee reviewed intelligence concerning Iraq's nuclear weapons capabilities. Paul feared that an invasion of Iraq was "a foregone conclusion," saying that the "testimony presented in the Committee focused not on the wisdom of such an invasion, but rather only on how and when it should be done."[2]

In September 2002, Paul delivered his case against invading Iraq on the floor of the House of Representatives. He believed that Iraq posed no threat to national security, calling the country an "impoverished third world nation 6,000 miles from our shores that doesn't even possess a navy or air force." He believed that the US military was overextended, and that invading Iraq would "dilute our ability to defend our country."

He further argued that the US should never go to war to enforce a United Nations resolution, and that it should never attack another country without a clear congressional declaration. He predicted that invading Iraq would wreak havoc on an already shaky US economy and ultimately hurt Republicans politically.

From a broader philosophical perspective, Paul opposed the war because of the growth of government and loss of liberty he believed would occur, noting that "many of the worst government programs of the 20th century began during wartime 'emergencies' and were never abolished."[3]

Predictably, his House colleagues ignored his warnings. On October 10, 2002, Congress passed a resolution giving President Bush the authority to wage war in Iraq at his discretion. Paul was one of only six House Republicans to vote against the resolution. He was irate at his colleagues' shirking of their Constitutional responsibility to declare war, accusing them of "lack[ing] the political courage to call an invasion of Iraq what it really is: a war."[4]

Less than a week after Paul's re-election, the UN Security Council passed a US-backed resolution demanding that Saddam Hussein allow weapons inspectors into Iraq or "face serious consequences."

Hussein immediately agreed to comply with the resolution, inviting UN weapons inspectors into Baghdad on November 18, 2002. On December 7, Iraq issued a 12,000-page report on its weapons programs to inspectors. The neoconservatives within the Bush administration almost seemed disappointed with the cooperation.

Within days, the US and UK accused Iraq of not declaring a full and complete report of its weapons programs. Chief UN weapons inspector Hans Blix said that pieces were missing from the report, but felt that progress was being made. US ambassador to the UN John Negroponte disagreed with Blix's assessment, saying that Iraq had "spurned its last opportunity to comply with its disarmament obligations."[5]

As the Bush administration's war rhetoric grew more confrontational, Paul continued to protest an invasion in weekly columns posted on his House website and in speeches on the House floor. In one speech, he listed the possible negative outcomes of war. He predicted that if the US were to invade Iraq, "al-Qaeda likely [would] get a real boost in membership."[6] He listed the problems associated with rebuilding a post-war Iraq and choosing leadership among Iraq's three major ethnic factions: Sunnis, Shi'ites, and Kurds. "Do we really believe that somehow we can choose the 'good guys' who deserve to rule Iraq?" he asked.[7]

Paul felt that invading Iraq would be yet another chapter in a long history of incoherent US foreign policy. He lamented the hypocrisy of the US claiming to support democracy in the Middle East, while helping overthrow the democratically elected leader of Iran in 1953 and befriending dictators like

Pakistan's Pervez Musharraf. Paul believed that America would be "best served by not interfering in the deadly conflicts that define the Middle East."[8]

On February 5, 2003, Secretary of State Colin Powell spoke to the UN Security Council, presenting evidence for the existence of illegal weapons in Iraq. Powell demanded that the Security Council come down aggressively against Iraq's violations of the 1991 cease-fire agreement it had signed following the first Gulf War.

Two Security Council members, France and Russia, continued to express reservations about authorizing an invasion.[9] The UN hesitance to support regime change in Iraq frustrated the Bush administration, who began to entertain the possibility of invading unilaterally.

Paul was irritated by the mixed signals from the Bush administration regarding the UN. He felt that if the US was willing to invade Iraq on its own, asking for UN approval in the first place was unnecessary. "The bizarre irony is while we may act unilaterally in Iraq, the very justification for our invasion is that we are enforcing UN resolutions," he said.[10]

Paul hoped that the anti-UN sentiment among Republicans at the time would ultimately lead to the US canceling its membership in the UN. On March 6, 2003, Paul introduced legislation that would do just that, but the bill never made it out of committee.[11]

On March 7, 2003, in a last-ditch effort to secure UN support for an invasion, the US presented the Security Council with a resolution demanding that Saddam Hussein disarm within ten days or face war. France and Russia vetoed the measure. By March 17, Iraq had apparently not met those demands, and the US, along with its pro-war allies Spain and Britain, abandoned efforts to seek UN approval to invade. War was imminent.[12]

The war began on March 19, as the US-led coalition launched *Operation Iraqi Freedom*. Within six weeks, coalition forces defeated Saddam's Republican Guard and took control of every major Iraqi city. On May 1, 2003, President Bush stood on the *USS Abraham Lincoln* in front of a banner that read *Mission Accomplished* and declared an end to major combat operations in Iraq.[13] This upset opinion makers in the media, who felt there were more battles to be fought in the Middle East.

In the months following the "mission accomplished" declaration, Iraqi rebels continued to kill and maim US troops in large numbers. Furthermore, coalition forces were unable to find the weapons of mass destruction (WMD) that the Bush administration had cited as justification for war. The President's approval ratings began to sink.

In June, several high ranking military officials predicted that rebuilding Iraq would cost the US hundreds of billions of dollars and require years of occupation. Paul feared that a long and costly nation building campaign in Iraq would drain Americans of their wealth and damage the economy.

He was disappointed in his Republican Party colleagues, who during Clinton's Presidency had claimed to believe in non-intervention in foreign affairs. They now endorsed an occupation of Iraq that threatened to claim thousands of lives and drain hundreds of billions of dollars from US taxpayers.

On July 10, 2003, in an impassioned speech on the House floor, Paul declared that the limited government movement in the US was dead. "There has not been, nor will there soon be, a conservative revolution in Washington," he lamented. It was one more disappointment following the squandered opportunity to shrink the size of government after Republicans had won control of Congress back in 1994.

Paul blamed this failure on the rise of neoconservatism within the Republican Party. Neoconservatives, Paul said, weren't conservatives at all, but rather big government liberals who favored using military force to impose the American way of life on the rest of the world. Paul feared that if the neoconservatives continued to control the Republican Party, "limiting the size and scope of government will be a long-forgotten dream."[14]

The neoconservatives were typically unabashed supporters of Israel who advocated reshaping the Middle East in Israel's favor, using US military might. They were admirers of Niccolò Machiavelli, the Italian philosopher who believed that government shouldn't be bound by morality, and Leon Trotsky, Lenin's number-two man in the Bolshevik Revolution.

In the middle of 2003, Ron Paul had a falling out with his longtime senior aide, Eric Dondero. According to Dondero, the break was directly caused by their differences on foreign policy. "Ron Paul and I agree on about 95% of all domestic issues," he later wrote. "We disagree on a myriad of foreign policy and defense issues."

Dondero was a heavyset former military man, having served four years in the United States Navy. In contrast to the reserved, polite disposition of Ron Paul, Dondero was outspoken, boisterous, and sometimes even crude. He would always speak his mind – a quality Paul respected. He was proudly Jewish and proudly Italian-American, occasionally signing his name *Eric Dondero Rittberg*.

When the neoconservatives began pushing for war with Iraq, the split between Paul and Dondero intensified. Saddam Hussein, an ally of the US in the 1980's, became an enemy to the Israeli cause when he announced his support for the Palestinians. Dondero believed the war with Iraq was justafied.

Dondero's support for the neoconservative agenda caused a rift too large to ignore. Although he claimed to be a libertarian, he seemed to equate supporting the troops (which Paul did) with supporting aggressive wars. As one columnist wrote, "being a pro-war or interventionist libertarian makes about as much sense as being a Christian atheist, a tee totaling alcoholic, or the much ballyhooed but nonsensical 'big-government conservative'"[15]

In the summer of 2003, Paul asked Dondero to accompany him on a ride to an event in Victoria, Texas; a two and a half hour drive from Lake Jackson. Paul wanted to discuss foreign policy, but Dondero remained aloof and evasive for most of the trip.

When they finally reached Victoria, Dondero released his pent up thoughts, heatedly telling Paul he thought he was wrong on the Iraq War. Paul, bristling with emotion himself, told Dondero, "I will have nobody working for me on my staff who supports the War in Iraq, even you."

For the next six months, neither man spoke to one another. Dondero virtually ceased work for Paul, although he remained on the payroll until 2004. According to Dondero, "Finally, Chief of Staff Tom Lizardo suggested that Ron and I not talking to each other was not helpful to the 'atmosphere' in the District offices. I offered to my friend Tom to resign. We discussed a date, two months out, and a compensation package and I agreed."

Although the disagreement was explosive, Dondero remained objective about Paul. Through the years, Paul's non-intervention policy had caused many to question whether his unsupportive attitude towards Israel was the same as being anti-Semitic. Dondero later wrote, "I've been asked by others if my former boss is an anti-Semite. My answer is an emphatic no. I am half Jewish. I am familiar with anti-Semites. Ron is not one of them." He added, "But I would say he's very insensitive to issues concerning Israel and for other concerns of Jewish Americans." This criticism stung, because Dondero knew Paul was not insensitive to Jewish Americans or Israelis. He was just equally sensitive. He treated them with the same respect as Hungarians, Egyptians, French, or any other nationality – all stemming from a policy to make friends with all nations, not to favor some at the expense of others.

Ron Paul himself did not remain sore at Dondero. While still an employee, Paul sent Dondero a gift of some banana trees. This later gave him a good excuse to call an old friend. According to Dondero, "...he called me for months afterwards just to shoot the shit, mostly about gardening and to check in on how his banana trees were doing." Dondero had little to say to Paul, however, and merely listened politely.

As the War in Iraq progressed, Dondero's attacks against Paul increased until Paul was forced to acknowledge Dondero's status as "a disgruntled former employee." It was a sad end to a relationship that, on a smaller scale, mirrored the differences that can occur between nations. Entangling alliances among friends had sown the seeds of unhappiness.

....

One possible threat to peace feared by Ron Paul, originally proposed by President Eisenhower, was the military-industrial complex. In his farewell speech in 1961, Eisenhower warned Americans of the threat posed by military contractors. The military, of course, needs weapons and they purchase their weapons from the private industry. Before the military can purchase weapons, Congress must approve military expenditures.

The system as described above is perfectly fine, according to Paul. However, it becomes problematic when military contractors pressure members of Congress in order to increase their orders. In severe cases, war might even be encouraged to increase demand for military products. It's a vicious cycle with no place in a free society.

Paul objects to the state giving welfare to any businesses: "Those who are on the receiving end of government contracts – especially in the military industrial complex during wartime – receive undeserved benefits."

Paul implicates his fellow Congressmen in the military-industrial complex. Curiously, Eisenhower's first draft of his farewell speech called it the military-industrial-*congressional* complex. It was reportedly changed to placate members of Congress.

As the Iraqi occupation dragged on, Paul demanded a debate in Congress on the merits of perpetual occupation at taxpayer expense. "It's not unpatriotic to ask how much Iraq is worth to us, and whether rebuilding it is more important than countless domestic priorities," he wrote.[16]

In September 2003, Bush asked Congress for an $87-billion supplemental funding bill to help finance the costs of the occupation. Paul noted that much of the bill was comprised of wasteful pork, including $900 million to import kerosene and diesel, even though Iraq had vast oil reserves. It was a sure indication of the military-industrial complex at work. The profligate spending inspired Paul to call Iraq "the most extensive nation-building experiment in history."[17]

Paul feared that the exploding costs of the Iraq war, in both monetary and human terms, might ultimately lead to the reinstatement of the military draft. On November 21, 2003, Paul gave a speech on the House floor opposing involuntary military service.

He felt that if occupying Iraq were truly a worthy cause, military officials would have no problem attracting enthusiastic recruits. The dwindling supply of volunteers proved to Paul that the Iraq war was not worth fighting, and amounted to little more than "teaching democracy to unwilling and angry Arabs."

He believed that the draft was in some ways worse than slavery. "Slaves were safer in that their owners had an economic interest in protecting their lives," he said. "Endangering the lives of our soldiers is acceptable policy." Paul argued that no government could be trusted to preserve liberty that would use the tyranny of mandatory military service. "The ends can never justify the means, no matter what the neo-cons say," he concluded.[18]

In February 2004, Paul gave a speech to his House colleagues criticizing the US policy of promoting democracy abroad with military force. For all the talk of building a democratic Iraq, Paul claimed the US seemed averse to democracy when it didn't suit its own interests. He noted the US government's hesitance to allow Iraq to hold free elections, suggesting that it feared a "national election in Iraq would bring individuals to power that the administration doesn't want." Paul offered an alternative solution: the US could promote democracy "through persuasion and example."[19]

On the one-year anniversary of the Iraq invasion, Paul reiterated his opposition to the war and questioned whether the war had improved anyone's lot. "The young men and women who were hurt or killed certainly are no better off. Their families are no better off. Taxpayers are no better off," he said. If sacrificing American lives to save a nation from one cruel dictator was justified, Paul wondered how many American lives should be sacrificed to free people from oppressive governments throughout the world.[20]

In the spring of 2004, six US soldiers were charged with abusing prisoners at the Abu Ghraib correctional facility near Baghdad. As Congress hurriedly assembled a resolution condemning the abuse, Paul objected. He suggested his colleagues were rushing to judgment, failing to allow the legal process to take place and "operating on the principle of guilty until proven innocent" in condemning soldiers before knowing all of the facts in the case.[21] Paul believed it was hypocritical for his fellow Congressmen to censure so quickly soldiers in the trenches when these same congressmen had voted to "put those soldiers into such a rotten situation in the first place."[22]

By 2004, popularity for the war was in rapid decline; and by 2007, 70% of Americans wanted out. Politicians who had previously supported the war became critics. However, many of these so-called critics were critical of the Bush administration rather than the decades-old policy of foreign intervention. They were condemning a scapegoat so they could reserve the "right" to launch more foreign interventions.

This was not unnoticed by Paul. "Some of today's critics were strongly in favor of going to war against Iraq when doing so appeared politically popular, but now are chagrined that the war is not going as smoothly as was hoped,"

Paul noted.[23] He was one of a few who had opposed the war from the start, not because he thought it would fail, but because of a consistent philosophy of libertarianism.

Lew Rockwell believed the failure of the Iraq war might help prevent future mistakes. "The total disaster of the Bush administration in its foreign policy and its domestic policy has taken the wind out of their sails, and now with Ron Paul I would say that freedom has got a real chance again," he said. July 11, 2007 AntiWar.com interview.

....

One of Paul's biggest fears was that the US invasion of Iraq would lead to meddling elsewhere. In July 2003, Paul proposed a resolution to keep the US military from intervening in the civil war in Liberia. While Paul sympathized with Liberians affected by the war, he strongly believed that the US had no national security interest and was already spread too thin around the world.[24]

In May 2004, the House considered legislation that threatened to "use all appropriate means to deter, dissuade, and prevent Iran from acquiring nuclear weapons." Paul was shocked that, in spite of the failure in Iraq, his colleagues were acting aggressively towards another Middle Eastern nation. Paul argued that the legislation, which called for strict economic sanctions against Iran, would do little to dissuade Iranian president Mahmoud Ahmadinejad from developing nuclear weapons. It would instead "sow misery among the poorest and most vulnerable segments" of Iran's population.[25]

In November, Paul spoke out against US involvement in the civil war in Sudan's Darfur region. He chided his colleagues for their eagerness to voice their opinions about a conflict they knew little about. Paul wondered whether there might be more to the US's desire to intervene than saving innocent Africans, noting that Sudan was "floating on a sea of oil."[26]

In December, a Pentagon study revealed the Iraq war had sparked an increase in terrorism in the Middle East. The war that had cost the US billions of dollars and thousands of lives was doing precisely the opposite of its alleged goals. Paul noted that many of those who opposed the initial intervention had succumbed to a belief the US had no choice but to remain mired in Iraq until democracy could take root. He insisted that the cure to America's foreign policy ills was a renewed policy of non-interventionism, "the foreign policy ideal of the Founding Fathers."[27]

....

As his term came to a close, Paul weighed in on the approaching Presidential election. Without mentioning him by name, Paul chastised Democratic candidate John Kerry's frequent talk of a "plan" for America. Paul wrote that "government is not supposed to plan our lives or run the country; we are supposed to be free," arguing that centrally-planned economies always lead to low standards of living.[28]

In one article, the one-time Libertarian presidential candidate defended Reform Party candidate Ralph Nader's presidential run and denounced those who would attempt to keep him off state ballots.[29]

Paul also fought against an accelerating trend toward police-statism during the 108th Congress, speaking out against a proposed National ID Card and the USA-PATRIOT Act. Paul criticized what he felt was excessive security at the US Capitol. Imposing drastic security measures on visitors to the Capitol was hypocritical, reasoned Paul, noting that "government rushes first to protect itself, devoting enormous resources to make places like the Capitol grounds safe, while just beyond lies one of the most dangerous neighborhoods in the nation."[30]

Though at odds with Republicans on foreign policy during his seventh term, Paul didn't completely break ranks with his party, instead siding with them on a number of fiscal issues. Paul joined Republicans in support of the President's proposal to cut double taxation of dividends.[31] He also spoke in favor of Bush's Tax-Free Savings Plan, arguing that the plan "could put millions of Americans on the road to self-sufficiency."[32]

However, Paul strongly opposed a Republican-supported Medicare prescription drug measure. He believed the bill should never have been backed by anyone claiming to be a fiscal conservative. Paul said the bill was consistent with the "New Deal and Great Society programs of the utopian left" and would leave "true conservatives ... wondering whether they still have a political home in the modern GOP."[33]

Paul's extended family added a new member during his seventh term in Congress. Daughter Joy Leblanc, the youngest child, gave birth to son Luke on June 22, 2004.

After Congress adjourned in October 2004, Paul took drastic measures to relieve his chronic knee pain.[34] The injury he had suffered while playing football in high school finally came to a critical juncture. Ron was physically active even compared to men half his age, but years of wear to his damaged knee finally caught up with him. Although biking didn't cause any problems, he was feeling pain while standing in the House of Representatives and walking to and from his office.

Ron and his doctor strategically timed his surgery so it would not interfere with his political duties. In October he had both his knee joints surgically removed and replaced with artificial joints composed of metal and plastic.

Post surgery, Paul spent less than a week in the hospital before rolling out in a wheel chair. For the next three weeks the housebound doctor limped around on crutches, often braving cooler temperatures in the swimming pool to help rehabilitate his knees and maintain joint mobility.

He had lots of time to read and write. Paul gave a back-cover endorsement to one book, The Politically Incorrect Guide to American History by Thomas Woods, Jr.: "Knowing our past is essential if we are to preserve our freedoms. Professor Woods's work heroically rescues real history from the politically correct memory hole. Every American should read this book." As the title suggested, the book was blatantly un-PC, and more than one opinion maker would later use the endorsement against him.

Eventually he was able to put his full weight on his new knees and he switched to limping about with a cane. By January 2005, Paul was fully healed and walking without aid, in time for his next term in congress. He would need his new knees if he wanted to continue standing on the House floor delivering impassioned speeches for freedom.

CHAPTER 22

BORDERS

2004-2006

Illegal Immigration

Immigration is the sincerest form of flattery.

JACK PAAR

By 2004, Ron Paul had fought his battle for decades, yet it seemed like the United States was no closer to the free society envisioned by its founders. In light of this, he saw no reason to give up his congressional seat after eight terms.

This would be his first election since 1988 without his campaign coordinator Eric Dondero by his side. Fortunately he would not require a campaign team this time around. In the 2004 general election, held on November 2 (concurrent with the presidential election), Ron Paul faced no opposition.

Paul was the only Texan from either party who ran unopposed and one of only 17 Republicans nationwide without a competitor. There were many possible reasons why no Democrat chose to run against him; after all, Texas' 14th district had mostly been a Democratic stronghold in the past. Statistically, between 15 and 50 House seats were unopposed every election due to a phenomenon called *regression towards the mean*, which virtually guarantees that every House seat will be unopposed at some point. Perhaps this time it was Paul's turn.

A political explanation is that Paul was among the most independent, non-partisan congressmen in the House,[1] therefore his seat was less important for the Democratic Party. On a tactical level, Paul had beat his Democratic opponent by increasing margins: 55% in 1998, then by 60% and finally with 68%. Thus his seat was likely seen as entrenched by the opposing party. Whatever the reason, Paul was naturally happy to continue his congressional work.

....

The 109th United States Congress, Ron Paul's ninth full term, began on January 3rd, 2005. The Senate consisted of 55 Republicans, 44 Democrats and one independent from Vermont, while the House of Representatives had 232 Republicans, 201 Democrats and one independent, again from Vermont. As George W. Bush had won the November election against Democrat John Kerry, it meant that the Republicans now dominated all three branches of the Federal Government.

If Republicans truly believed in limited government, it could have been an opportune time to undo the government largess of years past. Nothing could stand in their way. Sadly for Paul, neoconservatives now had a firm hold on his party and there was very little left of the Republican Revolution of 1994. Instead, Republicans proved to him how insincere they had been all along.

In early 2005, the housing prices had peaked and it appeared a housing bubble was about to burst. Paul gave an interview to the New York Times and vowed, "We will go back to the gold standard, even if it takes the near-destruction of the dollar to get there."[2] In November, Paul reaffirmed these beliefs in a speech at the Conference on Gold, Freedom, and Peace, a gathering organized by his old friend Burton S. Blumert.

During the 109th Congressional session the most important issues were the growing opposition against the Iraq war, the Hurricane Katrina disaster and immigration reform.

The immigration issue continued to intensify due to ongoing concerns in the aftermath of 9/11. Many Americans, fearful of terrorists crossing into the United States and undertaking further attacks, desired a tighter border. The immigration issue was further bolstered by a general anxiety of illegal immigrants taking American jobs, increasing crime and pushing down wages.[3] By 2004, estimates of illegal immigrants in the United States ranged from eight to twelve million.[4]

Lou Dobbs of CNN, the mild mannered host of Moneyline, was one of the first commentators to take up the issue seriously. He devoted roughly one-quarter of his airtime to immigration, which resulted in a substantial ratings increase for his show, Lou Dobbs Tonight. The topic consistently put his show at the top of CNN ratings, second only to Larry King Live.[5]

The immigration issue gained an even larger platform in 2005 when a group calling themselves The Minuteman Project began patrolling the US-Mexican border. These were private citizens who were so fed up with their government's lack of effectiveness in keeping out illegal immigrants that they took matters into their own hands.

Ron Paul's views on illegal immigration differed significantly from when he ran as a Libertarian in 1988. During his previous presidential run he stated, "As in our country's first 150 years, there shouldn't be any immigration policy at all. We should welcome everyone who wants to come here and work."[6] After the election, both Paul's views and those of libertarians began to shift.

Immigration has long been a divider issue among libertarians but it certainly is not the only one. The libertarian philosophy began to diverge during the late 1980s, resulting in a split between paleolibertarians and neolibertarians. The paleolibertarians emphasized property rights while the neolibertarians leaned more towards individual autonomy. This core difference shaped how both groups viewed the immigration debate.

Before the welfare state was born, the immigration issue was easily solved. As long as immigrants were not part of a hostile army, libertarians were generally open to unrestricted immigration. After the establishment of a welfare state, the question became more complex, raising doubts such as: do immigrants cross borders for the welfare benefits, and will immigrants reside on public property as beggars if open immigration is allowed?

Hans Hoppe, a critic of unrestricted immigration, noted that the libertarian immigration debate had diversified. According to Hoppe "three general strategies of dealing with immigration have been proposed: unconditional free immigration, *conditional* free immigration and restrictive immigration."[7]

Neolibertarians defended unconditional free immigration based on the fact that labor naturally moves to high-wage areas and business moves to low-wage areas, resulting in an equalization of wage rates and optimal localization of capital.

Some neolibertarians, such as Gary Becker, Milton Friedman, Thomas Sowell and Walter Williams, and many paleolibertarians have made the case for *conditional* free immigration. For example, Gary Becker[8] was worried about the fiscal impact of immigration and suggested a one-time $50,000 entrance fee to combat increasing expenditures due to immigrant use of government education and taxpayer health care.

Friedman agreed, saying, "In principle, you ought to have completely open immigration. But with the welfare state it's really not possible to do that. ... If there were no welfare state, you could have open immigration, because everybody would be responsible for himself."[9]

Sowell[10] and Williams,[11] on the other hand, were concerned about the burden on law enforcement illegal immigration had caused. They believed any proposed amnesty would whitewash an illegal act.

Some paleolibertarians followed the immigration debate to its other logical extreme and called for restricted immigration. According to Hoppe, open immigration should not be allowed even if the welfare state would cease to exist. He reasoned that the government would still own roads, parks and other public property and attract immigrants from the poorest areas of the world, who may be content to live on public property.

Ron Paul's beliefs were more consistent with the Founding Fathers, who came from a classic liberal tradition and often held favorable views towards immigration. Still, many Founders were skeptical towards unrestricted immigration and realized that it could jeopardize the existence of a free society.[12] They saw that the major issue with unlimited immigration was a possible cultural change in the population that the newly born Republic could not handle.

Thomas Jefferson provided the following thought experiment: "Suppose 20 million of Republican Americans [were] thrown all of a sudden into France, what would be the condition of that kingdom? If it would be more turbulent, less happy, less strong, we may believe that the addition of a half a million of foreigners to our present numbers would produce a similar effect here."[13]

Alexander Hamilton also showed immigration skepticism and wrote, in an ironic fashion, that the reason why American Indian culture lost to the European equivalent was because they suffered from a severe immigration problem. "Prudence requires us to trace the history further and ask what has become of the nations of savages who exercised this policy, and who now occupies the territory which they then inhabited? Perhaps a lesson is here taught which ought not to be despised."[14]

The generally favorable view of the classical liberals continued into the early 20th century and to Paul's mentor, Ludwig von Mises, who was once called the last knight of classical liberalism.[15] Still, even he was reserved towards immigration during some occasions such as war. "By removing migration barriers ... the Americas and Australia in admitting German, Italian, and Japanese immigrants would merely open their doors to the vanguards of hostile armies."[16]

Ron Paul was deeply influenced by the founders and by the late Ludwig von Mises.[17] His views on immigration could be best described as generally optimistic, with some reservations. In the welfare-warfare political culture of 2005, Paul supported conditional free immigration.[18] According to Paul:

> The immigration problem fundamentally is a welfare state problem. Some illegal immigrants – certainly not all – receive housing subsidies, food stamps, free medical care, and other forms of welfare. This alienates taxpayers and breeds suspicion of immigrants, even though the majority of them work very hard. Without a welfare state, we would know that everyone coming to America wanted to work hard and support himself. Since we have accepted a permanent welfare state, however, we cannot be surprised when some freeloaders and criminals are attracted to our shores. Welfare muddies the question of why immigrants want to come here.[19]

Pat Buchannan, who weighed in on the immigration issue frequently in 2005, believed it was the president's constitutional oath to protect and defend the borders. He noted, "The constitution says, and it's explicit, that the government of the United States shall protect the states from invasion. Now with 12 million people here illegally, three times the size of the American army in Europe after WWII, if that is not an invasion ... I don't know what it is."[20]

Buchannan held the same concerns as Sowell and Williams regarding the legality issue. Paul acknowledged this concern:

> The president [George W. Bush] claims that America lacks the political will to deport the eight to twelve million illegal aliens already here, so we have no choice but to grant them visas. But what message does this send to the rest of the world? If we reward millions who came here illegally, surely millions more will follow suit. Ten years from now we will be in the same position, with a whole new generation of lawbreakers seeking amnesty.[21]

Throughout the 20th century, the United States had found the political will to deport illegal aliens several times. In 1945, directly after World War II, President Dwight D. Eisenhower repatriated 130,000 illegal Mexican visitors.[22] Following this action, INS officials claimed an additional 1 to 1.2 million returned to Mexico of their own accord once it became clear the government would enforce the law. Before that, during the Great Depression, illegal aliens were repatriated by the US government when unemployment skyrocketed and welfare entitlements became an issue.

Paul favored enforcing the laws by deporting illegal visitors. He attacked Bush regarding his claim that America lacked "political will", a sentiment backed up by a 2006 opinion poll by Time Magazine that showed 89% of Americans believed illegal immigration in the US was a problem (30% "extremely serious," 33% "very serious," and 26% "somewhat serious").[23]

The first immigration related bill of the 109th Congress was HR 418, also known as the Real ID Act of 2005. On February 9th, Ron Paul delivered a speech titled "A National ID Bill Masquerading as Immigration Reform"[24] The House was quite empty when the speaker gave Paul permission to deliver his message.

Paul was furious about the bill. He demanded, "What are we doing with this bill? We are registering all the American people! And you want to register the criminals, and the thugs, and the terrorists! But why does a terrorist need a driver's license? He can just steal a car. ... So you are registering all the American people because you are looking for a terrorist and all the terrorists are going to do is avoid the law!"[25]

He looked sad when he ended the speech, saying, "I hope that there will be a few that oppose HR 418."[26] The Act eventually passed 261-161 on February 10th 2005. The national ID card, which he had fought against all these years, was now a reality.

A second immigration bill, the *Border Protection, Anti-terrorism and Illegal Immigration Control Act* (HR 4437), entered the House floor during 2005. If passed, the bill would enable the construction of a 700 mile fence on the US-Mexican border. It would also increase penalties for both human trafficking and employing illegal immigrants. Although Ron Paul never took a stance on this bill on the floor, he voted for the bill on December 16th when it passed by a narrow margin of 239 - 182.

Despite criticism from many libertarians, Paul stood firm on his decision regarding the Mexican border fence. During his 71st birthday in August 2006, he invited a special guest, Chris Simcox, the cofounder of another volunteer border patrol group, the Minuteman Civil Defense Corps. At the fundraising barbeque Paul gave an interview where he stated that securing the fence was not enough and that it needed to be accompanied by further immigration reform.[27]

The same year, a more specific bill on the border fence entered Congress; the Secure Fence Act of 2006 (HR 6061). This bill resembled the Border Protection bill of 2005, but instead of dealing with a broad number of immigration related subjects, the Secure Fence Act only dealt with the 700 mile long triple layered border fence and its future surveillance.

House Republicans supported the bill almost unanimously while only a third of Democrats favored it. Many Democratic congressmen criticized this bill and said that it resembled the Berlin wall, a wall the Soviets built around West Berlin after the Second World War in order to hinder East Germans from escaping. However, in this case the purpose of the fence was to defend the borders from illegal trespassers rather than locking citizens in.

As with the Border Security bill, Paul did not take a stance on the house floor. Instead, he voted for the bill, which passed with 283 votes for and

138 against on September 14th 2006. Paul said he favored the bill because "[w]hile the American people are demanding real immigration reform, many in Washington *lack the political will* to do what is required. That's why I've joined my colleagues in the House Immigration Reform caucus in demanding legislation this year that focuses on securing physical control of our borders while rejecting amnesty in any form. Congress has taken notice, and took an important first step last week by passing the Secure Fence Act of 2006 – legislation that provides physical security by lengthening border walls and creating a virtual border fence that extends thousands of miles."[28]

In total, the 109th Congress passed five immigration bills, but Ron Paul felt they did not truly address the problem of illegal immigration. "With the November elections looming, politics is taking priority over sensible policy," he wrote. "It appears congressional leaders have no intention of addressing the issue of illegal immigration this year, preferring not to tackle such a thorny problem for fear of angering voters one way or another."[29]

In his view, Congress was merely delaying true immigration reform, leaving the issue for the next Congress to solve. "The American people want something done about illegal immigration now – not next year. All sides in the immigration debate agree that the current, 'Don't ask, don't tell,' policy cannot continue."[30]

In order to solve the immigration problem, Paul has suggested six steps: 1. Physically secure the borders and coastlines. 2. Enforce visa rules on those already in the country. 3. Reject amnesty. 4. End welfare-state incentive for illegals. 5. End birthright citizenship. 6.Improve the legal immigration process.[31]

Philosophically, Paul would like to abandon the entire welfare state and have almost no immigration restrictions. Because political consensus does not allow this, his plan includes a transition period. This transition period consists of gradually reducing dependency on welfare benefits, while the size and scope of the welfare state is incrementally reduced. Until this occurs, he believes immigration must be restricted.

Ron Paul's final speech for the 109th congress took place on September 7th 2006. In it, he restated his political beliefs, emphasizing that government solutions do not work and that congress has for the past 50 years mostly caused havoc in the economy and decreased American liberties. He also took a strong anti-war stance and declared that the problems of the day stemmed from foreign interventionism. In order to restore a sound economy and American freedom, Paul suggested that politicians should resist PACs and lobbyists, while seeking guidance from the constitution.[32]

CHAPTER 23

NOW OR NEVER

2006-2007

Ballot Access

If ever a time should come, when vain and aspiring men shall possess the highest seats in government, our country will stand in need of its experienced patriots to prevent its ruin.

SAMUEL ADAMS.

Republicans in the 2006 congressional election knew they were in for a difficult fight due to the unpopular national sentiment pervading the Iraq war. Paul had been opposed from the war from the start, so he would likely remain popular in November for the general election. However, he had taken the position of opposing a Republican President's war, making him potentially vulnerable among Republicans in the primary race.

Paul's opponent in the primary race was Cynthia Sinatra, a 52 year old international attorney and ex-wife of Frank Sinatra Jr., the son of the legendary entertainer. Sinatra Jr. even campaigned at her side.

Cynthia accused Paul of not supporting President Bush. Regarding the war in Iraq, she told voters, "I support the president and Dr. Paul doesn't. … The world looks to us as a shining example for democracy."[1] The tactic failed to win her much support. Paul won the 14th district with nearly 80% of the vote, indicating solid Republican support in his district.

In the general election held in November, Congressman Paul would face Democrat Shane Sklar, a 30 year-old conservative Democrat and former Executive Director for the Independent Cattlemen's Association of Texas. In

1999-2000 he worked for Democratic Congressman Chet Edwards, but had never run for elected office himself.[2]

A poll of 500 voters in the 14th District, conducted in April of 2006 by the Sklar campaign indicated that Ron Paul was out of step with his constituents and they were ready for a change. The poll also indicated that when voters were exposed to Paul's voting record, and Shane Sklar's profile, they preferred Sklar 54% over Paul's 30% (with 16% undecided).[3] However, Ron Paul's name recognition was 88% in his district compared to Sklar's 25%.

The Sklar campaign moved forward with a strategy to emphasize Paul's libertarian label, which many voters perceived as negative, and Paul's voting record, which Sklar said was evidence that Paul was promoting his own personal ideological agenda over bringing federal money and jobs back to the 14th District.

As the elections drew near, Congressman Paul's dedicated base of support did not fail. With 97% of his donations coming from individuals, Paul out-raised Sklar $1.2 million to $600,000. He went on to win the general election, defeating Sklar by a 20% margin.[4]

....

Paul began his tenth term in Congress the same way he ended his ninth term: vocally opposing the War in Iraq. In January 2007 alone, he addressed the House three separate times concerning the country's foreign policy. Though the war had already dragged on for 45 months, he was still one of the few Republican voices of opposition to prevailing foreign policy in Iraq. Paul told his colleagues, "Military victory in Iraq is unattainable, just as it was in the Vietnam War."

The Democratic Party had managed to capture a majority in the House of Representatives, primarily due to the growing anti-war sentiment in America. However, rather than discussing ways to scale back the war, talk immediately began of the need for a surge of an additional twenty thousand troops and one hundred billion dollars. "The talk of a troop surge and jobs program in Iraq only distracts Americans from the very real possibility of an attack on Iran," Ron said. "Our growing naval presence in the region and our harsh rhetoric toward Iran are unsettling. Securing the Horn of Africa and sending Ethiopian troops into Somalia do not bode well for world peace. Yet these developments are almost totally ignored by Congress."

It was becoming apparent that neither the current administration, nor the newly elected Democratic majority in the House, intended to do anything other than escalate the existing war and perhaps embroil the United States in a new war with Iran. "Rumors are flying about when, not if, Iran will be bombed by either Israel or the US - possibly with nuclear weapons," warned Paul. "Our CIA says Iran is ten years away from producing a nuclear bomb and has no delivery system, but this does not impede our plans to keep 'everything on the table' when dealing with Iran."[5]

A perfect storm was gathering force in American politics that made a Presidential bid seem more plausible than ever. Sitting President George W. Bush was finishing his second tem and Vice-President Cheney had no intention of entering the race. For the first time since 1952, there would be no incumbent president or vice-president to run against in the general election. From a strategic standpoint, it was either now or never.

On November 22, 2006, 15 days after Ron's congressional victory, Chris

Elam, a former Washington staff intern for Ron Paul, registered the domain name RonPaul2008.com.[6]

The race was wide open on the Republican side. With no presumptive front-runner, a crowded field of initial candidates began forming exploratory committees. By the end of January 2007, a total of ten candidates would announce their intention to run for the Republican nomination. Though he was in his tenth term as a Congressman, the GOP had never fully embraced Ron Paul as a Republican and they still considered him an outsider. If history was any indication, he would receive little financial support from traditional Republican Party donors, nor endorsements from more nationally recognized GOP leaders.

At 71 years of age, Paul had no interest in running as a protest candidate or to simply inject often neglected issues into the debate. If he was going to do this, he would be in it to win. On January 7th, Paul attended a house party in Pembroke, New Hampshire thrown by libertarian Kevin Roll. It was a gathering of about 100 participants in the Free State Project, a movement to concentrate libertarians in one state. At the party, Paul confidentially told participants he was forming an exploratory committee for president. Three days later, after serious consideration with his family, and in response to many requests, Congressman Paul officially formed an exploratory committee.[7]

Paul had the full support of his family, and the first official member of the campaign team was his son, Rand Paul. Rand, like his father, was a physician, and would speak on Ron's behalf numerous times during the course of the campaign.

Ron Paul recruited Kent Snyder as the chairman of the committee. Kent grew up in Kansas and later attended Golden Gate University in San Francisco, where he pursued an undergraduate degree in political science. The openly gay political operative had been a longtime fan of Congressman Paul, having researched his congressional career during his graduate level studies.[8]

The two first met in 1987 when Snyder, a 28-year old martial arts master with a black belt in Kajukenbo, was working on Paul's Libertarian presidential campaign. Ron Paul described Snyder as a "gentle man who carried himself with quiet dignity."[9] From that time forward, they worked together on many liberty-oriented projects. He was the executive director of the Liberty Committee, a caucus of liberty-minded US House Representatives. Snyder saw his involvement in the Liberty Committee as a way to "ensure that the Constitution is seen neither as a dead letter, nor living document but rather the law of the land to be respected and obeyed."[10]

In 1995, Snyder left a position in telecommunications managing the San Francisco office of *United Communications* in order to serve as a Congressional staff member for Ron Paul when he returned to Congress.

In 2006, Snyder was integral in convincing Ron to run for president as a Republican. "It was Kent, more than anyone else, who urged me to run for president," said Ron. Snyder, 49 at the time, stepped into the role of chairman of the presidential campaign.

As they constructed their campaign strategy, the election team began to understand the difficulty of their task. "There's no question that it's an uphill battle, and that Dr. Paul is an underdog," Snyder said. "But we think it's well worth doing and we'll let the voters decide."[11]

As further evidence of the uphill nature that the campaign would face, a

CNN opinion poll from February of 2007 indicated that Ron Paul had the lowest name recognition of any Republican candidate who would ultimately seek the nomination.[12] In order to help overcome the obstacle of name recognition, Jesse Benton was tapped as the Communications Director. At 29 years of age, Benton was a self-described "conservative Republican hack" prior to his involvement in Ron Paul's Presidential campaign.[13] He was an economics major in college, and afterward worked for a number of prominent conservative groups, including Americans for Tax Reform and the American Conservative Union. He eventually became disillusioned when the rhetoric of limited government and personal liberty was not always backed up with real action. "I got to play with some big boys on the insider conservative movement and got to see how that works, and how, unfortunately, a lot of Beltway conservatives don't practice what they preach," he said.[14]

Jesse used his political experience to start a private communications firm, with the Paul campaign becoming one of his clients. "I'd been an admirer of Paul for many years," said Benton "They needed some press work getting off the ground when they were just a two-person operation." He would become the third staff member of Ron Paul's formal campaign team.

To succeed in his campaign, Ron would have to win over different voting blocks within registered Republicans, who can vote in the primaries. Snyder would need to identify the different groups and then begin an assault to win those groups to Ron's side. It would involve a constant process of high-profile attacks, measuring the effects through polls and focus groups, and then re-planning another assault on that target group, much as Karl Rove had done years earlier for George W. Bush.

Snyder knew that if they were to campaign against men with more name recognition and more resources, he would need to devise a radically different campaign strategy. He remarked, "This is going to be a grassroots American campaign. For us, it's either going to happen at the grassroots level or it's not."[15]

This grassroots campaign resulted in some unorthodox tactics employed by the Ron Paul Campaign. For example, Snyder often coordinated campaign activities with local groups around the country using video conferencing over the Internet.[16] The meetings required little money, yet helped to build a solid core of supporters within each state.

Jesse Benton credited much of their early success to the use of the Internet and other non-traditional forms of media. "Ron is the type of candidate who needs more than a thirty-second sound bite to be able to communicate his message." Benton said.[17] The campaign relied on Social networking websites such as Myspace and Meetup, along with online video streaming YouTube, to provide a more detailed forum for the positions that would become synonymous with Ron Paul Republicans.

In just over a month's time, the exploratory committee had gathered over $500,000 with very little effort, and Ron Paul formally announced his Presidential Bid on March 12, 2007 on C-SPAN's Washington Journal. Though he was reluctant to run again for President, it was never because he doubted the strength of his message. He knew that the message was good and that it could unite people across the nation. However, he was initially unsure that he was the right candidate to deliver the message. It was also difficult to judge the size of his supporters nationally. He wondered if this remnant of freedom-minded voters, no matter how small, would rally around him.

In his early appearances, Paul never appeared overly-eager to become president. His political aspirations were not that of a career politician, but of a burning desire to uphold the Constitution. "Almost all of our problems have been created by ignoring the rule of law," said Ron, "so almost every problem we have can be eliminated by returning to the Constitution. Conventional wisdom says that we have to have a president who should run things. What I would like to be is a president who doesn't even have a goal of running your life, the country, or running the world."

Though he ran as a Libertarian in the 1988 Presidential race, Paul was adamant from the beginning that he had no intention of running in a third party. He felt that not only are the ballot access laws biased against third-parties, but that there would be no chance of getting the necessary media attention or a spot in any of the major debates.

In the past, third parties thrived because there were no election laws to discriminate against them. Citizens were free to form new parties as they saw fit, and the government did not give preferential treatment to either the new or old parties. In 1854, the newly formed Republican Party sent more representatives to the House than any other. This was only possible because there were no ballot access laws until 1888. Ironically, the Republican Party was later partly responsible for changes to ballot access laws, which would have prevented its own existence much earlier.

Standardized, printed ballots didn't exist early in the republic either. People simply generated their own ballots, and voted for the candidate of their choice. When the government began printing ballots in 1888, there was a spot left for a write-in vote. This was just the beginning of a slippery slope of government intervention into the election process. It was only a matter of time before legislators of the established parties began to make ballot access more restrictive for new parties, ensuring the re-election of their own party's candidates. As with much government regulation and intervention, ballot access laws have become incrementally restrictive. In 1924, only 50,000 signatures were required to place a new party on the ballot in 48 states. By 1994, this number would jump to over 1.5 million signatures to accomplish the same goal.

Congressman Paul had long been an advocate of ballot access reform, having introduced HR 1941, the Voter Freedom Act, in 2003. The act would have created uniform ballot access laws for independent and third party candidates in Congressional elections. Shortly after he introduced HR 1941, he addressed the House.

"Candidates able to comply with onerous ballot access rules must devote so many resources to simply getting on the ballot that their ability to communicate ideas to the general public is severely limited," he said. "Perhaps the ballot access laws are one reason why voter turnout has been declining over the past few decades. After all, almost 42% of eligible voters have either not registered to vote or have registered as something other than Democrat or Republican."[18]

Each state has its own laws concerning who can appear on the ballot. The Constitution specifically addressed this in Article 1, Section 4, which says that the time, place and manner of federal elections are up to each State, unless Congress legislates otherwise. This was an opportunity for the Congress to legislate in an entirely Constitutional manner, for the benefit of all people, and the political process as a whole.

"The United States Constitution gives Congress the authority to regulate the time, place, and manner of federal elections," said Ron. "Thus, ballot access is one of the few areas where Congress has explicit constitutional authority to establish national standards. In order to open up the political process, I have introduced the Voter Freedom Act (HR 1941). HR 1941 established uniform standards for ballot access so third party and independent candidates can at last compete on a level playing field." The 2003 bill did not pass. However, Ron Paul was not dissuaded and he introduced similar legislation again in 2007.

....

It would take money and supporters in order to have a genuine chance of winning the Republican nomination. With this end in mind, Congressman Paul held one of his first significant fundraising events in Austin, Texas on May 19th, 2007.[19] There he gave a speech that set the tone for the message he would eventually deliver throughout the campaign. Unlike most presidential candidates, Congressman Paul just walked up to the podium without any note cards or teleprompter. His message stayed the same regardless of the audience. It was a message based on three key issues: foreign policy, economic policy, and personal liberty.

It was soon apparent from his rallies that Ron Paul was truly a unifying candidate. His supporters came from all different political affiliations: there were Independents, Libertarians, Democrats, and "even a few Republicans," as Ron would often joke. The audiences that came to hear him speak were a representative cross section of the American people. They were hard working, blue collar laborers. They were single mothers. They were college students. They were business owners. They were senior citizens. They were retired veterans and active military. They were people of all races and religious backgrounds.

"The art of politics is to bring people together, not to be divisive." Paul observed. "You have to bring coalitions together." While other candidates and political parties often exacerbated the differences between groups of people, or pandered to specific interest groups, Ron chose instead to address his audiences as individuals. He told them, "Personal liberty is not a special interest."

Although Paul tried hard to bring people together, one former employee became increasingly antagonistic towards Ron Paul. In May 2007, Eric Dondero announced, "I am this morning, declaring my candidacy for Congress in the GOP primaries against Ron Paul. If he does not resign his seat, and if another Republican candidate does not declare against him, I will run a balls-to-the-wall campaign for Congress in Texas [Congressional District] 14. I am the guy that got Ron Paul elected to Congress in 1996. I can and will defeat him in 2008."

The threat never materialized as another Republican ended up running against Paul in the primaries. However, Dondero actively campaigned for Paul's opponent, Rudy Giuliani.

Throughout the campaign, Paul would frequently pepper his speeches with quotes and references from Frederic Bastiat and Thomas Jefferson, as well as contemporaries like economist Ludwig Von Mises, and the former head of the CIA's bin Laden unit, Michael Scheuer. Citing John Adams, he discussed the importance of maintaining a moral society in order for freedom to truly work. "We have lost respect and confidence in how liberty works," he said. "Freedom works."

The issues of a weak dollar and the possibility of a recession were starting to make headlines as the sub-prime mortgage crisis began to surface. Having built his reputation over the previous thirty years as a proponent of free markets and sound money, Paul used his public speaking engagements to educate the American public on these and other economic issues. "Most Americans believe in the free enterprise system," said Ron. "The real big welfare in the system that we have goes to the military industrial complex and the big banks." He added that, if we had the proper size government, we wouldn't need the IRS or the 16th amendment.

And to Ron's surprise, beginning with his dedicated base in Texas, people were actually listening. In a few short weeks, people from all over the country, the liberty-minded remnant in America, began watching videos of his speeches on the Internet, joining Meetup groups, and sending thousands of dollars through the campaign website. The revolution was about to begin.

CHAPTER 24

THE INTERNET AND RON PAUL

2007

Regulations

We have it in our power to begin the world over again.

THOMAS PAINE

L ong before an official announcement, news that Ron Paul was exploring a run for president leaked out across the Internet. The official story that broke the news was a short blurb on January 11, 2007 by the Associated Press titled 'Texas Congressman Seeks Presidency.'[1] In just over 200 words, it explained that Paul had filed papers to form an exploratory committee for a presidential run.

In the pre-Internet era, such a story might be buried in the back pages of the local newspaper if it made the news at all. If one of Paul's hundreds of thousands of supporters scattered across the nation were to stumble across the news, he would certainly be delighted. But then what? Unless he already knew of other supporters personally, he would have no way of contacting them.

The Internet changes all of that. While not receiving the same level of coverage on television or in print as his competitors, the Ron Paul Revolution (as it came to be known) developed through the unregulated freedom of the Internet. The campaign clearly demonstrated the battle between the vested powers of the traditional *old media* and the vibrant rising power of Internet-based *new media*.

Paul had long recognized the importance of new communications technology. In the eighties, he created a cable television series to promote his constitutional message. He operated a premium-rate phone service to provide weekly updates to freedom loving Americans. He used early Apple Macintosh personal computers to print his newsletters. Paul understood that improvements in communications could improve freedom, and now he would use the Internet to his advantage.

Although Paul did not have a detailed technical understanding of the Internet, he grasped the importance of keeping the Internet free from government interference. "He is really interested in the Internet," said Jesse Benton in 2007. "He recognizes the power of the Internet and the need to make sure that the Internet is not regulated and not interfered with by government because it is one of the last true vehicles of liberty."[2]

A few weeks after the AP article debuted on the Internet, Paul gave an online audio interview about the impact the Internet would have on the 2008 presidential race. At the time, Hillary Clinton seemed like the presumptive Democratic nominee. Paraphrasing something he read online about his candidacy, he said, "This is not a contest between Ron Paul and Hillary Clinton so much as it is a real challenge between the people who get their information from the Internet in a quiet sort of way vs. the major networks."

Paul was already anticipating the battle that would take place between the old media and the new. "The numbers of people out there who are sick and tired of what they're getting are strong enough that we can have a real impact and be very competitive," he said. But in order for the campaign to be effective, he knew it would have to ignite at the grassroots level. "We live in a new and modern age and nobody has truly measured this. I think Howard Dean got around the edges two years ago and did pretty well ... but the technology continues to improve. The ability to reach millions of people at a very low cost is very intriguing."

Dean's 2004 run for president had set the prior standard for grassroots activism and Internet organization.[3] But greatly improved technologies – including many that didn't exist during Dean's run – would catapult Paul's campaign to an entirely new level. Technologies such as YouTube and MySpace allowed average people to participate in the national debate in ways that were impossible during the previous campaign season.

These technologies were the difference between vested powers telling Americans, "Good evening. Here is the news," and people finding and sharing what they believed to be important.[4] The shift was one from passive consumers of news and opinion to active participants that challenge, question and *create* news and opinion.

....

The central issues that Ron Paul has championed during his twenty years in Congress – freedom, liberty and limited government regulation – have been central to the Internet's explosive growth. Paul has therefore never voted to regulate the Internet, a major contributing factor to his solid, existing online base.

As a relatively new technology, the Internet remained mostly unregulated as Paul made his 2008 presidential bid. Anyone with basic computer literacy could set up a website. No special permission from the government was required and Paul wanted to keep it that way.

Throughout his tenth term, which began in January 2007, Paul would oppose any attempt to regulate the Internet. "The Internet is a powerful tool, and any censorship of Internet activity sets a dangerous precedent," he explained to his House colleagues. "Many Americans rely on the Internet for activities as varied as watching basketball games, keeping up on international news broadcasts, or buying food and clothing. In the last few years we have seen ominous signs of the federal government's desire to control the Internet. The ostensible reasons are to protect Americans from sex offenders, terrorists, and the evils of gambling, but once the door is open to government intrusion, there is no telling what legitimate activity, especially political activity, might fall afoul of government authorities."[5]

Paul opposed one such bill, HR 2046, which was introduced April 27, 2007 by House Democrat Barney Frank to control Internet gambling. Paul believed the bill violated basic freedoms, saying, "The ban on Internet gambling infringes upon two freedoms that are important to many Americans: the ability to do with their money as they see fit, and the freedom from government interference with the Internet."

He also feared it would turn businesses into de facto employees of the government, much as the income tax turned every employer in the United States into government tax collectors. "The regulations and underlying bill also force financial institutions to act as law enforcement officers," he said. "This is another pernicious trend that has accelerated in the aftermath of the Patriot Act, the deputization of private businesses to perform intrusive enforcement and surveillance functions that the federal government is unwilling to perform on its own."[6]

Paul wanted the Internet open and free, with no licenses to apply for, no proof of ID to show, no taxes to pay, and no government forms to fill out. This would allow expressions of creativity to continue unhampered and advance new cultures and ways for individuals to interact with one another. Ron Paul, with his consistent message as the defender of liberty, was a natural online favorite.

One issue frequently asked of Paul during the campaign was whether he supported government imposed *Network Neutrality*. The proposed regulations would supposedly prevent favoritism of Internet bandwidth by forcing Internet providers to treat all data packets that passed through their nodes equally, prevent providers from limiting content to their customers, and prevent tiered services. Network Neutrality proponents believed those individuals owning Internet infrastructure must be *forced* by the government to be fair to all data flowing through their network. It was obvious how Paul saw the issue.

Of the individuals who fathered the Internet, only one, Vinton Serf, supported regulated Network Neutrality. The others, such as Robert Kahn[7] (who co-developed TCP/IP with Serf) and Richard Bennet (inventor of WiFi) opposed it.[8] The reason for the almost uniform opposition, aside from property rights issues, was because they believed regulations would stifle innovation and technological advancement, as regulations have in the past. Khan warned that "nothing interesting can happen inside the net" if regulations passed.[9]

Like early wireless telephones, the Internet undoubtedly had a long way to evolve. Paul believed that if this evolution was going to continue, it must remain regulation free.

In mid-March, the campaign switched its simple exploratory committee site to the new RonPaul2008.com. However, the new site was widely panned by Paul's Internet savvy supporters as being old fashioned and unprofessional in appearance.[10] There was no way for supporters to interact with one another, no forums, no chat rooms, and no way for bloggers to communicate with the world. The extent of interaction was the ability to send email to campaign headquarters. Information about the campaign was left largely to an eclectic collection of independent blogs and websites that regularly posted Paul's writings.

This was in sharp contrast to Howard Dean's 2004 campaign website, which hosted all such features. The redesign employed by Paul's in-house design team was unique to his decentralized philosophy. Rather than mimic Dean's strategy, the Paul website outsourced the most vital functions. The official blog was kept at Typepad, videos were hosted on YouTube, and the calendar kept on Eventful.com. Supporters were encouraged to use social news sites like Digg and Reddit to popularize Ron Paul related news items.

At the time, it seemed odd for an official campaign to rely so heavily on third-party tools. In retrospect, the decision was made from necessity; the campaign had little money at the time. But it was also an extraordinary step that demonstrated just how frugal a campaign for president could be. Most importantly, it empowered supporters to promote Ron Paul's candidacy in the free market of ideas.

The only site at the time dedicated exclusively to Ron Paul's presidential bid was the DailyPaul.com,[11] a site created by blogger Michael Nystrom ten days after Paul filed his election papers. In keeping with the Internet's freewheeling nature, it was started without the knowledge or express permission of the campaign. It was the free market of ideas at work.

Paul's eldest grandson, Matthew Pyeatt, credits the site as "serving a vital function in the early months of the campaign, as it was the only central gathering place for Ron Paul supporters to communicate with one another."

By early spring of 2007, old media coverage of the campaign remained sparse as online activity continued to grow. Supporters began exploiting the Internet to share their skills and ideas about how to promote Ron Paul in the physical world. Posters and stickers in support of Paul were designed, uploaded and made freely available for anyone to download, print and distribute.[12]

In early March, Paul was excluded from a Pajamas Media website poll because he was reportedly polling at less than one percent at the time.[13] After a flurry of e-mails from Paul supporters, the website later relented and included Paul, who quickly rose to the top of the online poll. This resulted in accusations that Paul's supporters were *spamming* comment sections and stacking online polls.[14] It was a slight misuse of the term, which generally means to send out bulk e-mail messages.

Later in the year, Paul's online supporters were accused of actual e-mail spamming by Wired magazine when thousands of pro-Paul e-mail messages were sent to random recipients, further embarrassing the campaign. Spokesperson Jesse Benton answered Wired Magazine, saying, "If it is true, it could be done by a well-intentioned yet misguided supporter or someone with bad intentions trying to embarrass the campaign. Either way, this is independent work, and we have no connection."[15]

By early April, even online enthusiasm seemed to level out. Supporters began looking for ways to boost Internet traffic and activity via social networking sites to raise Paul's visibility. From this came the idea to encourage people to "Google Ron Paul" by putting up signs and banners in neighborhoods around the United States.

In late April, something happened that could have only taken place in the Internet era: the first ever interview of a presidential candidate from a college dorm room.[16] It was conducted by James Kotecki and posted to YouTube, a video sharing website, where it received hundreds of thousands of views. There was no capital investment required from the undergraduate. He used his computer, a web cam and an agreeable candidate. It was astonishing that an enterprising college student could so easily pull off an interview with a national politician.

....

Paul's campaign received its first major boost from the old media. In May 2007, at the first nationally televised GOP debate, Paul gave a performance that differentiated himself from the other nine candidates on stage. His positions – ending the war, abolishing the IRS, questioning the fundamental role of government, and giving possibly the first explanation of the *inflation tax* that many people had ever heard – were easy for the old media to dismiss.

At the debate, Paul was asked whether he trusts the mainstream media. "Some of them," he replied. "But I trust the Internet a lot more. I trust the freedom of expression, and that is why we should never interfere with the Internet."

This first debate performance caught the attention of many who had never heard of Ron Paul. Unfortunately for his campaign, post-debate news coverage all but ignored him; standard treatment for candidates with low polling numbers. The old media replayed no Ron Paul sound-bites, instead choosing to focus their attention on the candidates they already favored. The *New York Times* article covering the debate said nothing of Paul other than merely to mention that he was in attendance.[17]

By necessity, those looking for more information turned to the Internet. But even the ABC-news sponsored post-debate poll excluded Ron Paul. After vociferous email complaints by supporters, he was finally added and handily won the online poll,[18] in addition to those at MSNBC and CSPAN.

The war between the old media and the new was on. Within hours after the debate had finished, someone had edited the footage into a Ron Paul highlights reel and uploaded it to YouTube.[19] Internet based discussion picked up dramatically.

This and a second Fox News debate marked a turning point for the campaign. By the end of May, Paul became the most requested candidate on Eventful.com, and had twice as many YouTube supporters as all the other GOP candidates combined.[20]

In May, Ron Paul Forums debuted. It was the brainchild of an ordinary American, Josh Lowry, a professional realtor. This website would go on to have a major impact on the campaign, allowing users to discuss strategies, organize campaign activities, and inform people of upcoming events.

Along with Daily Paul, Ron Paul Forums also helped to promote news articles to the front page of social news sites like Digg and Reddit. These websites operate by allowing users to vote for news stories they find interesting. If a story is popular enough, it becomes promoted to the front page. The large numbers of Paul supporters resulted in dozens of Ron Paul news stories receiving millions of viewers.

The campaign immediately recognized the power of this new breed of Internet site. "Digg is real cool," commented Jesse Benton. "I wouldn't say it's a central nerve but it's part of our strategy. It's real cool because if people dig an article about Ron Paul it goes to the front of Digg.com and it's in a place where a lot of people can check it out and read it."[21]

Following the second debate, in which Paul took on Rudy Giuliani, the campaign began to make some ripples among the old media. Paul was discussed on the afternoon women's talk show the View, on CNN, and on comedian Bill Maher's HBO show. These clips were captured and uploaded to YouTube for the benefit of those supporters who had given up on television.

In May, a more videos began to emerge and spread virally. They were, for the most part, simple, homemade affairs featuring headshots of people talking into their web cameras. One featured an attractive young woman in *Confessions of a Ron Paul Junkie.*[22] "Hi Internet! My name is Rachel and I'm a junkie - a Ron Paul junkie!" she announced. "It started right after the debates in South Carolina. Ron Paul just inspired me so much and said so many of the things I've been wanting to hear from a politician for so long. And there he was on the stage saying them, blatantly… Ever since then I'm just totally hooked." Paul had awakened a segment of the population previously turned off by politics.

As the campaign continued, increased funds became available and Paul was more able to promote his candidacy. Following the criticisms of his frugal official campaign site, the team was determined to get it right. This time they hired a professional design consulting group, Terra Eclipse, to redesign the site. On June 5, they re-launched the website to positive acclaim from Paul supporters.

....

Paul's campaign appearances were another matter. Earlier in the year he didn't know who would show up to his appearances across the nation. As it turned out, his rallies attracted young people in droves. Everywhere he went, there were throngs of young voters screaming and cheering at his speeches. On June 15 in Kansas City, the campaign booked the Uptown Theater, a small venue that resulted in supporters spilling into the aisles.[23] He had never experienced anything like it. It was an incredible contrast to his earlier years as a congressman, and the crowds would only get bigger.

The abundant support affected Paul greater than he could have imagined. Since the events in 2001, Paul had carried around an air of pessimism. He had been fighting for freedom since the early 1970s, but his ideas had not been accepted in significant numbers. Now, in 2007, the ideas he espoused were becoming more fully understood.

The old media took notice. Articles began appearing in mainstream publications. He had a smattering of appearances on television. Each time he appeared, the media made a pointed effort to make clear that he had no chance of being elected. In one particularly egregious episode during July, ABC News correspondent (and former Bill Clinton advisor) George Stephanopoulos asked Paul, "What is success to you?" "Well, to win..." was the beginning of Paul's reply. But before he could finish his sentence, Stephanopoulos declared, "That's not going to happen."[24]

Rather than discussing his message, much of the old media focused their curiosity on his Internet support, something they never seemed to fully understand. By September, Time Magazine called him the top Internet candidate based on traffic flowing to his site.[25] But even as the old media began to comprehend the existence of a Ron Paul movement, the important news about his campaign was only available online. Paul began placing favorably in local GOP straw polls across the nation, yet the news was mostly ignored by the old media.[26]

At the Iowa straw poll, Paul's grassroots supporters organized an "adopt-an-Iowan" program to help pay for tickets so that locals could vote in the Iowa straw poll. Supporters organized a full-page ad to be placed in the Ames Tribune. Drafts of the ad, which featured a bust of Paul made up by a mosaic of supporters' faces were posted online at Ron Paul Forums, critiqued, and improved through several iterations. It was group collaboration on a massive scale by passionate individualists. Supporters across the country sent in money to pay for the ad.

Surprisingly, the official campaign was hardly involved in organizing these online movements, or even in fundraising. Supporters organized themselves. The grassroots organization was spontaneous and effective as the campaign took a laissez faire attitude towards these projects. They were neither encouraged nor discouraged by Paul, though he liberally acknowledged his supporters.

Politicians know that money is a key factor in a successful campaign, but it is not the only factor as an unfortunate Rudy Giuliani would later find out. In mulling his run, Paul was certain he would have support, but he wasn't sure if it would be enough to offset the wealth of his establishment opponents. "When you talk dollar-wise, that is a different story," said Paul. "Because for those individuals, groups and companies that have a special interest – the military industrial complex and other organizations; the Haliburtons of the world - this is high stakes politics."[27]

In August, the campaign held its first effort to harness the fundraising power of Ron Paul's regional support. It held a Meetup group contest to see which group could raise the most money for the campaign.[28] Competition was spirited, intense, and encouraging.

But the official campaign's first real breakthrough in harnessing the fundraising power of the online community came on September 17th - Constitution Day. In order to celebrate the birth of the constitution in 1787, the campaign set a goal to secure 1,787 donations by Friday September 21st. An online counter was set up on the official site to show the number of donations that had been made, and it was updated each time a new one came in. This first fundraising campaign was a modest success, with the number of donations exceeding the goal by several hundred.

Emboldened, the campaign set an ambitious goal to raise $500,000 in the final week of the 3rd quarter. A new real-time counter was added to the campaign website to record donations as they came in. The $500,000 level was achieved so quickly – within days – that the campaign upped the ante. It raised the goal to one million dollars, which also was surprisingly easily achieved.

Building on this success, the campaign set an even more ambitious target of $12 million for the new quarter. A revised counter was placed on the website. This was the campaign's true innovation: real time, open donation counting. It had never been done in a political campaign before. Data on the donations was made publicly available so that other sites, notably RonPaulGraphs.com were able to repackage and display the data in interesting ways.

In the first few weeks of October, fundraising was lagging behind the $12 million goal. Then the grassroots movement generated a new tactic. They targeted one specific day for fundraising: November 5th, inspired by the recent Hollywood film *V for Vendetta*.

The original concept came from Paul supporter James Sugra[29] who conceived of the idea and created a video that suggested 100,000 people donate $100 each for a $10 million day. The concept was first brought to the Ron Paul Forums by Trevor Lyman, an Internet entrepreneur, where it was discussed and fleshed out.[30] Lyman produced a website, with the help of other designers across the net. Someone else produced promotional banners to use on other websites. A separate artist created a flash countdown clock. Soon, news of the upcoming event quickly spread across the Internet.

Although the November 5th campaign failed to achieve the stated $10 million goal, the results were staggering nonetheless: $4.3 million was raised in one day, the largest amount ever by a candidate in a one-day online fundraising event until that time.[31] But the best was yet to come.

Paul's tremendous online success overshadowed the other candidates in 2007 (Republican or Democrat) in almost every category: Most Myspace Friends (later surpassed by Barack Obama); most cumulative YouTube video views of any candidate; Most Facebook supporters (again, later surpassed by Obama), most demands by Eventful, the most popular website of any GOP candidate, and the most Meetup members. Paul had 88,576 members in 2007, while Barak Obama, the leading Democrat, had 3,643.

Paul's Internet success soon changed his perception among his House colleagues. In an interview with Morning Joe, host Joe Scarborough noted, "When we were members of congress, a lot of the time you would go on the floor, you would sit alone. People treated you like you had the plague. ... But now you say that when you walk onto the floor, you're a popular guy. Republicans surround you and they want to know about one thing: how are you raising all that money?"

Paul chuckled at the genuine truth of those words. "They do ask me about it. Democrats are interested too," he said. "But they're asking the wrong question. It isn't a technique, it's a message."[32]

With the primaries rapidly approaching, the campaign was anxious to see whether this impressive show of online support would translate into votes.

CHAPTER 25

DEALING WITH THE MEDIA

2007

Media Bias

For the great majority of mankind are satisfied with appearances, as though they were realities, and are often more influenced by the things that seem than by those that are.

NICCOLO MACHIAVELLI

In the years leading up to his 2008 Republican presidential campaign, Congressman Ron Paul had occasionally appeared as a guest commentator on news programs and talk shows, but to most of the American public, he had not yet become a household name. A few memorable exchanges on national television would soon change that.

Conventional wisdom dictates that gaining the attention and tacit support of the mainstream media is a make-or-break matter for a political candidate. Additionally, it is asserted that there is ultimately no such thing as bad publicity. What matters is getting and keeping the media's attention—no matter how that is accomplished.

However, Paul did not achieve his notoriety because of the mainstream media, which played only a marginal role in his popularity. The television program *PBS Now* noted this relationship, observing, "Ron Paul has managed to not just impress people, but change them from apathetic observers to active supporters. And he hasn't done it with hugs and handshakes or the help of the mainstream media. The Ron Paul movement was borne on the power of the Internet."[1] Between August 2006 and August 2007, Paul was mentioned 4,695 times on television news and cable shows – 13 times per day. During the same period, fellow Republican contender John McCain was mentioned 95,005 times.[2]

The issue of attaining frequent media coverage was a prominent one in Ron's 2008 campaign. Supporters were known for calling and emailing television shows, asking for more coverage of Paul. Many of them were demonstrably frustrated with what they saw as an unfair bias against Paul in the major media – for example, He won a poll conducted by text message after a Fox News debate on September 5th, 2007, but newscasters largely ignored the win and dismissed it as a fluke caused by multiple entries from a few ardent Paul supporters.[3]

Many Americans maintain a certain sense of awe when it comes to the mainstream media. For the mainstream media to reject or ignore that which some people have passionately embraced is painful to them. When the mainstream media, as supporters saw it, blocked out their candidate, supporters turned to other forms of media: Internet activism, local campaign groups, and word of mouth.

In early 2007, Ron Paul's communications director Jesse Benton gave an optimistic interview with Dome Nation. "I don't think we are being completely bypassed," he mused. "The mainstream media has been covering us more and more." Benton commented on the amount of coverage Paul received, saying, "I think it's legitimate that a candidate has to make some buzz before the mainstream media starts to pay attention." To succeed, Ron Paul would have to make some buzz. But when the buzz happened, would the media respond?

The Ron Paul campaign initially received national exposure in March 2007, when he was invited as a guest on *Real Time with Bill Maher*, a political talk show on HBO. Paul gave a five minute interview via satellite.

Maher had on previous occasions described himself as a libertarian. However, his support for gun control, regulation of business, and opposition to home schooling brought that claim into question. "I've always thought I was a Libertarian but I'm Chairman Mao compared to you," Maher began his interview. "You think we should get rid of the CIA! ... I would feel naked without the CIA."

Paul had earlier endorsed the 2002 book, The Real Lincoln: A New Look at Abraham Lincoln, His Agenda, and an Unnecessary War by Thomas DiLorenzo. The thesis of the book is that the war was fought to prevent the southern states from declaring independence from the Union; not primarily to eliminate slavery.

The skeptical host took special issue with Ron Paul's belief that the Civil War was unnecessary and could have been avoided. "I've read that you said that you don't think we should have fought the Civil War!" said Maher.

Paul replied, "I think there would have been a better way. Every other major country of the world was able to get rid of slavery without a civil war. The Civil War wasn't fought over slavery. The Civil War was fought over unifying and making a strong, centralized state." To Progressives like Bill Maher, this was an alien idea.

"What about global warming? Are you on the page that there is such a thing as global warming?" Maher asked.

"Yeah, I think it's been around for a long time, and it's probably going to be here for a while longer," began Paul, referring to rises in temperature that began largely before automobiles came into use. "I don't think everybody knows everything about global warming, because you have reputable scientists on both sides of that argument…"

Stunning his audience, Maher cut in and yelled, "No you don't!"

Unperturbed, Paul changed tactics and explained his view that oil companies are essentially subsidized by the government via wars in the Middle East to protect their oil properties. The response garnered an enthusiastic round of applause. The obviously bothered host prodded back, "But still against the Civil War."

On May 15, 2007, Paul was in Columbia, South Carolina for the Fox News debate at the Koger Center for the Arts. The concert hall was packed to capacity with over 2000 people, with many more outside. At this early debate, the questions gave Paul a launching point to explain his positions. When asked which departments Paul would eliminate from the federal government, he answered that he would start with the Department of Education, Department of Energy, and Department of Homeland Security. He also pointed out that President George W. Bush ran on a platform of non-intervention eight years earlier, and in the interim had reversed that policy.

A tense moment occurred when a Fox News moderator asked Paul if he was suggesting the United States invited the attacks on 9/11. Paul answered that the terrorists attacked because the United States bombed Iraq for the previous 10 years and set up military bases on Middle Eastern soil. He added, "If China was doing the same thing to us, how would we feel?"

An infuriated Rudy Giuliani jumped in and called it "an extraordinary statement" and "absurd", receiving riotous and sustained applause from the audience. Giuliani then asked Paul to withdraw his statement.

It was the most electric moment of the debate, with the audience attention fixed on the two candidates. Paul later described it as a "lonely moment."[4] Carefully, he explained the CIA findings and gave a succinct description of the concept of "blowback." "If we think we can do what we want around the world and not incite hatred, then we have a problem. They don't come here to attack us because we are rich and free, they attack us because we are over there."

The exchange cemented Paul's reputation as the maverick in the race, stealing the mantle from John McCain. That week, Maher seemed to find Paul more interesting. "I watched the Republican debate, and I saw this guy Ron Paul. He's my new hero," said Maher.[5]

Although Paul had gained some attention in the debate, many members of the media seemed unaware of his platform. When New York Times columnist Paul Krugman wrote about the May 15th debate, he stated that John McCain was the only candidate opposed to torture.[6]

The Ron Paul campaign created some buzz by arranging a press event on May 24th, 2007. It was staged at the Washington Press Club, a popular venue for such events. During his time with the press, Ron Paul brazenly presented Rudy Giuliani (who was in absentia) with a reading list of books, including the 9/11 Commission Report.[7] This event was intended as showmanship, but it did gain Ron coverage on major media outlets such as CNN. On the popular video website YouTube, the video received over 100,000 views within hours.

On May 25th, 2007, Bill Maher invited Paul to his show for a second appearance, where Paul received sustained cheers and applause from the mostly liberal audience. Maher opened the interview saying, "We had you on in late March, and I think we just scratched the surface. And that's really my fault. I should have scratched it more. But after I saw you in the debate, I said, 'You know what? This is a person who I really want to talk to a lot more.' And there's so many things I want to ask you."

The second appearance allowed Paul to introduce his views on foreign policy. "I have been very supportive of what I call a non-interventionist foreign policy," he told Maher. "Mind our own business and stay out of the internal affairs of other nations." Once again, Paul's ideas received riotous applause from the audience. It was an indication that Americans of all political stripes might be ready for libertarian ideas.

One week later, Paul was in New York for an appearance on the Daily Show with John Stewart, a politically themed show on the cable TV network Comedy Central. Before the show, Paul was met by hundreds of supporters waving placards on the sidewalk.

Stewart was respectful of Paul. When asked how he would spread the ideas of liberty, Paul replied, "I think it's a good message, but I don't believe in spreading it with guns. We should spread it by setting a good example and get others to emulate us, but not to try to force it on other people."

Paul's statements were warmly received. Stuart remarked, "You seem to practice what you preach and you seem to preach it consistently. Even though people might disagree with the message, they can't argue that you're a man of consistent principles."

Stewart closed the interview saying, "You continue to bring excitement to the process, because I think that's what's lacking sometimes. It's nice to see guys just throwing their ideas out there for whatever it is and being principled." Despite the genial nature of the interview, segments throughout the rest of the year continued to cover only the accepted top tier candidates, with no further mention of Paul.

Nine days later, on June 13th, 2007, Paul was back in New York for an appearance on the Colbert Report, another Comedy Central show. Stephen Colbert was a character who hosts the Colbert Report, poking fun at Republican news commentators by imitating them. Stephen Colbert the character was played by an actor of the same name; the true Stephen Colbert is a registered Democrat.[8] Ron Paul, who had never watched the show before, indulged the audience in the joke by engaging the Colbert character. Colbert had this to say about Paul: "I usually like to come to my guests with a head full of steam either on their side or against them. I'm not sure how to feel about you, but I'm passionately ambivalent. ... You voted against the Patriot Act. You voted against the Iraq war. But you also hate taxes and you hate gun control. You are an enigma wrapped in a riddle nestled in a sesame seed bun of mystery."

The appearances on these three popular comedy-themed shows did much to attract a young, national audience to Ron Paul's campaign. And those who could not immediately watch his appearances had a chance to watch them on YouTube. The Paul campaign was gaining momentum.

Much of the mainstream focus on Paul was the result of the televised Republican debates. Paul participated in four major debates in the 3rd quarter of 2007 and five in the 4th quarter. Most were hosted by major networks such as MSNBC, CNN, and Fox News.

However, when it came time for the Republican Jewish Coalition candidate's forum on October 16, 2007, Paul was not invited to attend. According to the Jewish Telegraph Agency, Paul was excluded due to his "record of consistently voting against assistance to Israel and his criticisms of the pro-Israel lobby."[9] Rudy Giuliani, Mitt Romney, Fred Thompson, John McCain, Sam Brownback, and Mike Huckabee were all invited, though Huckabee declined the invitation.

The PBS debate focusing on African-American issues on June 28th, 2007, hosted by commentator Tavis Smiley, was almost the exact opposite of the Republican Jewish Coalition debate. All of the major Republican candidates were invited, but only Ron Paul and Mike Huckabee accepted.

It seemed like the "Ron Paul Revolution," as supporters called it, would warrant a good deal of media attention. He had energized the New Left, the Old Right, and the Disaffected Middle. Unfortunately, the media did not see a story in Ron Paul worthy of consistent coverage.

Reason Magazine editor David Weigel summarized the media's view of Paul: "The press has storylines," he says. "The storyline for McCain is that he's a maverick who speaks the truth. The storyline for Obama is that he is God's only son sent to sacrifice himself for us, and the storyline for Hillary Clinton is that she is this terrible Glen Close in Fatal Attraction shrew. The storyline for Ron Paul is what a nice old, old man. He's raising lots of money but he won't matter though. So the questions were never very respectful."[10]

Paul fielded a follow-up question to his earlier exchange with Rudy Giuliani during the September 5, 2007 Fox News debate in Durham, North Carolina when moderator Chris Wallace presented him with a partisan question. "So, Congressman Paul," Wallace said, "you're basically saying that we should take our marching orders from al-Qaeda? If they want us off the Arabian Peninsula, we should leave?"

Paul rumbled back, "No! I'm saying we should take our marching orders from the Constitution! We should not go to war without a declaration. We should not go to war when it's an aggressive war. This is an aggressive invasion. We've committed the invasion and it's illegal under international law. That's where I take my marching orders, not from any enemy."

Overall, Ron Paul was happy with his treatment in the debates, though he would have liked to receive more time. In an official campaign video, he admitted, "I think we've had a decent shake. They could have excluded us from the debates. But we never got an even amount of time." Paul's observation that he received less time than other candidates was not inaccurate. In a later MSNBC debate, Romney was allotted 22 minutes compared to Ron Paul's six.[11]

On September 10, 2007, Ron Paul made an appearance on The O'Reilly Factor, a political commentary show on Fox News hosted by Bill O'Reilly. The two sparred throughout the interview, making for a lively debate. Both Bill O'Reilly and Ron Paul appeared flustered at times, with O'Reilly interrupting Paul at least twice.

After the appearance, O'Reilly received hundreds letters from Paul supporters complaining about the interruptions. O'Reilly responded by saying that if he feels the interviewee is dodging his questions, he cuts them off. "He started to give a history lesson we didn't have time for," said the commentator. "I have a six minute window. If Ron Paul wants to give me a 20 minute history lesson on the Middle East, I can't let him."

During the October 9th, 2007 CNBC/Wall Street Journal debate in Dearborn, Michigan, opponent Mitt Romney answered moderator Chris Mathews' question on whether Congressional authorization is needed for an attack on Iran. Romney said, "You sit down with your attorneys and [they] tell you what you have to do." This generated another classic Paul rebuttal. "This idea of going and talking to attorneys totally baffles me. Why don't we just open up the Constitution and read it? You're not allowed to go to war without a declaration of war."

By October 25th, 2007, Ron Paul was enduring several attacks from the media. The Lone Star Times, a minor Republican-leaning newspaper from Texas, created a grim story about Ron Paul linking him with racism. They reported that a Florida resident named Don Black, the owner of a white supremacist website, had contributed $500 towards the campaign. The story was soon picked up by major media outlets, including MSNBC, CNN, PBS and Fox News.

Several watch-dog groups, such as the Anti-Defamation League, began applying pressure on Paul to return the donation. Surprisingly, Paul did not cave to their demands. Campaign spokesman Jesse Benton explained, "If people who hold views that the candidate doesn't agree with... give to us, that's their loss."[12]

In a December 19th, 2007 interview with Neil Cavuto on Fox News, Ron was again questioned about his decision. "I don't endorse what [Don Black] endorses... I see no purpose in screening everyone who sends me money. It's impossible to do and it's a ridiculous idea that I should screen these people."

In same month, the New York Times blog took the attack one step further by alleging that Ron Paul regularly meets "with members of the Stormfront set, American Renaissance, the Institute for Historic Review and others."[13] None of these accusations were true, and the paper later posted a retraction, admitting their "unverified assertions" should never have been made.

Ron Paul found himself seated in The Tonight Show with Jay Leno greenroom on October 30th, 2007, anxiously awaiting an appearance in front of mainstream America. It was the largest national coverage he would receive. Things looked good for Paul as he sat watching the show backstage. Every time Jay Leno mentioned Ron Paul's name the audience went wild.

After a warm introduction, Paul told Leno, "It's not me, it's the message." Of course, this was untrue. Paul had a homey charisma that Americans identified with.

Leno, however, assumed a vague air of doubt about the whole Ron Paul phenomenon, despite Paul's clever comment that there was "probably a risk" that he could win the presidency.

The show continued when Leno introduced the evening's musical act, the anarchist punk rock band The Sex Pistols, prefacing his introduction by telling Paul, "We have a band that is just right for you."

The Sex Pistols performed their signature song, Anarchy in the UK, whose lyrics begin, "I am the anti-Christ..." Lead singer Johnny Rotten yelled to Paul during the song, "Hello Mr. Paul" and later "When are you getting out of Iraq, Mr. Paul?" and "Mr. Paul! Anarchy! Mr. Paul!" Had Leno been more familiar with Ron Paul's religious and socially conservative nature, he may have avoided grouping the two together. But Ron was used to being misunderstood.

Afterward, Paul was happy to greet the band and shake hands, even though most politicians would have shuddered at the thought of any association with the Sex Pistols for fear of scaring away half of Middle America.

After November 5, 2007, the day Paul raised over $4.2 million largely in online donations, he began to receive even more press coverage. The fundraising milestone created buzz for the campaign among the media and energized his supporters. Most of the commentators seemed curious how Paul did it, but as he was quick to point out, he didn't do it – it was the message of freedom that was generating so much support.

Perhaps looking for a way to spin a positive story into something negative, some members of the media attempted to link Ron Paul's record day to terrorism because the money was raised on Guy Fawkes Day, a day commemorating Fawkes attempt to blow up the British parliament buildings. Furthermore, they didn't like the concept of the "money bomb," a term Paul's supporters had coined to describe the day of mass donation, because it contained the word "bomb" in it. Neither of these images sat well in the post-9/11 climate.

On November 28, 2007, Paul was in St. Petersburg, Florida for the CNN/YouTube Debate. The format consisted of users submitting questions to the candidates via videos. Paul appeared to be well suited to the debate format, given his popularity on YouTube (Paul had thousands of subscribers to his YouTube channel at that time). However, rather than allowing users to vote on the questions that would be asked, CNN chose the questions.

The initial question attempted to link Paul to conspiracy theorists. A viewer from Texas asked, "I've met a lot of your supporters online, but I've noticed that a good number of them seem to buy into this conspiracy theory regarding the Council of Foreign Relations, and some plan to make a North American union by merging the United States with Canada and Mexico."

It was true, Ron Paul did have misgivings that North America was headed for an arrangement similar to the European Union that would result in a loss of sovereignty for the United States. However, his beliefs were far from conspiratorial.

Paul explained in his answer that while organizations such as the Council on Foreign Relations and the Trilateral Commission exist, the real issue is an ideological battle between those who would prefer larger, more centralized, perhaps even international government bodies, and those who instead value national sovereignty.

Although the question was a poor opening to the debate for Paul, the implied accusation was not completely unwarranted. Ron Paul's candidacy did attract a significant number of conspiracy theorists; Paul's distrust of government made him their logical choice. That was enough to win him the support of such groups as the "9/11 Truth Movement," for better or for worse.

The 9/11 Truth Movement believed, among other things, that the US government deliberately planned the World Trade Center disaster. Paul clearly disagreed with this position, having stated that it was government ineptness and poor foreign policy that brought on the attacks. However, even with this disagreement, Paul viewed these "Truthers," as they called themselves, as Americans who are just as important as any other Americans.

At the same YouTube debate, Paul sparred with John McCain, with McCain maintaining that, in the Vietnam conflict, US soldiers wanted the government to "let them win." Paul hit back, asking McCain, "Why do I get the most money from active duty officers and military personnel?"

McCain called Paul an isolationist, but Paul asserted that McCain did not understand the difference between non-interventionism and isolationism. "I want to trade with people, talk with people, travel, but I don't want to send troops overseas using force to tell them how to live."

Ron Paul supporters continued to evolve their strategies throughout the remainder of 2007 in an impressive show of creativity. As big as the November 5th event was, it was merely a prelude to what the community had planned for December 16th – the 234th anniversary of the Boston Tea Party. Organized by Trevor Lyman entirely over the Internet, the "Boston Tea Party" was not only a fundraiser, but a day of celebratory events held across the nation.

A total of 58,407 donors combined to give a total of $6.04 million, setting the record for the biggest one day political donation at the time.[14] These two fundraisers – organized independently, online – led the campaign to raise nearly $20 million for the quarter, exceeding the original $12 million goal by over 60%.

The tremendous fundraising day resulted in a December 23rd, 2007 appearance on the MSNBC program <u>Meet the Press</u>. Host Tim Russert had previously worked for the respective senatorial and gubernatorial campaigns of Democrats Daniel Patrick Moynihan and Mario Cuomo. Russert was known for asking tough questions. Just two weeks earlier, he had conducted a particularly hard interview with former New York mayor Rudy Giuliani.

Now it was Ron Paul's turn. Despite suffering from a cold at the time, Paul performed well early on and was able to convey his major positions on taxation and foreign policy, addressing Russert's doubts on pulling troops out of Korea and the Middle East.

One of Russert's main concerns was over Israel, and he asked, "So if Iran invaded Israel, what do we do?"

Paul replied, "Well, they're not going to. That is like saying 'Iran is about to invade Mars.' I mean, they have nothing. They don't have an army or navy or air force. And the Israelis have 300 nuclear weapons. Nobody would touch them."

Russert followed up by asking, "Would you cut off all foreign aid to Israel?"

Paul replied, "Absolutely. But remember, the Arabs would get cut off, too, and the Arabs get three times as much aid altogether than Israel."

Later in the interview, regarding the reasons terrorists attacked the United States, Russert asked, "It sounds like you think that the problem is the United States, not al-Qaeda."

Paul replied, "No, it's both. … It's sort of like if you step in a snake pit and you get bit, who caused the trouble? Because you stepped in the snake pit or because snakes bite you?"

Russert then pointed out that Paul's district received almost $4 billion in Federal Payments, among the highest in Texas. Of this amount, Paul himself added $400 million in congressional *earmarks* – amendments to bills that direct funds for specific projects within a district. Ron Paul requested funds for several projects in Brazoria, a coastal district, for such things as removing a sunken ship from Freeport Harbor and money for improving the Gulf Intracoastal Waterway. Considering Paul's objection to pork barrel spending, it seemed hypocritical.

Paul explained that he has never voted for earmarks, although he was forced to admit he added earmarks for his district. According to Paul, he saw it as representing people who wanted some of their money back from the Federal Government, almost like a tax credit. "I vote against it, so I don't endorse the system," he said. The explanation did not sit well with Russert.

Russert also brought up the Civil War. When questioned on whether Abraham Lincoln could have avoided it, Paul replied, "Absolutely. Six hundred thousand Americans died in a senseless civil war. No, he shouldn't have gone to war." Russert then made the claim that in 2008, without the Civil War "we'd still have slavery," sparking Paul to reply, "Oh, come on, Tim. ... Every other major country in the world got rid of slavery without a civil war."

Though Paul was applying his traditional anti-war stance to the American Civil War, explaining that there would have been more constructive ways to abolish slavery without the expenditure of lives and resources made during the Civil War, his comments were taken out of context. The *Meet The Press* appearance provided fodder for other journalists who were unsympathetic to the Paul campaign.

Days later, Paul appeared on *Morning Joe* on MSNBC (the eponymous Joe Scarborough was absent). Paul was introduced: "Now joining us by phone, Republican Presidential Candidate Ron Paul, who made some remarkable comments about Abraham Lincoln on Meet the Press this past Sunday."

The host immediately put Paul in the hot-seat. "Some of your supporters were expressing some frustration that you would suggest that Abraham Lincoln started the Civil War, and also that Abraham Lincoln went to war just to enhance and get rid of the original intent of the Republic. Would you like to publicly take this opportunity to take back those remarks?"

Paul took a breath and replied, "Well I wouldn't mind discussing them." The next seven minutes were spent in a heated debate, with Paul on the defensive.

Paul ended the debate, saying, "The total irony of this is this distraction in a campaign that I'm running for - this esoteric point which came up on purpose. I did not even bring it up in the first place, but of course I'm going to respond. This idea of avoiding the catastrophic war that is going on right now because you want to re-fight a war 150 years ago that neither of us can change or deal with, this is misdirection."

....

But despite some conflicts with media personalities, in late 2007, Paul had a growing group of enthusiastic supporters who were excited to promote his candidacy. Trevor Lyman, the man behind the money bombs, had a creative idea that would serve this purpose. He wanted to fly a Ron Paul blimp over election states. It was certainly not a focused attempt to target Republican Party members, but it would be hard to miss and would likely to awaken others to Paul's message. It was big, it was bold, and, he thought, it would likely create some buzz.

However, the media did not respond in kind. There was very little coverage of the blimp.

Paul's mixed treatment by the media in 2007 was offset by a new milestone for his family. In 2007 his oldest grandson Matt Pyeatt and wife Kym had their first child, Collin. Carol and Ron were ecstatic about their new roles as great-grandparents.

CHAPTER 26

THE PRIMARIES

2008

The Environment

Nobody believes a weather prediction twelve hours ahead. Now we're asked to believe a prediction that goes out 100 years into the future? And make financial investments based on that prediction? Has everybody lost their minds?

MICHAEL CRICHTON

January of 2008 heralded the start of a new year and a new primary season. Ron Paul had been hard at work campaigning for the past year. Despite his overwhelming Internet popularity, however, polls of registered Republicans showed that he was only enjoying 5 to 10% of the support from likely voters.[1]

The Ron Paul campaign tended not to focus much on polling. Early on, the campaign's budget dictated that it had to make maximal use of its resources; polling was not a top priority. Internet buzz suggested that polling Republicans might not be the best strategy for the Paul campaign anyway, given that Paul attracted voters from many different political stripes, and not just registered Republicans. Additionally, messages that resonated with Ron Paul's growing group of supporters didn't always appeal to tried and true Republican Party voters.

The campaign began 2007 with six paid staff members, and only later expanded when a surge of donations came in late 2007. The campaign could not hire someone like Frank Luntz, a Republican pollster who had helped

George W. Bush's campaigns in 2000 and 2004, to carefully test sound bites and speeches on voters. Indeed, pandering to the "party base" was not on Ron Paul's agenda. As he had previously demonstrated in the Republican debates, he was willing to state his true beliefs no matter who was listening. Instead of pandering, Paul's message to the Republican Party was, as he famously said at the Republican debate in South Carolina, that it had "lost its way"[2] - a message that did little to win over those who strictly towed the Republican party line.

At the dawn of 2008, John McCain was roughly tied in national polls with Mike Huckabee.[3] Mitt Romney enjoyed a small lead over them both, and seemed the likely front runner. The press, however, didn't seem to care much for Romney, which would be difficult for him to overcome.

The January 3rd, 2008 Iowa Caucuses marked the start of the delegate selection process. Just months earlier, Romney had won an unofficial straw poll in Iowa with 32%, with Huckabee in second place at 18%.[4] Ron Paul and John McCain had been tied neck and neck with 7% each. But on this night, Mike Huckabee took the lead. Many credited his surprise win to an appearance on the Tonight Show with Jay Leno the previous evening, in which he played guitar with the Tonight Show Band.[5] Huckabee walked away with seventeen delegates to Romney's twelve. McCain received three delegates, and Paul two.

Ron Paul received 10% of the popular vote compared to McCain's 13%. The fourth place finish for Paul was not a spectacular start, but it was not devastating either, since most people looked to New Hampshire as a better indicator of how the country would vote.

On January 4th, 2008, Ron Paul had a positive interview with Bill Moyers on PBS. Fox News, however, was much less friendly. The station had earlier announced they were excluding Ron from attending their New Hampshire forum with the other candidates, despite his virtual tie with McCain and Huckabee in recent polls. Fox maintained that Paul was excluded because their portable studio wasn't big enough to hold six candidates.[6]

The Paul campaign website issued the following statement: "Given Ron Paul's support in New Hampshire and his recent historic fundraising success, it is outrageous that Paul would be excluded. Paul has consistently polled higher in New Hampshire than some of the other candidates who have been invited." The statement was referencing the lower poll numbers of Rudy Giuliani and Fred Thompson, both of whom had been invited to the Fox debate.

The New Hampshire Republican Party sided with Paul, officially withdrawing support of the Fox event. While he was disappointed with the exclusion, Paul acknowledged that, as a private business, Fox News was under no obligation to include him. "I realize they have property rights and I'm not going to crash the party," he later said.[7]

To combat this omission, the Paul campaign hurriedly organized a forum on the same night as the Fox News debate. During the unscripted question period, Paul faced an email question about global warming. The writer asked, "What would you do to help reduce global warming?"

Ron Paul viewed global warming with some skepticism. "I think there's plenty of debate about global warming, and there's debate on both sides of this," he stated,[8] setting out in a politically incorrect direction. He also suggested a link between climate change and global governance, arguing that an issue like global warming is a good excuse for international governmental agencies like the United Nations to seize more power.

Paul's skepticism about global warming made him hesitant to become alarmed that it would have catastrophic effects, as some of his political colleagues had done. He was unconvinced that humans were the cause of global climate change, and similarly dubious about the notion that humans could actively stop global warming from occurring. Furthermore, he recognized the possibility that if the earth warmed, as it had during some historical periods, it may not be the disaster that some made it out to be.[9]

Although there has been a significantly increased frequency and stridency of calls for governments to "do something" about the threat of man-made global warming, it's notable that the decade after 1998 experienced a slight cooling of average worldwide temperatures.[10] Paul was a lone voice among his fellow candidates. "I think some of it is related to human activities, but I don't think there's a conclusion yet," he said. "If you study the history, we've had a lot of climate changes. We've had hot spells and cold spells. They come and go. If there are weather changes, we're not going to be very good at regulating the weather."[11]

Those concerned with climate change maintain that global temperatures can hit a tipping point, after which the earth can not recover from increasing temperatures.[12] This tends to create a sense of urgency that something must be done before it becomes too late. However, global warming skeptics argue that the earth's temperature has been far hotter in the past and has reverted back to the comparatively cooler temperatures of the 21st century. For example, diversity of life thrived in the Jurassic period when temperatures were about ten degrees Celsius warmer than today;[13] and mass extinctions only occurred after the temperatures decreased.

Paul had opened his answer to that viewer question in New Hampshire by saying, "As a President, I wouldn't be president of the world".

Paul disagreed with the sentiment he heard from his colleagues in Washington, DC that "we have to close down everything in this country and in the world because there's a fear that we're going to have this global warming and that we're going to be swallowed up by the oceans."[14] This presumption was embodied in the 1997 Kyoto Protocol, which then-Vice President Al Gore signed but the United States Senate never ratified.

Former European Environment Commissioner Margot Wallstrom provided evidence that the motivations behind the Kyoto protocol, at least for some, were about more than just the issue of climate change. She said that Kyoto "isn't about whether scientists agree" on the issue, but "about leveling the playing field for big businesses worldwide."[15] It seemed to Ron as though Europe's leaders saw global warming as an excuse to impose equality on the developed world - not by freeing up their own economies, but by hampering that of the United States with extra regulations.

Paul's skeptical view on climate change was not meant to ignore the possibility that it could and should be addressed on an international level. Paul noted, "I think negotiation and talk and persuasion are worthwhile, but [not] treaties that have law enforcement agencies that force certain countries to do things."[16]

When it came to action on environmental issues, Paul made clear during the campaign that he would pursue proven approaches to environmental protection.

Domestically, Paul objected to energy subsidies, including those given to oil companies. In his view, they did more to distort the markets than help consumers. In his New Hampshire reply, Ron said, "We spend hundreds of billions of dollars protecting oil which compounds our problem." With this position, he found agreement from those on the political left – but not necessarily on the principle of opposing government subsidies in general, just on that of opposing subsidies to oil companies.

Ron opposed subsidies of any kind because he saw them as taxes forcibly taken from Americans and handed to politically favored companies. If there were really a demand for any product or service, he believed, the market would naturally offer incentives to businesses that produced them in the form of profits. Government subsidies were not necessary, and furthermore, the centrally planned distribution of subsidies often ended up encouraging companies to produce certain products that might not have truly been the best options (that is, the options that the customers wanted most).

After all, government can never know what products are best, because it does not receive that information via the market in the form of prices and demand. Its decisions about which products are best are political, not based on what sells and what does not. In a free market, if a company produces a bad product, it will not sell. The product will be discontinued, or the company will fail. But government subsidies, believed Ron, can send a false signal to companies that bad products are actually good – and as a result, they can stifle innovation and leave consumers with fewer options.

For example, government ethanol subsidies had recently been granted to several producers under the assumption that they would encourage production of ethanol as a cleaner and more sustainable alternative to gasoline. However, consumers quickly realized that ethanol was not the miracle fuel it was purported to be. Ethanol was relatively expensive for the energy it provided, even with the government subsidies. It was corrosive to car engines. Furthermore, since ethanol was largely produced from corn, the government-encouraged diversion of more corn away from animal feed and other corn-based products drove up the price of everything from meat to ice cream cones.[17]

Paul's anti-subsidy philosophy also applied to other "alternative" energy sources, like wind and solar power, which he believed would flourish in a free market without government support if they were truly sustainable and cost-effective. As history has amply demonstrated, mandates to force consumers to adopt new technology do not work. People in search of profits will deliver new sources of energy in a free marketplace; while government interventions simply chase investment in new technologies and innovation away.

....

Ron Paul had done a respectable job of presenting himself to voters in New Hampshire with his televised town meeting. However, the Fox News debate, which included all the other candidates, attracted more viewers. To viewers unaware of the controversy, it appeared as though Paul was not one of the true contenders.

News of the Fox snub spread to Tonight Show host Jay Leno, who had enjoyed Ron Paul's visit months earlier. He phoned Ron Paul on the evening of January 6th to invite him on the show the night before the New Hampshire primaries.[18]

Before introducing Paul, Leno said, "Let me tell you why Ron Paul is here. They had this Republican debate in New Hampshire and they did not let Ron Paul in the debate. He's tied with Giuliani and he's raised more money than the other candidates recently, so there's got to be a reason why Fox did not allow him in the debate."

During the interview, an animated Leno commented on the lack of coverage about the controversy. "I saw you interviewed by Wolf Blitzer on CNN and it wasn't mentioned. I didn't see it on MSNBC or any of the other cable channels. It seems like a big story!"

Although Paul's Tonight Show appearance ultimately would not have the same effect as it had with Huckabee, who faced no exclusion from Fox, it gave Paul a chance to air his views on freedom to an audience of millions.

On January 8th, 2008, the day of the all-important New Hampshire primaries, things got even worse for Paul when *The New Republic* magazine decided to reopen his 1996 newsletter controversy with a story titled, "Angry White Man" by self-described liberal journalist James Kirchick. Former staffer Eric Dondero was responsible for encouraging Kirchick to write the piece.[19]

The article featured a doctored photograph of Paul in a confederate uniform, complete with bars and stars tie. In the article, Kirchick cherry-picked the worst examples from thirty years of Ron Paul newsletters – ultimately only finding objectionable content in the years between 1989 and 1994, after the replacement of Ron Paul & Associates manager Nadia Hayes.

The scathing article ran with the newsletters' most politically incorrect statements. Kirchick took issue with comments such as, "blacks poured into the streets of Chicago in celebration. How to celebrate? How else? They broke the windows of stores to loot."[20] Most of the racially sensitive comments appeared in the early 1990s, around the time of the Los Angeles riots and the O.J. Simpson case.

The article castigated comments about Martin Luther King, such as describing King as "a comsymp [Communist sympathizer], if not an actual party member, and the man who replaced the evil of forced segregation with the evil of forced integration."

Kirchick, a contributor to *The Jerusalem Post*, was not enthusiastic about Ron Paul's proposal to end foreign aid, especially in regards to Israel. He objected to the newsletter labeling Israel as "an aggressive, national socialist state."[21]

The article criticized the tone of discussions about social issues of the day, preferring a more delicate treatment. He didn't like what he read about AIDS, race relations, welfare, or even banking criticisms. In one passage, the author took exception to the news letter "promoting his distrust of a federally regulated monetary system utilizing paper bills."[22] The article also took aim at Paul for appearing on the conspiracy-themed Alex Jones radio show and for writing an article for the John Birch Society newsletter, even though Paul himself was not a purveyor of the conspiracy theories espoused by Jones and JBS.

Paul maintained he did not write the statements in question, but took responsibility for them since they appeared in his newsletters. New York Times writer Christopher Caldwell accepted this explanation, "since the style diverges widely from his own."[23] Days later, speaking with Wolf Blitzer on CNN, Paul mused about why the attacks were coming then. "As a Republican candidate I'm getting the most support from black voters and now that has to be undermined," he said. "I defend the principle of libertarianism where ... every individual is defended and protected because they're important as an individual, not because of the color of their skin, but because of their character."

On January 8th, 2008, the day of the New Hampshire Primary, the one-two punches from Fox News and *The New Republic* made their mark. Paul finished with 7.8% of the vote and no delegates; a near tie with one-time front runner Rudy Giuliani. His momentum had ended; his numbers hadn't budged from New Hampshire polling numbers in late 2007.[24] McCain came out on top with seven delegates, Romney with four, and Huckabee with one.

On January 10th, however, it appeared that the tides were turning. Fox News held a debate at the Myrtle Beach Convention Center in South Carolina. Paul participated in the debate but declined to be interviewed by Hannity and Colmes afterwards. In the post-debate text poll the next day, Paul won with 32%, followed by Fred Thompson with 22%. Sean Hannity, who had been chased by a mob of Ron Paul supporters and pelted with snowballs the previous night, was understandably not won over by the poll results.[25]

After the primary polls closed, though, Paul came in fifth place in South Carolina with barely 4% of the vote, but ahead of sixth pace finisher Rudy Giuliani. The big winner of the night was John McCain, who won an upset victory over Mike Huckabee. Paul's results would improve over the next few weeks.

On January 15th, Ron Paul placed fourth in Michigan with over 6% of the vote. Mitt Romney decisively won the state where his father was once a popular governor.

Paul had higher hopes for Nevada, a state where many people embraced libertarian beliefs, but it was expected that Mitt Romney would carry the state because of the large Mormon population. Paul finished a surprising second with almost 14% of the vote, behind Mitt Romney. Very little news coverage was given to Paul's second place finish. The same day, Fred Thompson pulled out of the race, recognizing that he would have needed to win South Carolina to continue. At that point, there were five candidates left.

In Louisiana, Paul had a second place finish, behind John McCain. The Louisiana caucuses are notoriously complicated. The deadline for registration was January 10th, at which time Ron Paul appeared to be the clear front runner in Louisiana. However, the state's Republican Party decided to extend the deadline to January 12th.[26] Paul later commented, "We didn't get all our votes counted in Louisiana, and we believe we won that election clean."[27] The Paul campaign decided to contest the results, but by February it was clear that McCain would be declared the official winner.

Many saw Florida as a critical state, owing to its large population and its decisive role in previous elections. Competition was fierce; Rudy Giuliani put most of his campaign funds into advertising in the Sunshine State. The night before the Florida primaries on January 24, MSNBC held a debate at Florida Atlantic University in Boca Raton. Compared to his performances in other debates, Paul did not fare quite as well in the MSNBC debate. When given the opportunity to present Senator McCain with a question, he asked about the President's Working Group on Financial Markets – a topic with which few voters are familiar.[28]

The next day, a text message poll by the New York Times gave the debate to Romney with 41% and Paul with 40%. Despite these results, McCain edged out Romney at the polls in Florida with 36% compared to Romney's 31%. Because of the winner-take-all policy in that state, McCain won all fifty-seven delegates for himself. Giuliani, who was once considered a Republican front runner, withdrew from the race after a humiliating third place finish.

It was now an open slate until February 5th, a date known as "Super Tuesday." The trend among state Republican and Democratic Committees had been to shift their primaries to earlier and earlier dates, ostensibly to mitigate the hugely important impact of the first few caucuses and primaries – for example, Iowa and New Hampshire – in determining the party nominees. State parties determining dates for their primaries in late 2007, while New Hampshire's state law that mandates its primary be the first in the nation pushed the date of the New Hampshire primary back to January 8th, 2008. As a result of this trend, state primaries and caucuses in 2008 were happening earlier than ever before. Two dozen states would hold their primaries on Super Tuesday; pundits believed it was possible that the results of this day would conclusively determine the nominees for both parties.

Among the Super Tuesday states, California and New York were seen as critical states due to their respective sizes, and the large number of delegates they would carry in the general election.

The January 30th, 2008 CNN debate in Los Angeles, held at the Reagan Library, proved an interesting prelude to Super Tuesday for several reasons. It was down to four contenders seated close together: John McCain, Mitt Romney, Mike Huckabee and Ron Paul. The random seating arrangement had placed Paul in the center with John McCain. Questions came in a round-robin format, with each candidate having equal time to answer each question. The unique venue of the Reagan library, with host Nancy Reagan, included California Governor Arnold Schwarzenegger in the audience.

Janet Hook of the L.A. Times asked the first question: "Governor Schwarzenegger has proposed that California be allowed to implement much tougher environmental regulations on emission requirements than apply to the rest of the country. This is an initiative that conservatives generally oppose, and the Bush administration rejected California's request. Do you side with the governor or with the Bush administration?"

McCain received generous laughter when, in light of the former bodybuilder's presence, he replied, "Well, there's some physical danger." McCain, like the other candidates, stressed states' rights, a concept Paul agreed with.

However, Paul went even further, broaching the issue of personal property rights. "Yes, I think California should do what they want, and we all recognize that," he began. "But one thing that hasn't been emphasized here that should be emphasized when we're dealing with the environment and greenhouse gases is property rights." In Ron Paul's view, no one should be able to pollute property they do not own, including rivers and air. The problem, as he saw it, was an imperfect definition of property rights.

Citing his firsthand experience as a young man living in then-filthy Pittsburgh, Pennsylvania, Paul noted the improvements that the private sector achieved. Pittsburgh's industrial environment was heavily polluted during the "progressive" era. For nearly a century, examples of abuses in the name of the so-called greater good abounded, such as when Cleveland's Cuyahoga River was declared "for industrial use" by the state government, allowing companies to dispose of waste products in the river with no legal consequences.[29]

The truth, according to Paul, is that "governments don't have a good reputation for doing a good job protecting the environment. If you look at the extreme of socialism or communism, they were very poor environmentalists."[30]

Paul explained his position on environmental issues during a 2007 interview with Salon, touting legal remedies based on property rights:

> Imagine that everyone living in one suburb, rather than using regular trash service, were taking their household trash to the next town over and simply tossing it in the yards of those living in the nearby town. Is there any question that legal mechanisms are in place to remedy this action? ...For a good number of years, legislatures and courts have failed to enforce the property rights of those being dumped on with respect to certain forms of pollution. This form of government failure has persisted since the industrial revolution when, in the name of so-called progress, certain forms of pollution were legally tolerated or ignored to benefit some popular regional employer or politically popular entity.

> When all forms of physical trespass, be that smoke, particulate matter, etc., are legally recognized for what they are -- a physical trespass upon the property and rights of another -- concerns about difficulty in suing the offending party will be largely diminished. When any such cases are known to be slam-dunk wins for the person whose property is being polluted, those doing the polluting will no longer persist in doing so. Against a backdrop of property rights actually enforced, contingency and class-action cases are additional legal mechanisms that resolve this concern.[31]

Economists have noted that wealthier societies protect their land better than poorer, socialist societies such as pre-2000 China, India and Russia, which suffered high pollution levels in everything from rivers to soil.[32] Government or communal ownership of land makes individuals who use that land less accountable for it than are private property owners who use land that they themselves own. For example, compare and contrast buffalo and cattle in the 19th century United States. Western settlers hunted wild bison, which roamed freely and were not owned by anyone, to near extinction, while cattle were raised on private ranches, bred and cared for, and there was never a shortage of cows or beef.

Likewise, privately owned property is treated far better than communally or state owned land.[33] For example, the owners of private forests have an incentive to carefully monitor for fires and plant new trees each year so that they will have enough material to continue producing lumber or paper products. Government-owned forests, on the other hand, are more susceptible to fires and deforestation, because they are not owned by someone whose livelihood depends on the health of the forest. Environmental lobbyists can push for government protection of the forests, but they cannot protect the land directly, as could a private owner – they must go through the slow and often frustrating political process. Added to the equation are the opposing forces of those who would rather see the government-owned lands sold or used for logging. With publicly owned lands, two opposing interests can simultaneously push for opposite agendas – and the result is conflict and mismanagement of the land. According to Paul, the idea that property rights encourage better stewardship of the earth applies to the air as well as to natural resources. He told the audience at the CNN debate, "This idea that anyone has a right to pollute, with hydrocarbons or emissions, is wrong." Paul disagreed with solutions proposed by both the Republican and Democratic parties. "Instead of going back to a property rights solution, they go for more bureaucracy. With the EPA, everyone is guilty until proven innocent. They write laws without congressional approval and think they're going to solve this problem."

When asked if property rights could be easily applied to things like air and water, Paul said, "If you have a mill next door to me, you don't have a right to pollute my air -- that can be properly defined by property rights." Paul went on to explain that property rights could apply to bodies of water; a person could own part of a lake, or part of a river. "Even oceans can be defined by international agreements," he said.[34]

Paul's was a rare voice articulating serious economic thought; Alone among political leaders, he had written extensively on the matter from a classical liberal perspective, advancing free markets, deregulation and competition.

Wealth is harmed by interventionism, which seeks to centrally plan activities. Central planning represents the "fatal conceit" as Friedrich Hayek described it; the belief that politicians can come up with a plan that will direct an economy so that there will be no losers.

Ron Paul's answer to global warming was similar to Governor Schwarzenegger's plan for California. Schwarzenegger himself was sympathetic to Paul's ideas of limited government – he introduced a rebroadcast of the famous documentary Free to Choose by libertarian economist Milton Freedman in the 1990s.

Two days later, on February 1st, 2008, Ron Paul was in New York city for the MTV-MySpace forum. The MTV audience was important to Paul, because many of his enthusiastic supporters were young. The candidates present at the forum included Barack Obama, Mike Huckabee, Hillary Clinton, and Ron Paul.

Outside, there were throngs of Paul supporters, yet inside the venue, the producer-picked audience was different. It seemed like their questions were indirectly supportive of big government and domestic and foreign interventionism, and, contrary to most appearances, Paul received little applause after his responses.

Questions ranged from how the US should intervene in Darfur to how the government should subsidize birth control costs to how to ensure that Russia doesn't use oil as a "weapon against peace and prosperity". One young man wearing a Democrat lapel pin gave a well-prepared statement, laden with statistics, demonstrating that young people support Democrats more than Republicans – a statement likely meant to downplay Ron Paul's reputation of young supporters. Ron turned the question around on the man, acknowledging that most Republicans had a well-deserved decrease in youth support because of the policies they supported. Then he said, "You should come to one of my rallies and see the youth support there."

Paul added, "I can bring tens of thousands if not hundreds of thousands of young people who are interested. ... There is a strong resistance in the

Republican Party not to accept the young Ron Paul people who are willing to vote Republican."

In the MTV-MySpace forum, Ron gave detailed responses. By the end of the half-hour debate, he was visibly gaining traction. A high point came when he passionately stated, "I want to be president not because I want to run your life - I don't even know how to run your life. ... Likewise, I don't want to run the economy ... What I want to restore is freedom and a sound currency." In the end, the MTV host prompted the audience and they gave Paul a long and enthusiastic round of applause.

In a MySpace poll asking, "Which candidate best connects with youth voters?" Ron Paul finished first with over 50% of the vote, followed by Barack Obama with 31%. It was an indication that Ron Paul had won the support of young people, an unusual feat for a Republican candidate.

Super Tuesday was rapidly approaching, and the candidates had all been pushing hard to win. Back in early January 2008, the Paul campaign began running a series of televised ads in California, Alabama, Colorado, Georgia, North Dakota, Louisiana, Maine and Florida.[35] Some Paul supporters were unenthusiastic about the new ads.[36] The official campaign ads, they thought, seemed lackluster compared to the inspirational videos that users had been turning out on YouTube.

Just prior to Super Tuesday, a few smaller states held their contests. First were the Maine caucuses, which ended on February 3rd, 2008. Ron Paul finished solidly in third place, with 18% to McCain's 21%. Mitt Romney dominated the state with over 52% of the vote.

However, the focus of news media and political observers rested on Super Tuesday. After all the votes were cast and tallied, John McCain emerged as the clear winner. In California he received 42% support, compared to Ron Paul's 4.2%. In New York, 52% compared to 6.5%. One highlight of the day was Montana, where Paul finished with 25%; a close second to Mitt Romney.[37]

The next day, Ron Paul's $6.04 million one-day fundraising record was broken when the Obama campaign announced they raised $6.2 million following super-Tuesday.[38]

A few days later, Ron Paul released a statement to his supporters, acknowledging that there was no possibility of a brokered convention now that McCain had won. He also addressed the issue of running as a third party candidate, something many supporters desired. "I am committed to fighting for our ideas within the Republican Party, so there will be no third party run," he stated. "I am a Republican, and I will remain a Republican."

During his last run in 1988, Paul had dreamed of being included in major debates, a dream that was realized two decades later. Although Ron Paul did not garner as many votes as he had hoped for in the 2008 Republican primaries, he had gotten his ideas in front of millions of people with national TV appearances and a strong presence on the Internet. He had amassed a politically and socially diverse group of supporters of all ages and from all walks of life; all this, with virtually no help from the mainstream media.

However, the overwhelming defeat at the polls had deflated the Ron Paul movement. Many voters now had little interest in Ron Paul or his campaign. It seemed like his supporters had no choice but to move on to other candidates. The Ron Paul movement was demoralized and would go the way of other failed presidential contenders. To most people, it looked like the revolution was over.

CHAPTER 27

THE FUTURE
OF AMERICA

No army can stop an idea whose time has come.

VICTOR HUGO (TRANSLATED)

During the Wars of Scottish Independence, the English were slowly conquering Scotland by generously bribing the ruling Scottish noblemen. Most Scottish citizens did nothing and accepted their fate. However, one patriot decided to take on the vastly superior English army. His name was William Wallace. The nobleman achieved a minor victory by using his outnumbered troops to flank his opponent when they attempted to cross Stirling Bridge.

As his nation faced defeat, Wallace had managed to pull off an unconventional victory against a larger, well equipped enemy using radically new tactics. After this small victory, likeminded young men across Scotland began to gather together under his banner. One by one, they began destroying English fortresses until they had driven the English out of Scotland.

The corrupt nobles of yesterday have become the establishment politicians of 2008, willing to sell off America's freedom to anyone who will help reelect them and shower them with rewards. But someone has challenged them, and now likeminded young men and women are flocking under his banner. There are many entrenched fortresses to destroy – the IRS and the Federal Reserve will be the most difficult.

The Wars of Scottish Independence eventually led to freedom for Scotland and brought about the Scottish Enlightenment, which produced breakthroughs in science, technology, politics, education, and economics - things we collectively call prosperity - not just for Scotland, but the entire Western world. A new freedom movement promises to do the same.

....

On February 11, days after John McCain's victory, Ron Paul released a video on his website in which he asked his supporters to march on Washington. "At this point we have to do something major. ... We ought to make a grand display. We ought to have a march to show our true numbers." This was different for Paul, who normally did not ask anything specific of his supporters. Notably, he did not indicate a particular person or group to organize such an event nor any date. Instead, he would let the free market of ideas take over.

It was a bold request; one that could fail publicly. "This is risky," he acknowledged. "But a march on Washington ... could be very valuable. It would send a powerful message that the media could not ignore. At the same time, if nobody shows up, it might mean there weren't enough of us or we didn't have enough energy."

Within a few months, Ron's video amassed 800,000 views on YouTube and over 22,000 comments. Quickly a website came to prominence, RevolutionMarch.com, and organizers materialized. The date was set for July 12, 2008. Over 15,000 people pledged to attend the rally, although estimates of the actual march put the total number in the neighborhood of 10,000 attendees.[1] Paul's college-age supporters were the largest group who turned out, arriving from across the nation at their own cost. The large turnout was an impressive feat; especially considering the march received no national media coverage before or after the event.

....

After John McCain's victory, Paul turned his attention towards his congressional seat. The Republican primary would be held on March 4, less than a month after Super Tuesday. In recent years, strong support in Brazoria County had been enough to ward off potential competitors. This year, with Paul now plainly challenging the Republican establishment, it was clear someone would attempt to unseat him. Even diminishing support in his district could be used against him. Paul acknowledged this in the same post-Super Tuesday video, saying, "If I were to lose the primary for my congressional seat, all our opponents would react with glee, and pretend it was a rejection of our ideas. I cannot and will not let that happen."

Paul would be squaring off against fellow Republican Chris Peden for his party's nomination. Peden was the mayor of Friendswood, a small city in Ron's 14th district. Neither the National Republican Party nor the Texas Republican Party endorsed Peden or helped him financially, perhaps for fear of incurring the wrath of Paul's many supporters. As a result, most of Peden's funding came from personal loans to his campaign from himself and donations from family members.[2]

However, much of the local establishment supported Peden. Two newspapers in his district, the <u>Victoria Advocate</u>[3] and <u>Galveston County Daily News</u>,[4] endorsed Peden. <u>The Lone Star Times</u>, a newspaper which had been instrumental in digging up negative stories about Ron Paul in the past, also threw their support behind Peden.[5]

Polls showed Paul ahead of his rival 63% to 30%.[6] In one Lone Star Times article days before the election titled, "Can Chris Peden beat Ron Paul", writer David Benzion cited his reasons why he thought Paul was vulnerable, adding, "In other words, I'm highly skeptical of a +33 point Paul margin." He was right, the margin was incorrect. Paul ended up carrying the district with 70.18% of the vote.[7]

The Democrats had no plans to contest the seat in November, knowing popularity towards Paul was overwhelming. Ron Paul's congressional seat was now assured and he could continue campaigning for liberty rather than for his position in government.

....

On the same day as Paul's primary victory, John McCain secured enough delegates to guarantee his nomination. Days later, Paul released a video on his website reiterating that there was no realistic way to win the nomination. Many interpreted this to mean he would stop campaigning, but he specifically noted he would contest the remaining delegates. Once again, his purpose was to continue spreading the message of freedom and to contrast his position with McCain's.

Ron's reluctance to endorse McCain surely frustrated many Republicans, who would prefer him to throw the weight of his Ron Paul army against the Democrats. According to the Washington Times, National Republican Congressional Committee chairman Tom Cole wanted to see Paul's supporters stay in the Republican Party and "help expand the party's ranks."[8] This would have been a real possibility if McCain offered Paul a key position in his presidency. After all, his supporters would fight hard knowing their man would gain more influence in government.

This idea was presented in a commentary on WorldNetDaily, a conservative news site. "Rather than repeat the Bush policies, McCain needs to make it clear that he has no intention of continuing them," wrote the editorial board. "He can do so by announcing at the Republican convention that Rep. Paul, Gov. Huckabee and Mr. [Warren] Buffett will be on his economic team."[9]

The editors envisioned a role suitable for Paul. "Paul could be director of management and budget in charge of finding ways to cut federal spending," they suggested, "If Sen. McCain picks this team, not only would he win the presidential election, but he would also preside over an economic boom after the election." However, McCain extended no such offer.

In the aftermath of the primaries, with Paul no longer focused on his election, he began to change his strategy. He would attempt to displace the neoconservative movement within the Republican Party and replace them with a freedom movement. Paul said of the neoconservatives, "We don't agree with them. We agree with the Old Right, and they're the New Right, which is 'The Wrong,' [because] the New Right has morphed into neoconservative."[10]

The next phase of the Ron Paul Revolution would be a takeover of the Republican Party. In 2008 there would be almost 40 "Ron Paul" candidates.[11] Some have met with success, such as William Lawson, who supporters affectionately dubbed Ron Paul Jr. due to a background in medicine and physical resemblance. The rookie candidate won his Republican primary easily, but the next battle against Democratic incumbent David Price in November was guaranteed to be much harder because the fourth district in North Carolina was historically Democratic.

Libertarian writer Ben Novak noted in early 2008, "Already Ron Paul supporters are becoming prominent in the Republican Party across the nation, beginning at precincts and moving up to state level. Soon they will be in positions to educate others in the Party."[12]

As was typical for the Ron Paul movement, a website sprung up to support this effort, PaulCongress.com. For many of these Pauliticians, one of the main motivations was to work side by side with Paul in congress to change the shape of the debate and eventually change America. Many of these campaigns were thrown together on short notice and with little strategic planning, but writers such as Ben Novak expect the real push for Ron Paul candidates to come in the following congressional election year. He writes, "By 2010, there will be several Ron Paul–educated members of Congress, and Ron Paul will no longer be alone. The movement is growing and will continue to grow."

The battles that will be fought over the Republican Party were previewed in the spring of 2008. During the earlier Nevada caucuses in January, Mitt Romney won, with Ron Paul in second place and McCain in third. The Nevada Republican Party held their state convention on April 26 to elect the delegates they would send to the September Republican National Convention. The previous night, an earthquake hit Nevada, but the real seismic shift occurred at the convention.

Approximately two-thirds of the thousand plus attendees were Paul supporters. Both Mitt Romney and Ron Paul presented speeches to rally the Republican troops, amiably chatting together before their respective appearances. However, the presence of so many Paul supporters mixed with the neoconservative leadership caused pandemonium.

The Republican leadership was represented by chairman Robert Beers. The agenda of the day was to elect 31 delegates to send to the convention. However, because the majority of the attendees were Ron Paul supporters, they could dominate the agenda through their voting power. Their first act was to vote on a change to the Nevada Republican rules so that delegates could support who they wanted.[13] It passed, setting up a situation in which they could vote all or most of the 31 delegates in favor of Ron Paul.

It was a clever maneuver that would ensure they could demand some attention at the National Convention later in the year, and it was all done according to party rules. Of course, it would be a nightmare for Republicans hoping to consolidate support around John McCain. A band of loud, cheering, shirt wearing Paul supporters was not what they wanted to see at the September national convention. Although Paul supporters had the numbers, the Nevada Republican Party leadership had experience.

Voting began, and the early delegates were chosen for Ron Paul. Beers hastily called a recess and went into discussions with his council. When deliberations finally resumed, Beers closed down the convention, claiming they went past the 5:00 pm time limit for their hall rental. The Ron Paul movement had been outmaneuvered.

The packed room went silent for several seconds, and then chaos erupted. Shouts of "Baloney" and "Beers, you're finished" flooded the hall. Party Chairman Sue Lowden quietly snuck out the back door. Beers stuck around for a few moments to exchange words. Although he was in no immediate physical danger, he was soon escorted from the hall by concerned security guards.[14]

As it turned out, the hall owners had allowed the convention to continue until 8:00 pm.[15] However, after the announcement and amid the ensuing pandemonium, too many people had left in disgust. Paul supporters attempted to continue voting, but they needed 674 attendees to meet the quorum and they were 100 short. The coup was over, at least for the moment. The Nevada delegate selection was in stalemate. "Our supporters started winning the votes and we were going to have the delegates," Ron Paul later noted. "They closed down shop before the delegates were nominated, so I guess it's up in the air."[16]

Ron Paul spokesman Jeff Greenspan, a 21-year veteran in politics, remarked, "I've seen factions walk out, but I've never seen a party walk out."

After the fracas, two contingents booked separate venues in an effort to resume the convention. The Ron Paul contingent scheduled a convention for June 28, without Robert Beers support. The pro-McCain faction, with Beers and his council, scheduled a convention for July 26. In order to make the proceeding legal, one of the conventions would need enough attendees to meet a quorum; however, it was likely the National Republican Party would only recognize the results from the July 26 convention.[17] Unfortunately, neither contingent met the required quorum, and party officials decided to nominate delegates in a teleconference.

The coup is a sample of what will come for the Republican Party. Even in mid-2008, the Washington Times recognized that "his supporters have all but taken over at least one state Republican Party — in Montana — and some county Republican parties in Texas."[18] The state-by-state takeover of the Republican Party will be fraught with conflict. Ron Paul supporters easily out-organize the older neoconservative party members when it comes to technology, but the Republican establishment has more experience. It will be difficult for the old Republican Party to resist these new upstarts.

It's worth noting that Paul has stated that he does not want to crash the party or disrupt Republican functions. He just wants to get their attention and make his point that if they want to survive they will have to look more seriously at true freedom. And there are signs the beaten down Republican Party is receptive to this idea. Maryland state party Executive Director John Flynn says, "We welcome everyone to the Republican Party. ... Two years ago we didn't even field candidates for two of these races, so the Ron Paul Republicans are really adding something."[19]

....

While the campaign wound down, Ron Paul continued giving interviews to everyone from CNN to local radio stations. Most of his interviews took place from Washington, often on the steps of the Capital Building. Behind the scenes, Paul was hard at work putting the finishing touches on a new book, The Revolution: A Manifesto. It was a statement of his principles, outlining a vision for America based on the constitution. Even before release, the book dominated all other political books on Amazon.com.

The book was released on April 30 and quickly rose to the top of Amazon, as well as reaching number one on the New York Times best seller list (non-fiction) by its second week. It was an incredible accomplishment. Normally political and celebrity books only reach the New York Times best seller list due to massive, choreographed appearances with the major media: Larry King Live, Oprah, Good Morning America, Time Magazine, and the New York Times itself. Ron Paul received none of that support, yet still managed to climb his way to the top. The surprise hit reestablished that, although the primaries were over, Ron Paul remained a powerful force in politics.

Although the Republican primaries were pushed to the sidelines, Paul continued racking up impressive numbers. In Pennsylvania he received 16%, with Huckabee taking 11% and McCain 73%. The protest votes made it clear not everyone in the party was happy with McCain.

As the trend continued, New York Times columnist Alex Williams wrote, "Mr. Paul was supposed to be a memory by now. But in the Oregon primary last week, he won 15 percent of the vote, and the campaign appears to be growing into something beyond a conventional protest campaign."[20]

As the months went by, it became clear Paul was hoping to secure a speaking position at the Republican Convention in September. Unfortunately, the Republican Party did not extend an offer to Paul. Instead, his campaign planned to host a parallel gathering at same time in Minneapolis.

By June 12 there were no more primaries to contest, and Ron Paul announced the end of his campaign. However, he stated his intention to continue the fight. "We'll make our presence felt at every level of government, where just a few people with our level of enthusiasm can make a world of difference. We'll keep an eye on Congress and lobby against legislation that threatens us," he wrote.[21] "We'll identify and support political candidates who champion our great ideas against the empty suits the party establishments offer the public. We will be a permanent presence on the American political landscape. That I promise you."

On the same day, Paul launched the Campaign for Liberty, along with a website campaignforliberty.com, in order to coordinate his supporters. His first goal was to sign up 100,000 members by September 1. He received over 35,000 members on the first day, and 38 days later the membership was over 70,000. With this new organization, Paul will attempt to create a permanent revolution.

Paul's enthusiasm for the new campaign was tempered by personal concern for one of his closest staff members, Kent Snyder. Tragically, on June 26th, 2008, Snyder lost a two month battle with pneumonia. Paul had lost not only the man who devised the strategy for his campaign, but a close friend. He noted of his ally, "During difficult times, Kent was always a calm at the center of the storm."[22]

Snyder's passing did not go by without controversy. Two months of lying on a hospital bed produced over $400,000 in medical costs, and Snyder was uninsured, leaving his family with the bill.[23] While some, such as Huffington Post, thought it was an argument for universal healthcare,[24] others thought it was an argument that free market medicine would have been far cheaper, with improved medicine that might have provided a cure.

Paul himself received some criticism for not offering health insurance to his staff, but the practice was not typical for frugal campaigns. As Jesse Benton observed, "As a general practice, virtually no political campaigns offer health insurance. It's just not done. A campaign is a temporary organization that could disband at any minute."[25]

....

With Paul's presidential campaign over, it was time to assess his successes and failures. Paul himself admits the campaign could have been better. "Some of it was because we weren't as organized as we could have been or should have been," he said.[26]

Some of the most pointed criticisms of his campaign came from an old adversary. While acknowledging that the media did not give favorable coverage to Paul, former senior aide Eric Dondero noted, "One of the reasons Ron Paul failed is because his staff ran a miserable campaign. They had more money than Huckabee but they didn't do the right things with the money, including hiring professional campaigners, which is something they should have done."[27]

Reason Magazine contributor David Weigel describes how the media calculates who is viable and who is not. "There is an eternal calculus for who has a chance and who does not have a chance," he says. "To be fair to them, some of that calculus was, 'Well, Mitt Romney has hired these guys that have won 12 elections and Ron Paul hasn't.'"[28] If Paul wants to impress the media in future contests, he will need seasoned campaign professionals.

Candidates also benefit from the support of high-profile national figures. Many pundits of the 2008 election credit Chuck Norris for giving Mike Huckabee a boost in popular support. Paul himself made a startling political comeback in 1996 with help from baseball legend Nolan Ryan. Paul could gain attention with a high profile libertarian supporter, and it happens there are quite a few in Hollywood. Kurt Russell, whose film resume is at least equal to that of Chuck Norris', is an ideological match with Paul's ideas. In 2004 Russell told Fox News that his politics are "limited constitutional government. I believe in that. Freedom, freedom, freedom. Being a libertarian, I do believe that limited government is good."[29]

Paul's transformation into a national figure, with a young and passionate following, has opened up new possibilities for his drive for freedom. As of 2008 it is uncertain if he will attempt another run for president. In 2012, Paul will be 76 years old, which would make him the oldest president ever sworn into office, although Ronald Reagan was almost 78 while still in office. Yet Americans love an underdog, so his campaign could be seen as inspirational.

Whatever happens, Ron Paul has proved himself a powerful force in politics. And he usually accomplishes what he sets out to do – from setting state track records, to running a prosperous medical practice, to winning in politics against all odds. In 2008 he announced his intentions to revolutionize America, and if his movement can get enough like-minded individuals in congress, it might actually happen. As Paul warns his opposition, "The neocons, the warmongers, the socialists, the advocates of inflation will be hearing much from you and me."[30]

Paid Political Message

An Open Letter to the American People

In 1776 our Founding Fathers risked their "lives, fortunes, and sacred honor" to establish a free and prosperous nation.

They warned us that it was our responsibility to keep it that way, but we have strayed from their wise counsel.

We The Founding Fathers...

...**warned** of the dangers of foreign entanglements. Now the trusted friends and allies you support with generous foreign aid packages and weapons all too often become enemies who take the lives of your brave soldiers. ...**Ron Paul will order an immediate and orderly withdrawal of our troops in Iraq and keep us out of entangling alliances.**

...**warned** you to obey the Constitution because power corrupts. Now a secretive government can spy on you and detain you at will under the guise of "National Security." ...**Ron Paul will restore individual rights, liberty and habeas corpus.**

...**warned** of the dangers of excessive taxation. Now you must labor nearly six months of the year to pay your taxes at all levels as your economy groans beneath this cruel burden. ...**Ron Paul will reduce taxes and phase out the IRS.**

...**warned** of the dangers of government spending. Now your growing National Debt stands at nine trillion dollars and your children are in debt from the day they are born. ...**Ron Paul will stop spending beyond our means and insist on a balanced budget.**

...**warned** of the dangers of a Central Bank (The Federal Reserve) and a debt-based, fiat monetary system. Now your government borrows and spends endlessly while destroying the value of your savings. ...**Ron Paul will stop runaway inflation by restoring honest money.**

...**warned** you to keep your nation sovereign and independent. Now you submit to UN global authority and NAFTA "free trade" agreements at the expense of your independence and prosperity, as your borders are left open to legions of illegal aliens. ...**Ron Paul will secure our borders and put America and Americans first.**

Ron Paul will return the Government to the People • Ron Paul will put America and Americans first.
Ron Paul communicates honestly. • Ron Paul will restore the Founders' vision of this great nation.

For these reasons *We the People* support...

— Ron Paul —
The only anti-war, pro-national-defense,
small-government, fiscally-conservative
Republican running for president.

★ ★ ★ Ron Paul *for* President ★ ★ ★

Ron Paul has placed 1st or 2nd in 27 GOP straw polls across the country, and support for him is growing exponentially!

It's time to remind Washington DC that government in the USA works for the People—NOT the other way around!

Congressman Ron Paul...

- ✔ Advocates a strong US national defense.
- ✔ Opposes the doctrine of preemptive war.
- ✔ Voted against the war in Iraq, instead urged Congress to hunt down the terrorists responsible for 9/11.
- ✔ Will bring our troops home immediately to protect OUR national security and secure OUR borders.
- ✔ Is opposed to a preemptive attack on Iran. Advocates a humble, noninterventionist foreign policy.
- ✔ Has NEVER voted to raise taxes or for an unbalanced budget.
- ✔ Will stop spending US taxpayer dollars to build and police foreign nations.
- ✔ Will protect Social Security for seniors while allowing younger people to transition out.
- ✔ Will end "birthright citizenship" for illegal aliens, stop illegal immigration and secure our borders.

Vote for Ron Paul in Your Upcoming Republican Primary Election

★ **Together We CAN Change the World!** ★

When Ron Paul supporters raised a record $4.3 million in one day, that got everyone's attention.

— Now it's time to WIN! —

Help us make December 16th the largest ever, one-day political fundraiser in history.

Let YOUR voice be heard...
www.teaparty07.com

If not YOU, who? • If not NOW, when?

RON PAUL – a principled, honest man of integrity...

- ✔ During 10 terms in Congress, Ron Paul has never taken a government-paid junket, has never voted himself a pay raise, and has not participated in the lucrative congressional pension program.
- ✔ Ron Paul does not rely on lobbyists and special interest groups to fund his campaigns. His campaign is funded by ordinary Americans like YOU. Please donate!
- ✔ Ron Paul has received more donations from active military personnel than any other candidate.
- ✔ As a doctor, Ron Paul has delivered more than 4,000 babies. He has been married to his wife Carol for 50 years. They have 5 children and 18 grandchildren.
- ✔ Ron Paul served our nation as a flight surgeon in both the Air Force and the Air National Guard.

Freedom, Peace, and Prosperity

RonPaul2008.com • 1-877-Ron2008 • RonPaulLibrary.org • RonPaulNation.com

Paid for by Lawrence Lepard, a concerned American. lwlepard@gmail.com. Not authorized by any candidate or candidate's committee.
Graphic design by Linda Laguna, Merrimack, NH. Original concept by Max @ RonPaulForums.com

WHY DID I SPEND $85,000 TO SUPPORT PRESIDENTIAL CANDIDATE RON PAUL?

BECAUSE I CARE ABOUT MY CHILDREN AND YOUR CHILDREN.

Lawrence W. Lepard,
American Citizen.

Recently,I placed a full page ad in USA Today supporting the Presidential Candidacy of Congressman Ron Paul. Why? Because I believe Ron Paul is different from every other individual who carries the title "politician." In fact, he is a medical doctor by training and has delivered 4,000 babies. After medicine he entered politics and he is a true public servant. A "Mr. Smith goes to Washington", type of guy. No political lobbyists or vested interests will support him---but I will—and all honest Americans should too.

Given the troubling developments in our world, I firmly believe we face a very important choice at this time in the history of our nation. We need to make a decision as to what we want America to represent, and to become. History will record the outcome of our decision. If we make the wrong choice, many more innocent people will die, and history will not be kind. As I say to my closest friends, I do not want to have to explain to my children that I stood silent as others destroyed this country.

Please allow me to be very direct. The America that I grew up in believed in the rule of law, not the rule of men.

The America that I grew up in believed in telling the truth. The America that I grew up in believed in following Judeo-Christian values, and yet made room for those of different faiths and backgrounds. The America I grew up in had a religious flavor, but we were wary of those who wore their religion on their sleeves. The America that I grew up in believed in the golden rule: treat people the way we would like them to treat us. The America that I grew up in believed that you did not lie, cheat or steal. The America that I grew up in believed in the inherent goodness of most men, but recognized that evil exists.

Nevertheless, the America that I grew up in did not believe in an eye for an

eye, or retribution. **It believed in protecting oneself from evil, but in the process of doing so we were cautioned not to become what we were protecting against.**

In short, the America that I grew up in was a place where one could be proud of one's country, and thankful to the men and women who had sacrificed so much in the past to give us this heritage.

I wake up today as a 50 year old husband and father of three, and I wonder where that America has gone. I see a President who ignores the U.S. Constitution by issuing "signing statements" that have the effect of law. He replaced a President who blatantly lied to the American public. Admittedly, the lie was about something that was none of the public's business. However, when a country's President is a liar, it lowers that country's level of discourse and makes lying seem acceptable. It is not. In point of fact, that lie is a big part of the reason we have our current President. You see, actions have consequences. Are these the best leaders this Country can produce? I see that second President's wife running for President and now claiming she will end the war. Of course, she initially voted for the war, and recently voted for a resolution against Iran that makes another war more likely. Do Americans really believe she will act in our best interests given all the money she has received from lobbyists and the military industrial complex? Will she end the war, as she now has begun claiming in her political advertisements? Or is this just a tactic to gain anti-war votes now that her closest rival is breathing down her neck. Do we believe her current statement on the war? Or is this new position just another hard to believe statement, like the story she told us about how she traded "cattle futures" so successfully?

I see the U.S. involved in an aggressive, undeclared war against a country that did not represent a threat to us in any way. We were lead into this war using false and inaccurate information. In my opinion, we are far less safe now than we were before we invaded Iraq. This war has created more emotionally charged enemies who have more reasons to attack us than ever before.

Ron Paul voted against invading Iraq. Rather than attack an entire nation, he tried to convince Congress and our President to strategically target the terrorists responsible for 9/11. The current Administration has failed to capture and eliminate the criminals who perpetrated this crime against us. Those responsible are still at large, our borders are wide open, and our troops are spread thin all over the globe. We need a leader who will protect us with a strong national defense and keep us out of foreign entanglements that in the end, create more enemies than friends. We need a President who will put the national security of the American people, and the safety of our troops, before the interests of oil companies and the military industrial complex.

To date this war has lasted longer than World War II, and between 100,000 and 1.0 million innocent people have died. These figures are between 30 and 300 times the number of people killed on 9/11/2001. Do two wrongs make a right? Furthermore, the majority of the 9/11 hijackers were Saudis. Not Iraqis. We are allies with Saudi Arabia and yet Saudi Arabia is far from being a democracy. Yet we went to war to create a democracy in Iraq and set an example for the Middle East.

The hypocrisy is staggering. The mistakes that were made are enormous. Why anyone believes one thing that is said by the people who led us into this war is a mystery to me.

"We will be greeted as liberators." Wrong. "Oil revenues will pay the cost." Wrong. "A secular democracy will emerge and be an inspiration for other countries." Wrong. The list of misjudgments goes on and on.

Were the civilian Iraqis killed by our preemptive war "collateral damage" or is that just a euphemism for murder? Has anyone taken the time to look at their pictures on the Web? Does ignoring them make their deaths less real? I wonder how their relatives and friends feel about the United States? I wonder if they are more or less likely to become terrorists as a result of the actions of this Administration. I see a country that has violated the Geneva Conventions. I see a country that has violated the Christian Doctrine of Just War. I see a country that has started a war that is illegal under international law. As President Eisenhower said, "Preventive war was an invention of Hitler. Frankly, I would not listen to anyone who seriously talked about such a thing". I see a flock of Presidential candidates, most of whom voted for this war and many of whom believe "all options should be on the table" in dealing with Iran. For those who are not current on this subject, that language is code for: we should be prepared to attack Iran with conventional or nuclear weapons.

Think about that for a moment. Leaders in this Country are actually talking about using a nuclear weapon preemptively against a country that has not attacked us. Are they insane?

I hear Neocon pundits calling for the beginning of World War III. I see a Country that has suspended habeas corpus. I see a country that has stripped its citizens of the Constitutional protections against an overreaching government. I see a country that has sanctioned "rendition" which is just another term for the kidnapping of anyone, anywhere, throughout the world, and then spiriting them off to a remote location where they can be subject to "enhanced interrogation techniques," which we are told are not torture. Another lie. I see a country that has engaged in torture. One leading Presidential candidate wants to "double Guantanamo" and thinks his sons' campaigning for him is equivalent to serving in the military. Of course, that candidate got a deferment to avoid serving in Vietnam. Other candidates for the highest office in this land are not any better. I see a war hero candidate who sings "bomb Iran" to the tune of The Beach Boy's song, Barbara Ann. How can he make light of killing people? Joking about bombing a foreign country and killing innocent people is a disgrace. However, at least that candidate is a veteran. Most of the other top advocates of war have never fought in one. Worse yet, they sought and obtained deferments when others were fighting. You cannot make this stuff up. The irony is incredible. If, as I believe, you reap what you sow, - then the ultimate payback for these injustices will be staggering.

I see a Country that thinks that it owns and controls the world. I believe this is ethically wrong.

Furthermore, we cannot afford it, so even attempting to run the world is self-defeating. I see a country that thinks it should have bases in the Middle East for the next fifty years. I see a country where the dominant political group, the Neocons, believe the world is a dark and evil place. I believe the people who feel this way are projecting their own views onto the rest of the world. They need therapy, and their projection endangers us all!

In short, I wonder if America has lost its moral compass or soul? Out of malfeasance, fear, ignorance, or incompetence we have implemented the wrong policies and taken the wrong course. Since this is true, then effectively the terrorists are winning. God surely has a great sense of humor. Irony abounds.

As citizens, each and every one of us is somewhat responsible for the actions of our government. In fact, the Constitution states that we are the government. It has been said that all it takes for evil to flourish is for good people to do nothing. So, has America lost it soul: yes or no? I would submit that while the current U.S. Administration and the vast majority of the Senate and Congress have lost their souls, the American people have not. Nearly 70% of the American population is against this war, and yet the war goes on. The vast majority of the American people want peace. People know what is right, yet the government does the wrong thing. How can this be? We are supposed to be a government OF, FOR and BY the People. Are we? What do you think? Does our government really represent the American people? Do you think the U.S. government should kill innocent Iraqis or Iranians to make us safer? Would you advocate killing a man who lives down the street just because you think he might do you harm in the future, even though he has done nothing to you yet? I do not, and I believe most American agree with me.

The huge disconnect between what a majority of this country wants and what our government is doing is the elephant in the room that no one will discuss.

I cannot in good conscience condone or support the policies of the Neocons, the military industrial complex, or the oil industry. I do not believe in "Full Spectrum Dominance". I do not believe "We Are The Indispensable Nation". I do not believe we are "History's Actors." I do not believe we can "Make Our Own Reality". I do not believe we should be an Empire. I think we have great power and military superiority and we should use these abilities to protect ourselves. Furthermore, with these powers come enormous responsibility. We are a Constitutional Republic. I believe there is a power higher than my government and that the Founders drew upon this power when they drafted the Declaration of Independence and the U.S. Constitution. "We hold these truths to be self evident, that all men are created equal." That reads "all men." Not "all Americans." The Founders believed, as do I, that All men have God-given rights. Governments are made to protect these rights, not destroy them. Until recently, I believe the American government did a good job of protecting these rights for Americans. For many years now I believe the American government has used a different standard or play book when dealing with foreign countries and foreign citizens. But that is a story for a different essay.

If it sounds like I am mad, you're right.

I am mad that my money becomes worth less every year because the Federal Reserve can print money out of thin air. I am mad that the U.S. Government inflation statistics are a lie, thanks to Bill Clinton's changing of the CPI calculation. I am mad that this change and the Federal Reserve have put the economy on a roller coaster leading to boom and bust cycles that benefit financiers at the expense of the middle class, retirees and the poor. I am mad that Wall Street titans and speculators have been rewarded while savers and honest labor have been punished. I am mad that honesty is considered quaint and naive by the political classes. I am mad at the arrogance of those who hold power in Washington, DC. I am mad that the actions of some men in my country have taken away the moral high ground that the U.S. used to occupy. I am mad that my tax dollars are used for weapons rather than for peaceful purposes. I do not want the blood of innocents on my hands.

Individual Americans are great people. If 70% of them are opposed to the war, then there is still hope. Of course the mainstream media, the press and the vested industrial and political interests would have us all believe that we cannot make a difference. They say we need to listen to them as they tell us who the next President will be. We have to choose between the two war mongering candidates they will serve up to us. We are told who the two front runners are, and we are discouraged from looking elsewhere. Why bother, they say? No one else even stands a chance. Maybe so, ...but maybe not. This time I think they have gone too far. Americans may be slow to react, but we are not dumb. I would submit that the outcome of this election it is not so clear. The establishment dam has sprung a leak which is small now, but it is growing. It is growing exponentially. The word is spreading. The candidates who represent change are moving up. The candidates who represent the status quo are moving down.

The lines could not be more clearly drawn.

Ron Paul's message is clear and beautiful and true. It resonates with people. When you hear it you say, "that's right, that's what I believe".

This is why his poll numbers are rising faster than any other candidate. Yet, the media still ignore him and treat him poorly. It is beautiful irony that every attack on him only brings him more attention as intelligent Americans wonder, "who is this guy that everyone keeps attacking ... I wonder if there is a reason?" They say he cannot win. They say he is a fringe candidate. They say he will lose. I strongly disagree. They are wrong. First, I think there is a very good chance he will be our next President. Second, I think he has won already because he is standing up for everything that is good, right and true about America. He has won by putting forth the message of a Limited Constitutional Government dedicated to Freedom, and people like what they hear. The message he is spreading is like an uncontrollable wildfire. It cannot be stopped. I believe that history will record the Ron Paul Freedom Movement as an earth shattering event in the history of U.S. politics. If you want to see the future of US politics this is what it will look like.

It is an honor to support this man. We should be so lucky as to have him for our President.

Having said that, we could all help history along a little bit by supporting the Ron Paul campaign. My favorite movie is :It's A Wonderful Life. To me, the message of that movie is that we all make a difference. Individually, none of us have the power of the Neocons and the political classes, but collectively they are supposed to work for us. If we self-organize and unite, we have them greatly out numbered. They are terrified, and they should be. The growth in this movement is amazing. We can and will win this struggle. Anyone who tells you otherwise is a defeatist or is working to protect the status quo.. I ran the USA Today Advertisement because I wanted to plant a seed and make a difference. WE ALL MAKE A DIFFERENCE. Every conversation, every person converted, every e-mail , every effort; it all counts. The internet is what has made it possible.

What a beautiful thing. The trend is really changing and it is fun to watch the old guard struggle as their fortress crumbles.

So what can you do?

Join our effort to elect Ron Paul as the next President of the United States. Spread the word that we have an opportunity to elect an honest statesman with an impeccable record of voting in line with our Constitution. Vote for peace. Vote for freedom.

Donate to his campaign!

Each contribution represents another American who has said "enough is enough."

Every contribution helps. $10 is not too little. On December 16th, our collective voices were heard when grassroots supporters for Ron Paul succeeded in organizing the largest one-day fundraiser in political history. Over 58,000 ordinary Americans spoke with their wallets by donating more than $6 million dollars to the Ron Paul campaign in a single day. Together we are proving to be a force to be reckoned with.

Think about it. What is freedom worth? I would submit that it is priceless. If you care about the future of this country, I know that Ron Paul will not let you down. If you care about our troops, then you must vote for Ron Paul. He will bring them home to defend America instead of someone else's country. Ron Paul has received more donations from active military personnel than any other candidate. Why do you think that is? Have you heard about it from the Mainstream Media? I suspect that you have not.

This is it folks. A once in a lifetime opportunity. We may never see a candidate with more integrity and a better message or track record.

Has our country ever been so far off track. Our Founding Fathers pledged their lives, fortunes and sacred honors in order to establish this Nation. Perhaps we have taken for granted the risks they took and the sacrifices they made. But we are being called. We are being tested. How will we answer? Will we meet the test or will we fail? Each of us makes a difference.

So what are you going to do? Are you going to be a Loyalist or a Patriot?

Americans are brave people. I do not need the Federal government to take care of me, and neither do you. I want them to leave me alone. I believe we can set this country back on the right track and that America will experience a renaissance of Peace, Freedom and Prosperity. Vote Ron Paul for President.

The danger to our Republic is real. We must act now!

Remember, each one of us makes a difference. Please vote for Ron Paul in your state's Republican Primary and encourage your friends and neighbors to do the same.

You can also learn more atwww.RonPaulLibrary.org about Ron Paul"s positions on the issues that most concern you.

Sincerely,

Lawrence W. Lepard

END NOTES

CHAPTER 1

1   Author interview with Carol Paul. April 2, 2008.

2   Historical German insurance data: http://www.hvbg.de/e/pages/untern/grund.html

3   http://www.treasury.gov/education/fact-sheets/taxes/ustax.shtml retrieved on July 12, 2008.

4   NBC's Meet the Press, December 27, 2007

5   Ancestors of Ron Paul: http://www.wargs.com/political/paul.html

6   Author interview with Carol Paul. April 2, 2008.

7   Ibid.

8   Ancestors of Ron Paul: http://www.wargs.com/political/paul.html

9   Ron Paul, August 30, 2006 speech to Congress: http://www.lewrockwell.com/paul/paul342.html

10 Historical census of taxation: http://www2.census.gov/prod2/statcomp/documents/CT1970p2-01.pdf

11 Title 23 of the United States Code for Highways.

12 Ron Paul, "Cough Up", April 10, 2006: http://www.lewrockwell.com/paul/paul316.html

13 Senatorial deadlocks prior to 1905. http://www.venice.coe.int/docs/2008/CDL(2008)018-e.asp

14 Federalist No. 62, James Madison, 1788.

15 Ralph A. Rossum, *Federalism, the Supreme Court, and the Seventeenth Amendment* (2001, Lexington Books)

16 New Hampshire Union-Leader, February 26, 2007. "Libertarian candidate in '88, Paul eyes GOP nomination" by BENJAMIN KEPPLE

17 *Friedman, Milton; Jacobson Schwartz, Anna (1963). A Monetary History of the United States: 1867-1960.* Princeton: Princeton University Press.

18 *A History of Money and Banking in the United States* (2002, Ludwig von Mises Institute), Murray Rothbard

19 Calculate any date range using Consumer Price Index data: http://www.measuringworth.com/ppowerus/

20 "Our Economic Past" by Burton W. Folsom Jr. http://www.fee.org/publications/the-freeman/article.asp?aid=5603

21 Ron Paul. "Inflation and War Finance." http://www.lewrockwell.com/paul/paul364.html Posted January 30th, 2007. Accessed July 20th, 2008.

22 Ron Paul, August 30, 2006 speech to Congress: http://www.lewrockwell.com/paul/paul342.html

23 Author interview with Carol Paul. April 2, 2008.

24 Murray Rothbard, *America's Great Depression* (1963, D. Van Nostrand)

25 Ron Paul, September 10, 2002 speech to Congress, "Abolish the Fed": http://www.lewrockwell.com/paul/paul53.html

26 Ibid.

27 Author interview with Carol Paul. April 2, 2008.

CHAPTER 2

1   Gail Russell Chaddock, "Ron Paul: An Absolute Faith in Free Markets and Less Government," January 2, 2008, *The Christian Science Monitor*, http://www.csmonitor.com/2008/0102/p01s08-uspo. html accessed on June 16th 2008.

2   Dan Gilgoff, "Interview: Ron Paul's Christian Values: Pro-Life, Anti-War," January 25, 2008, *Faith in Public Life*, Washington, D.C., http://www.faithinpubliclife.org/content/news/2008/01/ron_pauls_ christian_values_pro.html, accessed on June 16th, 2008.

3   Gilgoff.

4   Gilgoff.

5   "Bill Moyers Talks with Ron Paul," *Bill Moyers Journal*, January 4, 2008, http://www.pbs.org/moyers/journal/01042008/transcript2.html, accessed on June 16th, 2008.

6   Garet Garrett, "The Church of Keynes," *American Affairs*, Volume VIII, Number 3 (July 1946), republished by the Mises Instiute, Auburn, Alabama, http://mises.org/story/2803, accessed on June 16th, 2008.

7   "WPA Home Survey, Allegheny County," Western Pennsylvania Genealogical Society c/o PA Department, Carnegie Library of Pittsburgh, 4400 Forbes Avenue, Pittsburgh, PA 15213-4080. http://www.wpgs. org/wpa_survey.htm, accessed on June 16th, 2008.

8   "How Green Tree Came to Be..." Green Tree Borough History, http://www.greentreeboro.com/history.html, accessed on June 16th, 2008.

9   Dan Treul, "An Interview with Ron Paul's Brother: Spreading the Good News (But Not from the Pulpit)" Huffington Post, November 6th, 2007, http://www.huffingtonpost.com/dan-treul/an-interview-with-ron-pau_b_71108.html, accessed on July 2, 2008.

10 Chaddock.

11 Chaddock.

12 Jacob Hornberger, "A Different Look at World War II," The Future of Freedom Foundation, August 2001, http://www.fff.org/comment/ed0801h.asp, accessed July 2nd, 2008.

13 Bloomberg TV, April 29, 2008: http://www.youtube.com/watch?v=3opx1wZysAY

14 Ron Paul, "February 14, 2007 Address at Farm Food Voices," Washington, D.C. http://www.ronpaulaudio.com/rpaudio/RonPaulFoodFarmVoices.mp3, accessed June 16th, 2008.

15 Ron Paul, "February 14, 2007 Address at Farm Food Voices," Washington, D.C. http://www.ronpaulaudio.com/rpaudio/RonPaulFoodFarmVoices.mp3, accessed June 16th, 2008.

16 Ron Paul, "Big Government Solutions Don't Work/The Law of Opposites" August 30, 2006 LewRockwell.Com, http://www.lewrockwell.com/paul/paul342.html, accessed on June 16, 2008.

17 http://www.nytimes.com/2007/07/22/magazine/22Paul-t.html

18 Treul.

CHAPTER 3

1   LinkedIn.com, Ron Paul, GOP Congressman & Presidential Candidate, http://www.linkedin.com/in/ronpaul; retrieved on April 28, 2008.

2   Author interview with Mr. Jesse Benton on April 25, 2008.

3   Ibid.

4   Carol Paul, "The Ron Paul I Know," LewRockwell.com, December 14, 2007, http://www.lewrockwell.com/orig8/paul-carol1.html; retrieved April 28, 2008.

5   Author interview with Mr. Jesse Benton on April 25, 2008.

6   LinkedIn.com, Ron Paul, GOP Congressman & Presidential Candidate, http://www.linkedin.com/in/ronpaul; retrieved on April 28, 2008.

7   Ibid.

8   Ibid.

9   "Profile: Republican Ron Paul," Seattle Times, Nation & World, July 29, 2007, http://seattletimes.nwsource.com/html/nationworld/2003810874_paul29.html;

retrieved on April 28, 2008.

10 Carol Paul, "The Ron Paul I Know," LewRockwell.com, December 14, 2007, http://www.lewrockwell.com/orig8/paul-carol1.html; retrieved on April 28, 2008.

11 Due to the lingering effects of his high school knee injury, Rep. Ron Paul underwent surgery again a few years prior to his 2008 presidential campaign. Author interview with Mr. Jesse Benton on April 25, 2008.

12 Carol Paul, "The Ron Paul I Know," LewRockwell.com, December 14, 2007, http://www.lewrockwell.com/orig8/paul-carol1.html; retrieved on April 28, 2008.

13 On The Issues, "Ron Paul on Education," http://www.ontheissues.org/2008/Ron_Paul_Education.htm; retrieved on March 21, 2008.

14 Representative Ron Paul Address to the US House of Representatives, "Introduction of the Family Freedom Education Act—Hon. Ron Paul," January 31, 2001, http://www.house.gov/paul/congrec/congrec2001/cr013101b.htm; retrieved on April 2, 2008.

15 On The Issues, "Ron Paul on Education," http://www.ontheissues.org/2008/Ron_Paul_Education.htm; retrieved on March 21, 2008.

16 John T. Woolley and Gerhard Peters, "Department of Education Organization Act Statement on Signing S. 210 Into Law," Press Release, The American Presidency Project, Santa Barbara, CA: University of California, October 17, 1979. http://www.presidency.ucsb.edu/ws/index.php?pid=31543; retrieved on April 22, 2008.

17 Ron Paul, "Issues: Education," Ron Paul 2008 http://www.ronpaul2008.com/issues/education/; retrieved on March 21, 2008.

18 Ibid.

19 According to the National Center for Education Statistics: "The results of the 2003 [National Household Education Surveys Program] survey reveal that the weighted estimate of the number of students being homeschooled in the United States in the spring of 2003 was 1,096,000, a figure which represents a 29 percent increase from the estimated 850,000 students who were being homeschooled in the spring of 1999. ... In addition, the estimated homeschooling rate—the percentage of the student population being homeschooled—rose from 1.7 percent in 1999 to 2.2 percent in 2003." http://nces.ed.gov/pubs2006/homeschool/; retrieved on 2008-03-31.

20 Ron Paul, "Paul Urges Colleagues to Improve Education by Expanding Freedom," Press Release, Office of US Representative Ron Paul, September 29, 2000, http://www.house.gov/paul/press/press2000/pr092900.htm; retrieved on March 31, 2008.

21 Ibid.

22 Ron Paul, "Paul Promotes Teacher Pay Raises," Press Release, Office of US Representative Ron Paul, July 14, 2000, http://www.house.gov/paul/press/press2000/pr071400.htm; retrieved on March 31, 2008.

23 Ron Paul, "The Psycho State," LewRockwell.com, September 14, 2004. http://www.lewrockwell.com/paul/paul203.html; retrieved on March 12, 2008.

24 Ibid.

25 Ibid.

26 GovTrack.us, "H.R. 609 [109th]: College Access and Opportunity Act of 2006," http://www.govtrack.us/congress/bill.xpd?bill=h109-609; retrieved on April 2, 2008.

27 Ron Paul, "The 'Academic Bill of Rights'," LewRockwell.com, April 28, 2006. http://www.lewrockwell.com/paul/paul320.html; retrieved on March 12, 2008.

28 Ibid.

29 Ibid.

30 Ibid.

31 Ibid.

32 GovTrack.us, "H.R. 1 [107th]: No Child Left Behind Act of 2001 (Vote On Passage)," http://www.govtrack.us/congress/vote.xpd?vote=h2001-145; retrieved on March 31, 2008.

33 Whitehouse.gov, "President Signs Landmark No Child Left Behind Education Bill," Press Release, The White House, January 8, 2002. http://www.whitehouse.gov/news/releases/2002/01/20020108-1.html; retrieved on April 22, 2008.

34 Representative Ron Paul Address to the US House of Representatives, "Statement on the Congressional Education Plan," May 23, 2001, http://www.paulonpaper.com/document.php?id=781; retrieved on April 1, 2008.

35 Ibid.

36 Ibid.

37 Ibid.

38 Ibid.

39 Representative Ron Paul Address to the US House of Representatives, "Are Vouchers the Solution for

Our Failing Public Schools?," LewRockwell.com, September 30, 2003, http://www.lewrockwell.com/paul/paul132.html; retrieved on March 10, 2008.

40 Ibid.

41 Ibid.

42 Ibid.

43 Ibid.

44 Ibid.

45 Author interview with Mr. Jesse Benton on April 25, 2008.

46 "The Korean War, June 1950 - July 1953—Introductory Overview and Special Image Selection," Department of the Navy, Naval History Center, February 6, 2001, http://www.history.navy.mil/photos/events/kowar/kowar.htm; retrieved on April 29, 2008.

47 Author interview with Mr. Jesse Benton on April 25, 2008.

48 Carol Paul, "The Ron Paul I Know," LewRockwell.com, December 14, 2007, http://www.lewrockwell.com/orig8/paul-carol1.html; retrieved on April 28, 2008.

CHAPTER 4

1 Author interview with Wayne Paul, June 4, 2008.

2 Anderson, Lisa. "Paul: A Seller of Ideas." Calendarlive.com <http://tinyurl.com/5dx7vc>.

3 Paul, Carol. "The American Dream." <http://www.ronpaul2008.com/articles/331/the-american-dream/>

4 Author interview with Wayne Paul, June 4, 2008.

5 Fusion, Jennn. "First Lady to Be: Carol Paul." VicePresidents.com. <http://www.vicepresidents.com/first-lady-be-carol-paul>.

6 "Alpha Xi Delta: Women's Fraternity." <http://tinyurl.com/4vrqeu>.

7 Author interview with Carol Paul on June 5, 2008.

8 Ibid.

9 Barrick, Chris. "Ron Paul's Presidential Bid." Cross and Crescent. <http://www.crossandcrescent.com/2007/11/ron-pauls-presidential-bid>.

10 "Gettysburg College – Facts & Figures." <http://www.gettysburg.edu/about/facts/>.

11 "Gettysburg College – College History." <http://www.gettysburg.edu/about/college_history/>.

12 Author interview with Lois Lewandowski on June 2, 2008.

13 Truel, Dan. "An Interview With Ron Paul's Brother." Huffington Post. <http://www.huffingtonpost.com/dan-treul/an-interview-with-ron-pau_b_71108.html >. <http://christianity.about.com/od/religionpolitics/p/ronpaulfaithss.htm>.

14 Paul, Ron. "The State vs. Doctors." Mercola.com. <http://articles.mercola.com/sites/articles/archive/2001/08/25/doctors-part-two.aspx>

15 Author interview with Carol Paul on June 5, 2008.

16 "Lambda Chi Alpha History." <http://lambda.students.mtu.edu/history.html>.

17 Faulstick, Ben. "Hazing's Culture." Cross and Crescent. <http://www.crossandcrescent.com/2006/11/hazings-culture>.

18 Barrick, "Ron Paul's Presidential Bid."

19 Author interview with Lois Lewandowski on June 2, 2008.

20 Ibid.

21 Barrick, "Ron Paul's Presidential Bid."

22 Ibid.

23 "Gettysburg College - College History."; Author interview with Carol Paul on June 5, 2008.

24 Author's interview with Lois Lewandowsky on June 2, 2008.

25 Chaddock, Gail Russell. "Ron Paul: An Absolute Faith in Free Markets and Less Government." Christian Science Monitor. <http://www.csmonitor.com/2008/0102/p01s08-uspo.html?page=2>.

26 Author's interview with Lois Lewandowsky on June 2, 2008.

27 Paul, "The American Dream."

28 "Gettysburg College - Bullet Hole."
<http://www.gettysburg.edu/about/offices/fa/dining/bullet_hole>.

29 "Jon Stewart Respects Ron Paul." ABC News Political Radar.
<http://blogs.abcnews.com/politicalradar/2007/06/jon_stewart_res.htm>.

30 US Constitution, Article I, Section 8.

31 Author interview with Wayne Paul on June 4, 2008.

32 "Raw Milk. What's In It?" Raw-milk-facts.com.
<http://www.raw-milk-facts.com/what_is_in_raw_milk.html>.

33 Paul, Ron. "Free Trade in Unpasteurized Milk." Lewrockwell.com.
<http://www.lewrockwell.com/paul/paul422.html>

34 Barrick, "Ron Paul's Presidential Bid."

35 "Ron Paul 2008 > Issues > Education."
<http://www.ronpaul2008.com/issues/education/>.

36 Author interview with Carol Paul on June 5, 2008.

37 Ibid.

38 Ibid.

39 Ibid.

40 "Ron & Carol Paul's Wedding Story." BridesDecide.com.
<http://www.bridesdecide.com/articles/a70830114256/ron--carol-pauls-wedding-story.aspx>.

41 Ibid.

42 Paul, "The American Dream."

43 Ibid.

44 Ibid.

45 Ibid.

46 Author interview with Carol Paul on June 5, 2008.

47 Ibid.

48 Ibid.

49 Ibid.

50 Lieberman, Brett. "Ron Paul campaigns in Gettysburg." The Patriot-News.
<http://www.pennlive.com/midstate/index.ssf/2008/04/ron_paul_campaigns_in_gettysbu.html>.

51 "Ron Paul Tours Alma Mater Gettysburg College." <http://video.aol.com/video-detail/ron-paul-tours-alma-mater-gettysburg-college/1034523749>

52 Author interview with Carol Paul on June 5, 2008.

53 Ibid.

54 Ibid.

55 Ibid.

56 Ibid.

57 Ibid.

58 Paul, Ron. "The Federal Marriage Amendment is a Very Bad Idea." Lewrockwell.com. <http://www.lewrockwell.com/paul/paul207.html>.

59 Peggy Pascoe, "Why the Ugly Rhetoric Against Gay Marriage Is Familiar to This Historian of Miscegenation." History News Network. <http://hnn.us/articles/4708.html>

60 "Ron Paul NH Meet and Greet Part 7."
<http://www.youtube.com/watch?v=ToCahPBG9sw>.

61 Paul, "The Federal Marriage Amendment is a Very Bad Idea."

62 Ibid.

63 Paul, Ron. "Government and Marriage." Lewrockwell.com.
<http://www.lewrockwell.com/paul/paul151.html>.

64 Ibid.

65 Ibid.

CHAPTER 5

1   Wereschagin, Mike "Presidential candidate Ron Paul drawing diverse crowds" Pittsburgh Tribune Review June 17, 2007 http://www.pittsburghlive.com/x/pittsburghtrib/news/cityregion/s_513029.html

2   The American Dream - Through the Eyes of Mrs. Ron Paul http://www.dailypaul.com/node/53

3   "A Brief Narrative History." Duke University. http://library.duke.edu/uarchives/history/narrativehistory.html Accessed July 8, 2008.

4   Lori Pyeat http://familytrees.genopro.com/JcMorin/RonPaul/default.htm?page=Paul-Lori-ind00004. htm ;Ronnie Paul 49 years old myspace page http://www.myspace.com/r_w_paul ; Carol Paul places Ronnie and Lori one year apart with Ronnie being the oldest in this video http://www.youtube.com/ watch?v=FgF-s1voM_Y

5   The American Dream - Through the Eyes of Mrs. Ron Paul http://www.dailypaul.com/node/53

6   Gail Russell Chaddock "Ron Paul: an absolute faith in free markets and less government" The Christian Science Monitor January 2, 2008 http://origin.csmonitor.com/2008/0102/p01s08-uspo.html?page=2

7   Linda Johnston, MD, DHt Congressman Ron Paul February 2002 http://www.lewrockwell.com/orig3/johnston6.html

8   Time Magazine "The Man on the Bandwagon" Friday, Jun. 12, 1964 http://www.time.com/time/magazine/article/0,9171,875856-8,00.html

9   Rep. Ron Paul "The Hidden Costs of War" Antiwar.com June 16, 2005 http://www.antiwar.com/paul/?articleid=6330

10 John F. Kennedy "Radio and Television Report to the American People on Civil Rights" June 11, 1963 http://www.jfklibrary.org/Historical+Resources/Archives/Reference+Desk/Speeches/JFK/ 003POF03CivilRights06111963.htm

11 Ron Paul "Rosa Parks's Heroism a 'Testament to the Power of Freedom'" Reuters Feb 4, 2008 http://www.reuters.com/article/pressRelease/idUS206214+04-Feb-2008+BW20080204

12 Time Magazine "Where Barry Stands" August 2, 1963 http://www.time.com/time/magazine/article/0,9171,870316-2,00.html

13 Tavis Smiley "CC Goldwater" September 26, 2006 http://www.pbs.org/kcet/tavissmiley/archive/200609/20060926_goldwater.html

14 Ron Paul 'Meet the Press' transcript for Dec. 23, 2007 http://www.msnbc.msn.com/id/22342301/page/4/

15 Ibid.

16 Time Magazine "The Man on the Bandwagon" Friday, Jun. 12, 1964 http://www.time.com/time/magazine/article/0,9171,875856-8,00.html

17 An Interview with Ron Paul's Brother: Spreading the Good News (But Not From the Pulpit) November 6, 2007 http://www.huffingtonpost.com/dan-treul/an-interview-with-ron-pau_b_71108.html

18 Ibid.

19 Ibid.

20 Paul, Ron "The Trouble With Forced Integration" http://www.lewrockwell.com/paul/paul188.html

21 Ibid.

22 Ibid.

23 Ibid.

24 Ibid.

25 Paul, Ron "The Trouble With Forced Integration" http://www.lewrockwell.com/paul/paul188.html

26 Ibid.

27 Ibid.

28 Paul, Ron Patriotism May 22, 2007 http://www.lewrockwell.com/paul/paul388.html

CHAPTER 6

1   Paul, Ron. "The State vs. Doctors." LewRockwell.com. August 16, 2001.
    <http://www.lewrockwell.com/orig/paul3.html>

2   Rothbard, Murray. "Making Economic Sense." Ludwig von Mises Institute.
    <http://mises.org/econsense/ch20.asp>

3   "Internal Medicine Residency Programs, Henry Ford Hospital, Detroit,MI."
    <http://www.henryford.com/body.cfm?id=37270>

4   Barrick, Chuck. "Ron Paul's Presidential Bid." Cross & Crescent. November 2007. <http://www.
    crossandcrescent.com/2007/11/ron-pauls-presidential-bid/>

5   Paul, Carol. "The American Dream - Through the Eyes of Mrs. Ron Paul." Daily Paul. March 16, 2007.
    <http://www.dailypaul.com/node/53>

6   Ericson, A.S. "Ron Paul, M.D. Speaks on Health Care." The Dartmouth Review. October 14, 2007.
    <http://dartreview.com/archives/2007/10/14/ron_paul_md_speaks_on_health_care.php>

7   Paul, Ron. "The State vs. Doctors." LewRockwell.com. August 16, 2001.
    <http://www.lewrockwell.com/orig/paul3.html>

8   Barrick, Chuck. "Ron Paul's Presidential Bid." Cross & Crescent. November 2007. <http://www.
    crossandcrescent.com/2007/11/ron-pauls-presidential-bid/>

9   "What is Austrian Economics?" Ludwig von Mises Institute.
    <http://mises.org/etexts/austrian.asp>

10 Ron Paul, Congress Speech, June 1, 2008.

11 Interview with Roger Ream, Mises Institute. Professor Dominick T. Armentano and Congressman Ron
    Paul discuss anti-trust and monopoly. July 13, 1983

12 Cockett, Richard. "The Road to Serfdom – Fifty Years On." History Today, Vol. 44.
    May 1994. <http://www.questia.com/PM.qst?a=o&se=gglsc&d=5000197144>

13 Rothbard, Murray N. "Biography of Ludwig von Mises (1881-1973)."
    Ludwig von Mises Institute. <http://mises.org/about/3248>

14 Hazlett, Thomas W. "The Road from Serfdom." Reason Magazine. July 1992.
    <http://www.reason.com/news/show/33304.html>

15 Powell, Jim. "The life and times of F.A. Hayek, who explained why political liberty is impossible without
    economic liberty." Libertystory.net. 2001.
    <http://www.libertystory.net/LSTHINKHAYEKLIFE.htm>

16 Hayek, F.A. "Tribute to Ludwig von Mises by F A. von Hayek." March 7, 1956. Ludwig von Mises
    Institute. <http://mises.org/misestributes/hayek.asp>

17 Ebeling, Richard M. "Wilhelm Ropke A Centenary Appreciation." The Foundation for Economic
    Education. October 1999. <http://www.fee.org/publications/the-freeman/article.asp?aid=4930>

18 Long, Roderick T. "Ayn Rand's Contribution to the Cause of Freedom."
    Ludwig von Mises Institute. February 2, 2002. http://mises.org/story/1738

19 Paul, Ron. "Ron Paul discusses Ayn Rand." YouTube. September 29, 2007.
    <http://kr.youtube.com/watch?v=MjwuGHPilwl>

20 Chambers, Whittaker. "Big Sister Is Watching You." National Review. December 27, 1957
    <http://www.nationalreview.com/flashback/flashback200501050715.asp>

21 Hicks, Stephen, R.C. "Ayn Rand 1905-1982)."
    Internet Encyclopedia of Philosophy. 2006. <http://www.iep.utm.edu/r/rand.htm>

22 William F. Buckley, Jr. "Miles Gone By: A Literary Autobiography". 2004.

23 "Getting It Right: A Conversation With Bill Buckley." Human Events. March 3, 2008.
    < http://findarticles.com/p/articles/mi_qa3827/is_20080303/ai_n24952703/pg_2>

24 Paul, Ron. "Has Capitalism Failed?" LewRockwell.com. July 9, 2002
    <http://www.lewrockwell.com/paul/paul42.html>

CHAPTER 7

1 Dr. Ron Paul address to the Robert Taft Club, Washington, D.C. on October 11, 2007, http://www.youtube.com/watch?v=j8cPoCcqL3U

2 "Our History of the 'Alamo Wing,'" 433rd Wing History Office, Lackland AFB, San Antonio, http://www.433aw.afrc.af.mil/units/433rdairliftwingstaffagencies/historyoffice/433historyofficeintroduction/433rdhistorysummary.asp, on December 17, 2007

3 Author interview with Matthew Pyeatt on December 6, 2007.

4 Ibid.

5 Ibid.

6 Christopher Caldwell, "The Antiwar, Anti-Abortion, Anti-Drug-Enforcement-Administration, Anti-Medicare Candidacy of Dr. Ron Paul," (*The New York Time Magazine*, July 22, 2007) http://www.nytimes.com/2007/07/22/magazine/22Paul-t.html, on July 9, 2008.

7 Ron Paul Roundtable with New Hampshire Supporters and Reporters, http://www.youtube.com/watch?v=DxppejbOgSw, on December 13, 2007.

8 Ibid.

9 Newsreel of President Kennedy's Address at the Brooks AFB Aerospace Medical Center on November 21, 1963. http://www.youtube.com/watch?v=Ep1ihYkemMY, on December 22, 2007.

10 Representative Ron Paul Address to the US House of Representatives, "Conscription – the Terrible Price of War," on November 21, 2003, http://www.house.gov/paul/congrec/congrec2003/cr112103.htm, on 22 December 2007.

11 Ron Paul, Freedom Under Siege: The US Constitution after 200 Years (Foundation for Rational Economics and Education, Lake Jackson, Texas: 1987) p. 38.

12 Representative Ron Paul Address to the US House of Representatives, "3.000 American Deaths in Iraq," on January 5th, 2007. http://www.house.gov/paul/congrec/congrec2007/cr010507.htm, on December 22, 2007.

13 Thomas Jefferson: 1st Inaugural Address, 1801. ME 3:321, Thomas Jefferson Digital Archive, University of Virginia Library, Charlottesville, Virginia. http://etext.virginia.edu/jefferson/quotations/jeff1400.htm, on December 10, 2007.

14 Representative Ron Paul Address to the US House of Representatives, "Removing US Armed Forces from Bosnia and Herzegovina," March 17, 1998, http://www.house.gov/paul/congrec/congrec98/cr031798.htm, accessed on December 22, 2007.

15 Paul, Freedom Under Siege, p. 60.

CHAPTER 8

1 http://www.greenjournal.org/cgi/content/abstract/34/2/235

2 *Ron Paul, National Right to Life Convention June 15, 2007, Kansas City.*

3 http://communities.justicetalking.org/blogs/day25/default.aspx

4 *Ron Paul, Abortion and Liberty (1983)*

5 http://www.merriam-webster.com/dictionary/fertilization

6 *Ron Paul, The Challenge to Liberty: Coming to Grips with the Abortion Issue, 1990.*

7 H.R. 760 [108th]: Partial-Birth Abortion Ban Act of 2003. http://clerk.house.gov/evs/2005/roll144.xml

8 Congressman Ron Paul in the US House of Representatives, June 4, 2003

9 *Ron Paul, Challenge to Liberty: Coming to Grips with the Abortion Issue (1990)*

10 The Medical Code of Ethics, Declaration of Geneva, 1948. http://www.euthanasia.com/belgium.html#code

CHAPTER 9

1   University of Texas Health Science Center at San Antonio. "History." http://www.uthscsa.edu/univrel/History.html Accessed on June 1st, 2008.

2   Author interview with Ronald E. Paul, MD. June 1, 2008.

3   Ibid.

4   Ibid.

5   Author interview with Llewellyn H. Rockwell, Jr. May 28, 2008.

6   Author interview with Ronald E. Paul, MD. June 1, 2008.

7   Ibid.

8   "The Ron Paul Story." www.youtube.com/watch?v=FgF-s1voM_Y, Accessed on May 24th, 2008

9   Author interview with Ronald E. Paul, MD. June 1, 2008.

10   Ibid.

11   Diana J. Kleiner. "Brazoria County." *The Handbook of Texas Online.* http://www.tshaonline.org/handbook/online/articles/BB/hcb12.html Accessed on May 28th, 2008.

12   Dow. "History of Texas Operations." http://www.dow.com/facilities/namerica/texops/about/history.htm Accessed on June 1st, 2008.

13   Author interview with Ronald E. Paul, MD. June 1, 2008.

14   Ibid.

15   Ibid.

16   "The Ron Paul Story."

17   Author interview with Llewellyn H. Rockwell, Jr. May 28, 2008.

18   Author interview with Ronald E. Paul, MD. June 1, 2008.

19   "Brazoria County."

20   http://www.linkedin.com/in/ronpaul

21   Author interview with Llewellyn H. Rockwell, Jr. May 28, 2008.

22   Author interview with Jack R. Pruett, MD. May 29, 2008.

23   Ibid.

24   "Brazosport Regional Health System." http://www.brhstx.org/bmh.nsf/View/AboutUs Accessed on May 29th, 2008.

25   Author interview with Jack R. Pruett, MD. May 29, 2008.

26   Author interview with Ronald E. Paul, MD. June 1, 2008.

27   Ibid.

28   "Interview with Ron Paul 7/19/2007 health care part 1" Kaiser Family Foundation. http://www.youtube.com/watch?v=IWLwJycOZqI Accessed on May 24th, 2008.

29   Author interview with Jack R. Pruett, MD. May 29, 2008.

30   Ibid.

31   Author interview with Ronald E. Paul, MD. June 1, 2008.

32   Author interview with Jack R. Pruett, MD. May 29, 2008.

33   Ibid.

34   Ibid.

35   Ibid.

36   Ibid.

37   Ibid.

38   Author interview with Llewellyn H. Rockwell, Jr. May 28, 2008.

39   "Interview with Ron Paul 7/19/2007 health care part 1."

40   Author interview with Llewellyn H. Roc kwell, Jr. May 28, 2008.

41   Author interview with Ronald E. Paul, MD. June 1, 2008.

42   Author interview with Jack R. Pruett, MD. May 29, 2008.

43   Ibid.

44   Author interview with Ronald E. Paul, MD. June 1, 2008.

45   Author interview with Jack R. Pruett, MD. May 29, 2008.

46   Ibid.

47   "Interview with Ron Paul 7/19/2007 health care part 1."

48   Ron Paul, MD. Address to the United States House of Representatives. February 27th, 2001. http://www.ronpaul2008.com/articles/903/blame-congress-for-hmos/ Accessed June 27th, 2008.

49   Author interview with Jack R. Pruett, MD. May 29, 2008.

50 Ron Paul. UT Austin TX Speech, 2008.

51 Ron Paul, MD. "Paying Dearly for Prescription Drugs." www.lewrockwell.com/paul/paul133.html Posted October 7th, 2003. Accessed July 15th, 2008.

52 Author interview with Llewellyn H. Rockwell, Jr. May 28, 2008.

53 Author interview with Jack R. Pruett, MD. May 29, 2008.

54 Ibid.

55 "The Ron Paul Story."

56 Ibid.

57 Author interview with Llewellyn H. Rockwell, Jr. May 28, 2008.

CHAPTER 10

1   Ron Paul, Mises and Austrian Economics: A Personal View (Ludwig Von Mises Institute, Auburn, Alabama: 2006) p. 3.

2   Linda Johnston, MD, DHt, "Congressman Ron Paul," October 28, 2004, http://www.lewrockwell.com/orig3/johnston6.html, accessed on March 04, 2008.

3   Ron Paul, Mises and Austrian Economics: A Personal View (Ludwig Von Mises Institute, Auburn, Alabama: 2006) p. 3.

4   Llewellyn H. Rockwell, Jr., "Libertarianism and the Old Right", http://www.lewrockwell.com/rockwell/oldright.html, accessed on March 12, 2008.

5   Christopher Caldwell, "Ron Paul Backs up New Ad with Straight Talk: GOP Rivals are Fake Conservatives," July 22, 2007, http://www.nytimes.com/2007/07/22/magazine/22Paul-t.html, accessed on March 04, 2008.

6   Ron Paul, "Big Government Solutions Don't Work", http://www.lewrockwell.com/paul/paul342.html, accessed on March 12, 2008.

7   Henry Hazlitt, "Economics in One Lesson", http://www.fee.org/library/books/economics.asp accessed on March 13, 2008.

8   Ron Paul, "Taxes, Spending, and Debt Are the Real Issues", http://www.lewrockwell.com/paul/paul347.html, accessed on March 12, 2008.

9   Ron Paul, "Do Tax Cuts Cost the Government Money?", http://www.lewrockwell.com/paul/paul348.html, accessed on March 12, 2008.

10 Ron Paul, "Tax Cuts and Class Wars", http://www.lewrockwell.com/paul/paul74.html, accessed on March 12, 2008.

11 Bruce Bartlett, "Not Your Average Republican Presidential Candidate" January 23, 2007, http://bartlett.blogs.nytimes.com/2007/01/23/not-your-average-republican-presidential-candidate, accessed on March 04, 2008.

12 Gary North, "True Confessions of 'Ron No's' Ron No", January 2, 2008, http://www.lewrockwell.com/north/north595.html, accessed on March 04, 2008.

13 Forbes, Steve: A New Birth of Freedom: A Vision for America, Regnery Publishing, Inc., 1999

14 http://www.lewrockwell.com/paul/paul316.html Accessed on June 15, 2008.

15 Economist Dr. Walter Williams. On cable show "At Issue", 1989.

16 Ron Paul, "Taxes, Spending, and Debt Are the Real Issues" http://www.lewrockwell.com/paul/paul347.html, accessed on March 12, 2008.

17 Ron Paul, "How Government Debt Grows" http://www.lewrockwell.com/paul/paul309.html, accessed on March 12, 2008.

18 Ron Paul, "Why Can't Congress Stop Spending?" http://www.lewrockwell.com/paul/paul187.html, accessed on March 12, 2008.

19 Ron Paul, "Government Policy and False Prosperity" http://www.lewrockwell.com/paul/paul75.html, accessed on March 12, 2008.

20 Ron Paul, "Are We Doomed To Be a Police State?" http://www.lewrockwell.com/paul/paul41.html, accessed on March 12, 2008.

21 Ron Paul 2008 Presidential Campaign Press Release, "Ron Paul Backs up New Ad with Straight Talk", http://www.ronpaul2008.com/press-releases/193/ron-paul-backs-up-new-ad-with-straight-talk-gop-rivals-are-fake-conservatives, accessed on March 04, 2008.

22 The Foundation for Rational Economics and Education, Inc., "Introduction to FREE and NEFL", http://www.free-nefl.com/html/introduction.html, accessed on March 04, 2008.

23 Ron Paul, Mises and Austrian Economics: A Personal View (Ludwig Von Mises Institute, Auburn, Alabama: 1984) p. 4.

24 Ron Paul, Mises and Austrian Economics: A Personal View (Ludwig Von Mises Institute, Auburn, Alabama: 1984) p. 23.

CHAPTER 11

1 Author interview with Dr. Pruett.
2 Author interview with Lew Rockwell.
3 Ibid.
4 http://www.npr.org/templates/story/story.php?storyId=15016924
5 http://www.cqpolitics.com/wmspage.cfm?docID=news-000002615198
6 July 11, 2007 AntiWar.com interview
7 Op cit., interview.
8 Op cit., interview.
9 "A Congressman Recalled as a Communist Hater," by Carl M. Cannon, *Philadelphia Inquirer*, September 2, 1983, p. A16.
10 Op cit., interview.
11 "The Swiss Report: A Special Study for Western Goals Foundation," Letter from the Chairman, March 1983.
12 *Congressional Record*, May 2, 1979, pp. 9600-01.
13 Ibid.
14 Ibid.
15 "House Members Ask Carter to Oppose Draft, Registration," by Dan Morgan, *Washington Post*, April 10, 1979, p. A1.
16 Op cit., interview.
17 Congressional Record June 4, 1997, p. H3336.
18 Ibid.
19 "On Capitol Hill" column, *Washington Post*, April 7, 1979, p. A5.
20 "Lengthening Shadows: From 1929 to the Present," *The New American*, September 16, 1996 (Second Edition), pp.20-23.
21 http://video.google.com/videoplay?docid=-4245169480003136735
22 Op Cit., interview.
23 *John Birch Society Bulletin*, March 1986.
24 Op cit., interview.
25 *John Birch Society Bulletin*, February 1984.
26 *John Birch Society Bulletin*, January 1984.
27 http://www.ontheissues.org/2008/Ron_Paul_Foreign_Policy.htm

CHAPTER 12

1 Hunt, Albert. "The Myth of Incumbent Protection." *Wall Street Journal*. New York. May 21st, 1979. p. 24
2 Compiled by Ladd E. Thomas under clerk of the House of Representatives, Henshaw L. Edmund Jr. "Statistics of the Congressional Election of November 4th, 1980." US Government Printing Office. Washington 1981
3 Paul, Ron. "Gold, Peace, and Prosperity." Foundation for Rational Economics and Education. Lake Jackson, Texas. 1981. p.36
4 Buffum. Richard. "Will Dollar Become Good as Gold?" *Los Angeles Times*. February 3rd, 1980. p. B2
5 Hobart, Rowen. "House Member Seeks to Revive Gold Standard" *Washington Post*. April 30th, 1981. p. A24
6 Paul, Ron. "Gold, Peace, and Prosperity." Foundation for Rational Economics and Education. Lake Jackson, Texas. 1981. p.11
7 Staff Writer. "Voting for Competition" *Wall Street Journal*. May 13th 1980. p. 24
8 Paul, Ron. "Gold, Peace, and Prosperity." Foundation for Rational Economics and Education. Lake Jackson, Texas. 1981. p.13
9 July 11, 2007 AntiWar.com interview.
10 Ibid.

11 P.L. 96-389

12 *Oversight Hearing Before the Subcommittee on Mines and Mining of the Committee on Interior and Insular Affairs, House of Representatives,* 96th Congress, October 2, 1980, Serial 96-40, p. 5.

13 Ibid, p.72.

14 Op cit., interview.

15 New York Times Magazine, July 22, 2007. http://www.nytimes.com/2007/07/22/magazine/22Paul-t.html?_r=4

16 Schwartz, Anna. "Reflections on the Gold Commission Report" *Journal of Money, Credit, and Banking.* Vol. 14, No. 4, Part 1. November 1982. p. 539

17 Ibid. p. 541

18 Evans, Rowland and Novak, Robert. "Enemies of Gold" *The Washington Post.* August 5th, 1981. p. A 23

19 Rowen, Hobart. "Reagan Might Just Join the New Gold Rush" *The Washington Post.* August 20th, 1981. p. A29

20 Perry, James. "'Gold Bugs' Confront Difficulties Finding, Er, a Silver Lining" *The Wall Street Journal.* December 10th 1981. p. 1

21 Ibid.

22 Staff Writer. "Gold Debate Program" *The Wall Street Journal.* September 19th, 1981. p. 30

23 Schwartz, Anna. "Reflections on the Gold Commission Report" *Journal of Money, Credit, and Banking.* Vol. 14, No. 4, Part 1. November 1982. p. 544

24 Ibid. p. 541

25 Ibid. p. 548

26 Ibid p. 548

27 Temin, Peter. "Transmission of the Great Depression" *Journal of Economic Perspectives.* Vol. 7, No. 2. Spring 1993

28 Atkinson, Caroline. "Disagreements Surface On a Commission Over Return to Gold Standard" *The Washington Post.* October 27th, 1981. p. D16

29 Atkinson, Caroline. "Gold Bugs Buzz, Don't Bite" *The Washington Post.* September 19th, 1981. p. D8

30 Perry, James. "'Gold Bugs' Confront Difficulties Finding, Er, a Silver Lining" *The Wall Street Journal.* December 10th 1981. p. 1

31 Staff Writer. "Gold 'Coin' Favored by US Board Group Rejects Gold Standard" *New York Times.* March 9th, 1982. p. D16

32 Compiled by Ladd E. Thomas under clerk of the House of Representatives, Guthrie, Benjamin J. "Statistics of the Congressional Election of November 2nd, 1982." US Government Printing Office. Washington 1983

33 July 11, 2007 AntiWar.com interview.

34 Associated Press. "Funny money from the Mint?" *Chicago Tribune.* November 29th, 1983. p. N5

CHAPTER 13

1 Balz, Dan. "Sen. Tower Won't Seek Reelection" *Washington Post.* August 24th, 1983. P. A1

2 Shapiro, Daniel. "An All-Out Battle for the Senate" *Newsweek.* January 16th, 1984. P. 21

3 King, Wayne. "Rivals for Senate Mix It Up in Texas." *New York Times.* February 3rd, 1984. P. 11A

4 King, Wayne. "Texas Politicians Are Scrambling to Succeed Tower in Senate." *New York Times.* January 30th, 1984. P. 13A

5 Staff Writer. "After Tower." *The Economist.* May 12th, 1984. P. 28

6 Malone, Julia. *Christian Science Monitor.* February 9th, 1984. P. 22

7 Staff Writer. "Texas; Big fight soon." *The Economist.* December 17th, 1983. P. 18

8 Staff Writer. "Congress' 'best,' 'worst' cost cutters" Industry Week. May 28th, 1984

9 Staff Writer. "Rep. Gramm is Texas Republican Senate Nominee." *New York Times.* May 5th, 1984. P. 27

10 Tayler, Paul. "3 Texas Democrats Vie for Senate; Man in Middle Seems To Have Safest Spot."
    Washington Post. May 2nd, 1984. P. A15

11 Paul, Ron. "Some Observations on Four Terms in Congress." *LewRockwell*.
    September 19th 1984. www.Lewrockwell.com P. 9

12 AP. "Rep. Paul of Texas Says Foes Used His Mail List." *New York Times*.
    April 26, 1984. P. 8 Sect. B

13 Staff Reporter. "Wayward List" *The Washington Post*. April 26th, 1984. P. A14

14 Paul, Ron. "Some Observations on Four Terms in Congress." *LewRockwell*.
    September 19th 1984. www.Lewrockwell.com P. 14

15 Paul, Ron. "Some Observations on Four Terms in Congress." *LewRockwell*.
    September 19th 1984. www.Lewrockwell.com P. 2

16 Paul, Ron. "Some Observations on Four Terms in Congress." *LewRockwell*.
    September 19th 1984. www.Lewrockwell.com P. 10

17 Ibid. P. 9

18 Ibid. P. 10

19 Ibid. P. 4

20 Ibid. P. 13

21 Paul, Ron. "Some Observations on Four Terms in Congress." *LewRockwell*. September 19th 1984.
    www.Lewrockwell.com P. 3

22 Ibid P. 1

CHAPTER 14

1   Matthew Pyeatt interview with author, December 4, 2007

2   Ron Paul, "Independence from England, Dependence on Washington?"
    http://www.lewrockwell.com/paul/paul109.html, accessed on March 12, 2008.

3   Ron Paul, "Independence from England, Dependence on Washington?"
    http://www.lewrockwell.com/paul/paul109.html, accessed on March 12, 2008.

4   Ron Paul, "Independence from England, Dependence on Washington?"
    http://www.lewrockwell.com/paul/paul109.html, accessed on March 12, 2008.

5   Paul, Ron. *Freedom Under Seige*, Foundation for Rational Economics and Education, Lake Jackson, TX,
    1987. ix

6   *Freedom Under Seige*. 1

7   *Freedom Under Seige*. 1

8   *Freedom Under Seige*. 2

9   *Freedom Under Seige*. 13

10 *Freedom Under Seige*. 3

11 *Freedom Under Seige*. 18-21; and "The War on Drugs is a War on Doctors"
    (May 17, 2004), "The Federal War on Pain Relief" (April 19, 2004), and "Rush Limbaugh and the Sick
    Federal War on Pain Relief" (February 12, 2004), www.ronpaullibrary.org

12 Matthew Pyeatt interview with author, December 6, 200

CHAPTER 15

1   *New York Times*, "Now for a Real Underdog: Ron Paul, Libertarian, for President," October 17, 1988.

2   Ron Paul in the US House of Representatives, April 2, 2003.

3   Ron Paul, Night Talk, Bloomberg TV, 04/29/2008.

4   Ron Paul in the US House of Representatives, March 10, 2004.

5   Tim Cridland, as quoted in Liberty Watch, Volume 3, Issue 6.

6   Houston Chronicle, "Campaign '88/Libertarian Party Candidate unfazed by certain loss, hopes `truth

7   Carol Moore, January 15, 2008: http://carolmoorereport.blogspot.com/2008/01/ron-lew-et-al-apologize-for-old.html

8   http://www.careerjournal.com/article/SB121521073192129407.html?mod=fpa_mostpop

9   Eric Dondero interview with Editor, July 2008.

10   http://libertarianrepublican.blogspot.com/2008/07/jesse-helms-dead-at-85-surprising.html

11   *New York Times*, "Now for a Real Underdog: Ron Paul, Libertarian, for President", October 17, 1988.

12   Ron Paul, Night Talk, Bloomberg TV, 04/29/2008.

13   http://cases.justia.com/us-court-of-appeals/F2/863/1368/

14   *New York Times*, "Some Republicans Back Foe of Bush", August 10, 1988.

15   The Daily Collegian, Penn State, "Libertarian party wants to rid gov't of 'Big Brother'," November 4, 1988.

16   Ron Paul in the US House of Representatives, March 10, 2004.

17   The Morton Downey Jr. Show, http://www.youtube.com/watch?v=IHB2I83_N_k, http://www.youtube.com/watch?v=MGGDVm4mmTo, and http://www.youtube.com/watch?v=waesMWjaqnU, July 1988.

18   Interview with Eric Dondero (Fmr. Travel Aid and Advance Man for the Ron Paul campaign) by Author in June 2008.

19   *American Libertarian*, November 1988.

20   Liberty Party News, "Rumors... And Reality," May/June 1989.

21   Major Gerrett, "Ron Paul aide target of fraud investigation." *The Houston Post*, July 8, 1989.

22   Ron Paul, Night Talk, Bloomberg TV, 04/29/2008.

23   *Houston Chronicle*, "Campaign '88/Libertarian Party Candidate unfazed by certain loss, hopes 'truth wins,'" November 2nd, 1988.

24   Ralph Z. Hallow, "Libertarians hold pre-'92 skirmish." *Washington Times*, August 30, 1991.

25   Interview with Eric Dondero (Fmr. Travel Aid and Advance Man for the Ron Paul campaign) by Author in June 2008.

CHAPTER 16

1   David Leip. "1988 Presidential General Election Results." http://uselectionatlas.org/RESULTS/national.php?year=1988&minper=0&f=0&off=0&elect=0 Accessed June 27th, 2008.

2   S.C. Gwynne. "Dr. No.," Texas Monthly Magazine. http://www.texasmonthly.com/2001-10-01/feature7-1.php October 2001. Accessed June 27th, 2008.

3   Author interview with Jack R. Pruett, MD. May 29th, 2008.

4   Author interview with Ronald E. Paul, MD. June 1st, 2008.

5   Author interview with Ronald E. Paul, MD. June 1st, 2008.

6   Author interview with Burton S. Blumert. June 27th, 2008.

7   "About Us." Ludwig von Mises Institute. http://mises.org/about.aspx Accessed June 27th, 2008.

8   Author interview with Burton S. Blumert. June 27th, 2008.

9   Ibid.

10   Ibid.

11   Ibid.

12   Ibid.

13   Ibid.

14   Carlson, Tucker. "Pimp My Ride." *The New Republic*. http://www.tnr.com/politics/story.html?id=83665295-1de6-4571-af9c-0a90f6d1fde0 Posted December 21st 2007. Accessed June 26th 2008.

15   Author interview with Burton S. Blumert. June 27th, 2008.

16   "Introduction to FREE and NEFL." http://www.free-nefl.com/html/introduction.html Accessed June 27th, 2008.

17   Ibid.

18   Editor interview with Eric Dondero, July 13, 2008.

19 Ibid.

20 Ibid.

21 "'At Issue' with Ron Paul." http://www.youtube.com/watch?v=WxmCMiAANpE
    Posted April 26th, 2008. Accessed July 14th, 2008.

22 Ibid.

23 Editor interview with Eric Dondero, July 13, 2008.

24 Ibid.

25 "'At Issue' with Ron Paul." http://www.youtube.com/watch?v=WxmCMiAANpE
    Posted April 26th, 2008. Accessed July 14th, 2008.

26 Ibid.

27 Ibid.

28 Ibid.

29 Ibid.

30 Ron Paul, MD. "CAFTA: More Bureaucracy, Less Free Trade." LewRockwell.com. http://www.lewrockwell.
    com/paul/paul254.html Posted June 7th, 2005.
    Accessed June 27th, 2008.

31 Ibid.

32 Ibid.

CHAPTER 17

1   Chris Barrick, "Ron Paul's Presidential Bid," Cross and Crescent, November 2007, <http://www.
    crossandcrescent.com/2007/11/ron-pauls-presidential-bid/>,
    accessed May 22, 2008.

2   Christopher Caldwell, "The Antiwar, Anti-Abortion, Anti-Drug-Enforcement-Administration, Anti-Medicare
    Candidacy of Dr. Ron Paul," The New York Times Magazine, July 22, 2007, < http://www.nytimes.
    com/2007/07/22/magazine/22Paul-t.html>,
    accessed June 1, 2008.

3   Jake Tapper, "Guns and Money," Salon.com, August 11, 1999,
    <http://www.salon.com/news/feature/1999/08/11/gun/index.html>,
    accessed May 22, 2008.

4   Evelyn Theiss, "Clinton Blames Losses on NRA," Cleveland Plain-Dealer, January 14, 1995, p. A1.
    The NRA also takes this view (see, e.g., "The Clinton Gun Ban Story" at <http://www.youtube.com/
    watch?v=SxBJaAioXEO>).

5   Author phone interview with Dr. Jack Pruitt, conducted June 11, 2008.

6   Author interview with Ronald E. Paul, MD. June 1st, 2008.

7   Caldwell, op. cit.

8   Ethan Wilenksy-Lanford, "A Shrewd Run for Congress: National GOP United Against Ron Paul in
    '96," The Concord (N.H.) Monitor, January 5, 2008, <http://www.concordmonitor.com/apps/pbcs.
    dll/article?AID=/20080105/FRONTPAGE/801050301>, accessed May 31, 2008.

9   Ibid.

10 Adam Clymer, "The Race for Congress: Texas' 14th District; Under Fire, a G.O.P. Convert Wins Party's
    Fierce Loyalty," The New York Times, April 8, 1996, < http://query.nytimes.com/gst/fullpage.html?res=9F
    03E5DE1039F93BA35757C0A960958260>, accessed May 31, 2008.

11 David Beiler, "Paul vs. Laughlin: Ron Paul's Campaign Against Representative Greg Laughlin,"
    Campaigns & Elections, June 1996, archived at < http://findarticles.com/p/articles/mi_m2519/is_n6_
    v17/ai_18535311/pg_1>, accessed May 31, 2008.

12 S.C. Gwynne, "Dr. No," Texas Monthly, October 2001,
    < http://www.texasmonthly.com/2001-10-01/feature7-1.php>,
    accessed May 31, 2008.

13 Howard Phillips interview with Ron Paul, 1997, Conservative Roundtable, archived on
    < http://www.youtube.com/watch?v=_suZvyB69YM>, accessed June 24, 2008.

14 Ibid.

15 Wilenksy-Lanford, op. cit.

16 Ibid.

17 Beiler, op. cit.

18 Wilenksy-Lanford, op. cit.

19 Gwynne, op. cit.

20 Wilenksy-Lanford, op. cit.

21 Beiler, op. cit.

22 Ibid.

23 Ibid.

24 Ibid.

25 Clymer, op. cit. The video, "The Ron Paul Story," can be viewed on the Internet at
    <http://www.youtube.com/watch?v=FgF-s1voM_Y>.

26 Caldwell, op. cit.

27 Beiler, op. cit.

28 Alex De Marban, "Paul-itically Incorrect: Ron Paul's Wacky Views Highlight a Bitter Race,"
    The Austin Chronicle, October 31, 1996, <http://www.austinchronicle.com/gyrobase/Issue/
    story?oid=oid%3A525510>, accessed June 1, 2008.

29 Ron Paul, *Conservative Roundtable*, op. cit.

30 Cary Wesberry, "Ron Paul Has Betrayed the GOP," April 18, 2007, Townhall.com blog entry, <http://afk.
    blogtownhall.com/default.aspx?mode=post&g=62e31d0c-9338-4b8d-8638-7042ac083cc0>, accessed
    June 25, 2008.

31 Ibid.

32 Catalina Camia, "Candidates Comments on Blacks Questioned,"
    The Dallas Morning News, May 22, 1996, archived at <http://www.criticalreactor.com/ronpaul/
    newsletters/1996_Dallas_Morning_News.html>, accessed June 1, 2008.

33 De Marban, op. cit.

34 Camia, op. cit.

35 Gwynne, op. cit.

36 Ibid.

37 "Congressional Election 1996 National Political Awareness Test," Project Vote Smart,
    < http://www.votesmart.org/npat.php?can_id=296#826>, accessed June 5, 2008.

38 Ron Paul, 1987, *Freedom Under Siege: The US Constitution After 200 Years*,
    Lake Jackson, Texas, Foundation for Rational Economics and Education, p. 27,
    <http://mises.org/books/freedomsiege.pdf>, accessed June 5, 2008.

39 Ron Paul, "Assault Weapons and Assaults on the Constitution,"
    Ron Paul's Texas Straight Talk, April 21, 2003, archived at
    <http://www.ronpaullibrary.org/document.php?id=301>, accessed June 9, 2008.

40 De Marban, op. cit.

41 Gwynne, op. cit.

42 Federal Election Commission, 1996 Electoral and Popular Vote Summary,
    <http://www.fec.gov/pubrec/fe1996/elecpop.htm>, accessed June 11, 2008.

43 Ron Paul, MD. "CAFTA: More Bureaucracy, Less Free Trade." LewRockwell.com.
    http://www.lewrockwell.com/paul/paul254.html Posted June 7th, 2005.
    Accessed June 27th, 2008.

CHAPTER 18

1 Office of US Representative Ron Paul, Press Release, Paul refuses to participate in "immoral" pension
   system, issued January 30, 1997, http://www.house.gov/paul/press/press97/prjan30.htm accessed on
   March 16,2008.

2 Office of US Representative Ron Paul, Press Release, Paul votes for every term limitation measure,
   issued February 12 1997, http://www.house.gov/paul/press/press97/prfeb12.htm accessed on March
   16,2008.

3 Congressional salaries of Congress: http://www.congressproject.org/congressionalsalary.pdf

4 Office of US Representative Ron Paul, Press Release, Paul votes against congressional pay raise, issued
   July 17, 1998, http://www.house.gov/paul/press/press98/pr071798.htm accessed on March 16,2008.

5 Office of US Representative Ron Paul, Press Release, Paul assigned to two banking subcommittees,
   issued February 5 1997, http://www.house.gov/paul/press/press97/prfeb5.htm accessed on March
   16,2008.

6   Office of US Representative Ron Paul, Press Release, Paul introduces Liberty Amendment to Constitution, issued April 28, 1998, http://www.house.gov/paul/press/press98/pr042898liberty.htm accessed on March 16,2008.

7   Office of US Representative Ron Paul, Press Release, Legislation brought forward to stop National ID, issued July 15, 1998, http://www.house.gov/paul/press/press98/pr071598.htm accessed on March 16,2008.

8   Office of US Representative Ron Paul, Press Release, If UN won't follow our laws, UN should leave, issued April 25, 1997, http://www.house.gov/paul/press/press97/prapril25.htm accessed on March 16,2008.

9   Ron Paul, *A Foreign policy of Freedom* (Foundation for Rational Economics and Education, Lake Jackson, Texas: 2007) p. 60.

10   Press release issued by Ron Paul, August of 2007

11   Office of US Representative Ron Paul, Press Release, Paul calls UN Meddling in US law enforcement unconscionable, issued August 22, 1997, http://www.house.gov/paul/press/press97/praug22.htm accessed on March 16,2008.

12   Office of US Representative Ron Paul, Press Release, Paul speaks in favor of amendment to cut phony UN debt, issued September 2, 1997, http://www.house.gov/paul/press/press97/prsept02.htm accessed on March 16, 2008.

13   Ron Paul, *A Foreign policy of Freedom* (Foundation for Rational Economics and Education, Lake Jackson, Texas: 2007) p. 65.

14   Office of US Representative Ron Paul, Press Release, Paul advises president to continue diplomacy and rule out force in Iraq, issued November 19,1997, http://www.house.gov/paul/press/press97/prnov19a.htm accessed on March 16,2008.

15   Ron Paul, *A Foreign policy of Freedom* (Foundation for Rational Economics and Education, Lake Jackson, Texas: 2007) p. 67.

16   Ron Paul, *A Foreign policy of Freedom* (Foundation for Rational Economics and Education, Lake Jackson, Texas: 2007) p. 71

17   Office of US Representative Ron Paul, Press Release, Paul introduces legislation to stop military action in Iraq, issued February 12, 1998, http://www.house.gov/paul/press/press98/pr021298.htm accessed on March 16,2008.

18   Ron Paul, *A Foreign policy of Freedom* (Foundation for Rational Economics and Education, Lake Jackson, Texas: 2007) p. 74-75.

19   Ron Paul, Texas Straight Talk weekly column. http://www.house.gov/paul/tst/tst2008/tst032308.htm

20   Ron Paul, *A Foreign policy of Freedom* (Foundation for Rational Economics and Education, Lake Jackson, Texas: 2007) p. 79.

21   Office of US Representative Ron Paul, Press Release, Clinton endangers troops to end-run impeachment, issued December 16, 1998, http://www.house.gov/paul/press/press98/pr121698.htm accessed on March 16,2008.

22   Office of US Representative Ron Paul, Press Release, Ron Paul votes for impeachment, issued December 16, 1998, http://www.house.gov/paul/press/press98/pr121998.htm accessed on March 16,2008.

CHAPTER 19

1   Gwynn, S. C. "Dr. No". *TexasMonthly.com.* http://www.texasmonthly.com/2001-10-01/feature7-3.php, accessed on May 23, 2008.

2   "Paul vs. Sneary". June 26, 1998. *Human Events.* http://findarticles.com/p/articles/mi_qa3827/is_199806/ai_n8799789, accessed on May 30, 2008.

3   Copeland, Libby. "Congressman Paul's Legislative Strategy? He'd Rather Say Not". *Washingtonpost. com.* http://www.washingtonpost.com/wp-dyn/content/article/2006/07/08/AR2006070800966_2.html, accessed on May 30, 2008.

4   Gwynn, S. C. "Dr. No". *TexasMonthly.com.* http://www.texasmonthly.com/2001-10-01/feature7-3.php, accessed on May 23, 2008.

5   Paul, Ron. "Protecting integrity of Social Security". Jan. 11, 1999. http://www.house.gov/paul/tst/tst99/tst011199.htm, accessed on May 26, 2008.

6   Paul, Ron. Feb. 9, 1999. http://www.house.gov/paul/legis/106/hr647.htm, accessed on June 14, 2008.

7   Paul, Ron. "Cosponsored Bills". *Texas Straight Talk.* http://www.house.gov/paul/tst/tst99/tst122099.htm, accessed on June 14, 2008.

8   http://www.govtrack.us/congress/bill.xpd?bill=h106-3636, accessed on June 16, 2008.
9   http://www.govtrack.us/congress/bill.xpd?bill=h106-4265, accessed on June 16, 2008.
10 Greenspan, Alan (2007). *The Age of Turbulence*. New York: The Penguin Press. 40, 52
11 Rand, Ayn (1967). *Capitalism: The Unknown Ideal*. New York: Signet. 101
12 Luskin, Donald. "The Greenspan Gadfly". *SmartMoney*. March 1, 2002.
    http://www.smartmoney.com/ahead-of-the-curve/index.cfm?story=20020301,
    accessed on May 28, 2008.
13 Paul, Ron. "The Maestro Changes His Tune". *LewRockwell.com*. Feb. 22, 2005.
    http://lewrockwell.com/paul/paul236.html, accessed on May 23, 2008.
14 Paul, Ron. "A Perennial Gift From Greenspan". *LewRockwell.com*. March 9, 2004.
    http://www.lewrockwell.com/paul/paul163.html, accessed on May 23, 2008.
15 Paul, Ron. "Questions for Greenspan". *LewRockwell.com*. July 22, 1999.
    http://lewrockwell.com/paul/paul253.html, accessed on May 23, 2008.
16 Paul, Ron. "The GSE Crisis". *LewRockwell.com*. Oct. 27, 2005.
    http://lewrockwell.com/paul/paul282.html, accessed on May 23, 2008.
17 Paul, Ron. http://www.house.gov/paul/legis/106/hr1148.htm, accessed on May 23, 2008.
18 Paul, Ron. "Bring Back Honest Money". *LewRockwell.com*. July 25, 2003.
    http://lewrockwell.com/paul/paul118.html, accessed on May 23, 2008.
19 Rand, Ayn (1967). *Capitalism: The Unknown Ideal*. New York: Signet. 97
20 CPI Inflation Calculator. http://data.bls.gov/cgi-bin/cpicalc.pl,
    accessed on May 23, 2008.
21 Hagenbaugh, Barbara. "New rules outlaw melting pennies, nickels for profit."
    USA Today. Dec. 14, 2006. http://usatoday.com/money/2006-12-14-melting-ban-usat_x.htm, accessed
    on May 26, 2008.
22 Paul, Ron. "Questions for Greenspan." *LewRockwell.com*. July 25, 2000.
    http://lewrockwell.com/paul/paul253.html, accessed on May 23, 2008.
23 February of 2004, House Financial Services Committee session.
24 Interview on Sean Hannity's radio show in January 2008
25 Paul, Ron. "The Electoral College Serves to Protect Liberty and Statehood."
    November 13, 2000. http://www.house.gov/paul/tst/tst2000/tst111300.htm

CHAPTER 20

1   http://www.noaanews.noaa.gov/stories/s367.htm accessed on Monday, May 12, 2008
2   Weekly Defense Monitor Volume 4 Issue 3 (http://www.cdi.org/weekly/2000/issue03.html) accessed on
    Thursday, May 15, 2008
3   IBID
4   Texas Monthly, October, 2001 (http://www.texasmonthly.com/mag/issues/2001-10-01/feature7-3.php)
    accessed on Monday, May 12, 2008
5   Economic Sanctions and the Effect on US Agriculture Hearing before the House Committee on
    Agriculture US House of Representatives (http://books.google.com/books?id=OHRW_InkH38C)
6   http://www.campaignmoney.com/committee.asp?pg=2&candidateid=H8TX14088&cycle=00&cnt=285&a
    mt=428596&cname=Loy+E+Sneary&prevpage=1
    accessed on Thursday, May 15, 2008
7   http://www.house.gov/paul/congrec/congrec2001/cr010301.htm
    accessed on Friday, May 24, 2008
8   http://www.whitehouse.gov/news/releases/20010129-2.html
    accessed on Sunday, June 1, 2008
9   http://www.house.gov/paul/congrec/congrec2001/cr061301C.html
    accessed on Monday, May 26, 2008.
10 http://www.capmag.com/article.asp?id=155
    accessed Sunday, June 1, 2008
11 http://www.house.gov/paul/congrec/congrec2001/cr091201.htm
    accessed Sunday, May 25, 2008.
12 http://www.freerepublic.com/focus/f-news/546659/posts -
    accessed Friday, May 23, 2008

13 http://www.freerepublic.com/focus/f-news/549655/posts
accessed Sunday, June 1, 2008

14 http://www.house.gov/paul/congrec/congrec2001/cr101001.htm
acessed Sunday, June 1, 2008

15 http://www.house.gov/paul/congrec/congrec2001/cr101201.htm
accessed Sunday, June 1, 2008

16 http://www.whitehouse.gov/news/releases/2001/10/20011026-5.html
accessed Saturday, May 31, 2008

17 http://educate-yourself.org/cn/patriotact20012006senatevote.shtml
accessed Sunday, June 1, 2008

18 http://www.house.gov/paul/congrec/congrec2001/cr102501.htm
accessed Sunday, June 1, 2008

19 http://www.house.gov/paul/congrec/congrec2001/cr121901.htm
accessed Thursday, May 15 2008.

20 Eric Dondero interview by editor in July 2008.

CHAPTER 21

1 CNN Election Results 2002 http://www.cnn.com/ELECTION/2002/pages/states/TX/H/14/race.html

2 Paul, Ron. Texas Straight Talk. "Will Congress Debate War with Iraq?" August 5, 2002, http://www.house.gov/paul/tst/tst2002/tst080502.htm, accessed on March 10, 2008.

3 Paul, Ron. Texas Straight Talk. "Arguments Against War in Iraq." September 4, 2002, http://www.house.gov/paul/congrec/congrec2002/cr090402.htm, accessed on March 10, 2008.

4 Paul, Ron. Texas Straight Talk. "Why Won't Congress Declare War?" October 14, 2002, http://www.house.gov/paul/tst/tst2002/tst101402.htm, accessed on March 10, 2008

5 King, Oliver and Paul Hamilos. The Guardian. "Timeline: The Road to War in Iraq" http://www.guardian.co.uk/politics/2006/feb/02/iraq.iraq, accessed on March 10, 2008.

6 Representative Ron Paul Address to the US House of Representatives, "Unintended Consequences," November 14, 2002, http://www.house.gov/paul/congrec/congrec2002/cr111402.htm, accessed on March 10, 2008.

7 Paul, Ron. Texas Straight Talk. "Why Won't Congress Declare War?" December 16, 2002, http://www.house.gov/paul/tst/tst2002/tst121602.htm, accessed on March 10, 2008.

8 Paul, Ron. Texas Straight Talk. "Our Incoherent Policy Fuels Middle East Turmoil" December 2, 2002, http://www.house.gov/paul/tst/tst2002/tst121602.htm, accessed on March 10, 2008.

9 King, Oliver and Paul Hamilos. The Guardian. "Timeline: The Road to War in Iraq" http://www.guardian.co.uk/politics/2006/feb/02/iraq.iraq, accessed on March 10, 2008.

10 Paul, Ron. Texas Straight Talk. "Time to Renounce the United Nations?" March 17, 2003, http://www.house.gov/paul/tst/tst2003/tst031703.htm, accessed on March 10, 2008.

11 Ron Paul Legislative Information, http://www.house.gov/paul/legis.shtml, accessed on March 10, 2008.

12 King, Oliver and Paul Hamilos. The Guardian. "Timeline: The Road to War in Iraq" http://www.guardian.co.uk/politics/2006/feb/02/iraq.iraq, accessed on March 10, 2008.

13 CNN. "Commander in Chief Lands on USS Lincoln" May 2, 2003, http://www.cnn.com/2003/ALLPOLITICS/05/01/bush.carrier.landing/, accessed on March 10, 2008.

14 Representative Ron Paul Address to the US House of Representatives, "Neo-Conned!" July 10, 2003, http://www.house.gov/paul/congrec/congrec2003/cr071003.htm, accessed on March 10, 2008.

15 Etherzone, "Pro-War Libertarians: Is There Such a Thing?" <http://www.etherzone.com/2007/phill060407.shtml>

16 Paul, Ron. Texas Straight Talk. "War and Red Ink," September 15, 2003, http://www.house.gov/paul/tst/tst2003/tst091503.htm, accessed on March 11, 2008.

17 Paul, Ron. Texas Straight Talk. "Your Money in Iraq," September 29, 2003, http://www.house.gov/paul/tst/tst2003/tst092903.htm, accessed on March 11, 2008.

18 Representative Ron Paul Address to the US House of Representatives, "Conscription: The Terrible Price of War," November 21, 2003, http://www.house.gov/paul/congrec/congrec2003/cr112103.htm, accessed on March 11, 2008.

19 Representative Ron Paul Address to the US House of Representatives,

"A Wise Consistency," February 11, 2004, http://www.house.gov/paul/congrec/congrec2004/cr021104. htm, accessed on March 11, 2008.

20 Paul, Ron. Texas Straight Talk. "Iraq One Year Later," March 22, 2004, http://www.house.gov/paul/tst/tst2004/tst032204.htm, accessed on March 11, 2008.

21 Shanker, Thom. "6 G.I.'s in Iraq Are Charged with Abuse of Prisoners," March 21, 2004, http://query. nytimes.com/gst/fullpage.html?res=9C05E2DD1E31F932A15750C0A9629C8B63&scp=11&sq=abu+gh raib+torture&st=nyt, accessed on March 11, 2008.

22 Representative Ron Paul Address to the US House of Representatives, "Statement on the Abuse of Prisoners in Iraq," May 6, 2004, http://www.house.gov/paul/congrec/ congrec2004/cr050604.htm, accessed on March 11, 2008.

23 Representative Ron Paul Address to the US House of Representatives, "Justifications for War," July 21, 2003, http://www.house.gov/paul/congrec/congrec2003/cr072103.htm, accessed on March 11, 2008

24 Representative Ron Paul Address to the US House of Representatives, "Stay out of Liberia!" July 23, 2003, http://www.house.gov/paul/congrec/congrec2003/cr072303.htm, accessed on March 11, 2008.

25 Representative Ron Paul Address to the US House of Representatives. "Don't Start a War with Iran!" May 6, 2004, http://www.house.gov/paul/congrec/congrec2004/ cr050604b.htm, accessed on March 11, 2008.

26 Representative Ron Paul Address to the US House of Representatives, "Stay out of Sudan's Civil War," November 19, 2004, http://www.house.gov/paul/congrec/congrec2004/ cr111904.htm, accessed on March 11, 2008.

27 Paul, Ron. Texas Straight Talk. "Ignoring Reality in Iraq," December 13, 2004, http://www.house.gov/paul/tst/tst2004/tst121304.htm, accessed on March 11, 2008.

28 Paul, Ron. Texas Straight Talk. "I Have a Plan," October 18, 2004, http://www.house.gov/paul/tst/tst2004/tst101804.htm, accessed on March 12, 2008.

29 Representative Ron Paul Address to the US House of Representatives, "End the Two Party Monopoly!" July 15, 2004, http://www.house.gov/paul/congrec/congrec2004/cr071504.htm, accessed on March 12, 2008.

30 Paul, Ron. Texas Straight Talk. "Police State USA," August 9, 2004, http://www.house.gov/paul/tst/tst2004/tst080904.htm, accessed on March 12, 2008.

31 Paul, Ron. Texas Straight Talk. "Tax Cuts and Class Wars," January 20, 2003, http://www.house.gov/paul/tst/tst2003/tst012003.htm, accessed on March 12, 2008.

32 Paul, Ron. Texas Straight Talk. "Support the President's Tax-Free Savings Plan," February 10, 2003, http:// www.house.gov/paul/tst/tst2003/tst021003.htm, accessed on March 12, 2008.

33 Paul, Ron. Texas Straight Talk. "GOP Abandons Conservatives," December 1, 2003, http://www.house. gov/paul/tst/tst2003/tst120103.htm, accessed on March 12, 2008.

34 Ron Paul Family Holiday Cookbook, December, 2004.

CHAPTER 22

1   Washington Post/ "The US Congress Votes Database." *Washington Post.* <www.washingtonpost.com>.

2   http://www.lewrockwell.com/dilorenzo/conf-schedule.html and http://www.nytimes.com/2005/06/05/ magazine/05GOLD.html?pagewanted=2&th&emc=th [especially page 2]

3   CBS News, January 8, 2004. "Skepticism Over Bush Migrant Plan" <http://www.cbsnews.com/stories/2004/01/06/politics/main591660.shtml>

4   "Mexico's Fox backs Bush immigration plan." Dallas Morning News, January 9, 2004.

5   "CNN Shifts Slot for Lou Dobbs", New York Times, Oct. 16, 2007. <http://www.nytimes.com/2007/10/16/arts/16arts.html>

6   Ron Paul interviewed on Meet the Press, Dec. 23, 2007. < http://www.msnbc.msn.com/id/22342301/page/3/>

7   Hoppe, Hans-Hermann. (2001). Democracy: *The God That Failed.* London: Transaction Publishers. 158.

8   Rockrohr, Phil. "*Gary Becker Explains the Benefits of Setting a Price for Immigration*". GSB News. Apr. 2, 2007. <www.chicagogsb.edu/news/>.

9   Varadarajan, Tunku. "The Romance of Economics". *The Wall Street Journal.* Jul. 22, 2006. <www.opinionjournal.com/>.

10 Sowell, Thomas. "Guests or Gate Crashers". Real Clear Politics. Mar. 28, 2006.
   <www.realclearpolitics.com>.
11 Williams, Walter E. "Illegal Immigration". *Human Events*. Jun. 10, 2007.
   <www.humanevents.com>.
12 For the discussion and sources below I am indebted to: Woods, Thomas E. Jr. (2007).
   33 Questions About American History You're Not Supposed to Ask. Crown Forum.
13 Waldstreicher, David, ed. (2002). Thomas jefferson *Notes on the State of Virginia*. Boston: Bedford/St.
   Martin's. 138
14 Lodge, Henry Cabot, ed. (1904). *The Works of Alexander Hamilton*. New York: G.P. Putman's Sons.
   8:217
15 Hülsmann, Guido Jörg. (2007). Mises: *The Last Knight of Liberalism*. Auburn: Ludwig von Mises
   Institute.
16 von Mises, Ludwig. (1998). *Human Action*. Auburn: Ludwig von Mises Institute. 821.
17 Paul, Ron. (1984). *Mises and Austrian Economics: A Personal View*. Auburn: Ludwig von Mises Institute.
18 The author's interview with Jesse Benton on April 18, 2008 confirms this view.
19 Paul, Ron. "Amnesty and Culture". *Lew Rockwell*. Jan. 13, 2004. <www.lewrockwell.com>.
20 Interview in 2006 with Alex Jones.
21 ibid.
22 "How Eisenhower solved illegal border crossings from Mexico" < http://www.csmonitor.com/2006/0706/
   p09s01-coop.html>
23 Time Magazine, Jan. 2006
24 Paul, Ron. "HR 418- A National ID Bill Masquerading as Immigration Reform."
   The United States House of Representatives. Feb. 9, 2005. <www.house.gov>.
25 http://www.youtube.com/watch?v=MCU2OJPZ4AM
26 ibid.
27 http://galvestondailynews.com/story.lasso?ewcd=dccf67f62a6b27c1
28 Paul, Ron. "Amnesty and the Welfare State." *Lew Rockwell*. Sep. 19, 2006
   <www.lewrockwell.com>.
29 Paul, Ron. "Immigration Reform in 2006?." *Lew Rockwell*. Sep. 12, 2006
   <www.lewrockwell.com>.
30 ibid.
31 Paul, Ron. "Immigration Reform in 2006?." *Lew Rockwell*. Sep. 12, 2006
   <www.lewrockwell.com>.
32 Paul, Ron. "Big Government Solutions Don't Work/ The Law of Opposites."
   The United States House of Representatives. Sep. 7, 2006. <www.house.gov>.
21 Paul, Ron. "HR 418- A National ID Bill Masquerading as Immigration Reform."
   The United States House of Representatives. Feb. 9, 2005. <www.house.gov>.
22 http://www.youtube.com/watch?v=MCU2OJPZ4AM
23 ibid.
24 Paul, Ron. "HR 418- A National ID Bill Masquerading as Immigration Reform."
   The United States House of Representatives. Feb. 9, 2005. <www.house.gov>.
25 Paul, Ron. "Don't Reauthorize the Patriot Act." *The United States House of Representatives*. Jul. 21,
   2005. <www.house.gov>.
26 http://www.lewrockwell.com/dilorenzo/conf-schedule.html and http://www.nytimes.com/2005/06/05/
   magazine/05GOLD.html?pagewanted=2&th&emc=th [especially page 2]
27 http://galvestondailynews.com/story.lasso?ewcd=dccf67f62a6b27c1
28 Paul, Ron. "Amnesty and the Welfare State." *Lew Rockwell*. Sep. 19, 2006
   <www.lewrockwell.com>.
29 Paul, Ron. "Immigration Reform in 2006?." *Lew Rockwell*. Sep. 12, 2006
   <www.lewrockwell.com>.
30 ibid.
31 Paul, Ron. "Immigration Reform in 2006?." *Lew Rockwell*. Sep. 12, 2006
   <www.lewrockwell.com>.
32 Paul, Ron. "Big Government Solutions Don't Work/ The Law of Opposites".
   The United States House of Representatives. Sep. 7, 2006. <www.house.gov>.

CHAPTER 23

1   http://thefacts.com/story.lasso?ewcd=d96491ceb90c68b4 retrieved on July 12, 2008.

2   State Races: Texas. Elections 2006. Cable News Network. http://www.cnn.com/ELECTION/2006//pages/results/states/TX/index.html Accessed on June 23, 2008

3   Sklar Poll Summary Memo. http://offthekuff.com/blog/misc/SKLAR_POLL_SUMMARY_MEMO.doc. Accessed on June 23, 2008.

4   State Races: Texas. Elections 2006. Cable News Network. http://www.cnn.com/ELECTION/2006//pages/results/states/TX/index.html Accessed on June 30, 2008

5   Escalation is Hardly the Answer, Ron Paul's Speeches and Statements, issued January 11 2007, http://www.house.gov/paul/congrec/congrec2007/cr011107.htm accessed on June 30, 2008.

6   Biography of Chris Elam, http://www.crpolitics.com/html/chris.html accessed on July 12, 2008.

7   RP PEC Video. Posted February 20, 2007. http://www.youtube.com/watch?v=FPIPT4bncq8 Accessed June 23, 2008.

8   http://www.gaywired.com/Article.cfm?Section=66&ID=19631

9   Paul, Ron. In Loving Member of Kent Snyder. Posted June 29, 2008. http://www.campaignforliberty.com/blog/?p=95 Accessed June 30, 2008.

10 Contributor Bio of Kent Snyder, Free Market News, Corp. http://www.freemarketnews.com/Writers-Bio-Analysis.asp?wid=76 Accessed June 30, 2008.

11 Texas Congressman Ron Paul files for GOP Presidential Bid. Dallas Morning News. January 11, 2008. http://www.dallasnews.com/sharedcontent/dws/news/politics/local/stories/011207dntswpaul.2114595.html. Accessed June 23, 2008

12 CNN/WMUR Granite State Poll, New Hampshire Primary Poll. USA Election Polls, February 2007. Published May 18, 2007. http://www.usaelectionpolls.com/2008/articles/ron-paul-unknown-in-new-hampshire.html. Accessed June 23, 2008.

13 Alex Jones interview with Jesse Benton, Infowars.com, June 6, 2008. http://alexjonesradioshow.blogspot.com/2008/06/friday-june-6ᵗʰ-2008.html Accessed June 23, 2008

14 Donadio, David. What's Your Story? Jesse Benton. AFF Doublethink Online, February 25, 2008. http://americasfuture.org/doublethink/2008/02/whats-your-story-jesse-benton/ Accessed June 23, 2008.

15 Snyder discussing presidential bid, January 11, 2007 http://www.libertythink.com/2007/01/texas-congressman-ron-paul-files-for.html retrieved on July 12, 2008.

16 Caldwell, Christopher. The Antiwar, Anti-Abortion, Anti-Drug-Enforcement-Administration, Anti-Medicare Candidacy of Dr. Ron Paul. New York Times, July 22,2007. http://www.nytimes.com/2007/07/22/magazine/22Paul-t.html?_r=4&ref=magazine&pagewanted=all&oref=slogin&oref=slogin&oref=slogin&oref=slogin. Accessed June 23, 2008.

17 Team Ron Paul's Jesse Benton. Dome Nation, Episode 5, Posted May 30, 2007. http://www.youtube.com/watch?v=hQ9NMbONSWU. Accessed June 23, 2008.

18 End the Two-Party Monopoly, Ron Paul's Speeches and Statements, issued July 15 2004, http://www.house.gov/paul/congrec/congrec2004/cr071504.htm Accessed on June 23, 2008.

19 Ron Paul Speech in Austin, TX May 19, 2007 Complete. Posted May 28,2007. http://www.youtube.com/watch?v=NDHCLpNbMmc. Accessed June 23, 2008.

CHAPTER 24

1   "Texas Congressman Seeks Presidency", Joe Stinebaker, The Associated Press, Jan. 11, 2007 http://www.washingtonpost.com/wp-dyn/content/article/2007/01/11/AR2007011101424_pf.html

2   Jesse Benton interview with Dome Nation. David All, Jerome Armstrong. 2007 http://www.youtube.com/watch?v=hQ9NMbONSWU

3   Trippi, Joe. "The Revolution Will Not Be Televised", William Morrow (publisher), 2004.

4   Adapted from John Van Dyk, "Drupal, Grassroots Political Activism and the Ron Paul Campaign", June 23, 2007. http://www.sysarchitects.com/node/49

5   Before the Financial Services Committee Subcommittee on Domestic & International Monetary Policy of the US House of Representatives, April 2, 2008: Hearing on Proposed UIGEA Regulations.

6   Ron Paul, "Hands Off Internet Gambling", April 4, 2008. http://www.lewrockwell.com/paul/paul450.
    html

7   "Father of internet warns against Net Neutrality", Andrew Orlowski, Jan. 18, 2007.
    www.theregister.co.uk/2007/01/18/kahn_net_neutrality_warning/

8   "How 'Saving The Net' may kill it", Andrew Orlowski, July 17, 2006. www.theregister.co.uk/2006/07/17/
    net_neut_slow_death/

9   Interview with Robert Khan http://archive.computerhistory.org/lectures/an_eveninig_with_robert_kahn.
    lecture.2007.01.09.wmv

10 "A New RonPaul2008.com - What would you like to see?", April 4, 2007.
    http://www.dailypaul.com/node/79

11 www.dailypaul.com

12 http://www.dailypaul.com/node/90 (Brochures) http://www.dailypaul.com/node/89 (stickers)

13 "USAT/Gallup Poll: Steady leads for Giuliani & Clinton". Mark Memmott and Jill Lawrence. USA Today
    blogs. July 9, 2007. http://blogs.usatoday.com/onpolitics/2007/07/usatgallup-poll.html

14 Jonah Goldberg, "Another Omen", National Review Online, May 4, 2007. http://corner.nationalreview.
    com/post?q=NGU2ZWYOMGZmYjAwYmU4NTg5MjJhOWRjMTg3MjZjMjc=

15 Sarah Lai Stirland, "'Criminal' Botnet Stumps for Ron Paul, Researchers Allege", Oct. 31, 2007.
    http://www.wired.com/politics/security/news/2007/10/paul_bot

16 James Kotecki interviews Ron Paul, posted April 26, 2007. http://www.youtube.com/
    watch?v=vjQwIcy4OTU

17 Adam Nagourney, Marc Santora, "Republican Candidates Hold First Debate,
    Differing on Defining Party's Future", New York Times, May 4, 2007.

18 Rick Klein, "The Ron Paul Effect", ABC News, May 7, 2007. http://abcnews.go.com/Politics/
    story?id=3165894&page=1

19 First GOP Presidential Debate at Reagan Library, May 3, 2007.http://www.youtube.com/
    watch?v=8Hfa7vT02IA

20 C.M. Paulson, "Presidential Candidate Ron Paul Gains Popularity on the Internet", May 30, 2007.
    http://www.associatedcontent.com/article/263850/presidential_candidate_ron_paul_gains.html

21 Jesse Benton interview with Dome Nation. David All, Jerome Armstrong. 2007

22 "Confessions of a junkie", posted May 22, 2007. http://www.youtube.com/watch?v=p8rsMhQUFkA

23 "Ron Paul in Kansas City", June 15, 2007. http://thecrossedpond.com/?p=806

24 http://www.youtube.com/watch?v=yAh9sp7ebdY retrieved Jan. 3, 2008.

25 Bill Tancer, "Ron Paul for President 2.0?", Time, Sep. 12, 2007 http://www.time.com/time/business/
    article/0,8599,1661290,00.html

26 "Straw Poll Results", retrieved Jan. 3, 2008. http://www.ronpaul2008.com/straw-poll-results/

27 Audio interview with the Korelin Report in late 2007 http://www.kereport.com/Congressman/RonPaul-
    0001.mp3

28 Ron Paul Meetup Page retrieved on January 6, 2008. http://www.ronpaul2008.com/meetup/

29 "We have the Power: Ron Paul, James Sugra, Trevor Lyman, and the iMoney Bomb? that Rocked
    America" http://ronpaulforpresident2008.com/editorials/james_sugra.html

30 "On Board the Ron Paul Blimp", posted Dec. 21, 2007. http://www.youtube.com/watch?v=TcaVshJnMXg

31 Fox News, Ron Paul Sets Online Fundraising Record with $4.2 million in One Day, November 06, 2007
    http://www.foxnews.com/story/0,2933,308404,00.html

32 December 18, 2007 Morning Joe, MSNBC.

CHAPTER 25

1   Bill Moyers, PBS Now, December 15, 2007.

2   BMS (Broadcast Marketing Services) statistics as reported by CNN Situation Room,November 7, 2007.

3   Ron Paul Wins 2nd FOX News Debate Despite Ridicule, Opposition. Posted September 6th, 2007.
    http://thinkrink.wordpress.com/2007/09/06/ron-paul-wins-2nd-fox-news-debatedespite-ridicule-
    opposition/

4   On Point with Tom Ashbrook, interview on NPR, June 21, 2007

5   Real Time with Bill Maher, May 25, 2007. http://youtube.com/watch?v=WUYDt7kC3Z0

6   "Who's Afraid of Ron Paul", Cathy Young, Reason Magazine, May 21,2007.
    http://www.reason.com/news/show/120309.html

7   CBS-New York (local), Coverage of Ron Paul presenting Giuliani with reading list. May 24, 2007. http://www.youtube.com/watch?v=KZGHey7anhl

8   Steven Daly. ìStephen Colbert: the second most powerful idiot in Americaî Posted May 5th, 2008. http://www.telegraph.co.uk/arts/main.jhtml?xml=/arts/2008/05/18/sv_stephencolbert.xml&page=3

9   "Paul not welcome at RJC event", Jewish Telegraph Agency, Sept. 26, 2007. http://jta.org/cgi-bin/iowa/breaking/104383.html

10   Eric Donderoís blogtalkradio show. May 16, 2008

11 "Final Speaking Times", Domenico Montanaro, Jan. 24, 2008. MSNBC Website. http://firstread.msnbc.msn.com/archive/2008/01/24/607248.aspx

12 "Ron Paul's Jewish Problem", Daniel Sieradski, November 9, 2007 http://www.jewcy.com/cabal/ron_pauls_jewish_problem

13 "The Ron Paul Vid-Lash", Virginia Heffernan, New York Times Magazine, Dec. 24, 2007. http://themedium.blogs.nytimes.com/2007/12/24/the-ron-paul-vid-lash/

14 Teaparty 2007 Official Site figures, retreived Dec. 23, 2007. http://www.teaparty07.com/

CHAPTER 26

1   Election 2008 Polls at Real Clear Politics. http://www.realclearpolitics.com/epolls/2008/president/national-primary.html Retrieved onMarch 23, 2008.

2   Transcript: Republican Presidential Debate in South Carolina.î Posted May 15th, 2007. http://www.nytimes.com/2007/05/15/us/politics/16repubs-text.html?pagewanted=all

3   "Thompson Skids While Romney-Paul Climb in NH Poll", retreived Dec. 15, 2007. http://politicalticker.blogs.cnn.com/2007/11/19/thompson-skids-while-romney-paulclimb-in-nh-poll/

4   "Romney Wins Iowa Straw Poll by a Sizable Margin", Aug. 12, 2007. New York Times. http://www.nytimes.com/2007/08/12/us/politics/12straw.html Retrieved on March 23, 2008.

5   "Jay Leno, Jon Stewart ó Why Mike Huckabee Can Win It All", Jan. 3, 2008. http://fundyreformed.wordpress.com/2008/01/03/jay-leno-and-huckabee

6   Ron Paul Excluded From Fox News January 6 Forum In New Hampshireî, 2008Central. net, December 29, 2007. http://2008central.net/2007/12/29/ron-paul-excluded-fromfox-news-jauary-6-forum-in-new-hampshire/

7   Ron Paul appearance on The Tonight Show with Jay Leno, January 6th, 2008.

8   "Conversation with the Candidate" in New Hampshire. The exchange may be viewed at http://www.youtube.com/watch?v=hVG4Ns2LZtQ

9   USA Today Magazine, June 2000. ìGlobal Warming May Be Beneficialî. http://findarticles.com/p/articles/mi_m1272/is_2661_128/ai_62685291

10 See, e.g., Professor Robert M. Carter, ìThere IS a problem with global warmingÖit stopped in 1998î, The Telegraph (UK), April 9, 2008. http://www.telegraph.co.uk/opinion/main.jhtml?xml=/opinion/2006/04/09/do0907.xml; see also NASA satellite data at http://www.atmos.uah.edu/public/msu/t2lt/tltglhmam_5.2.

11 Amanda Griscom Little. ìRon Paulís free, green marketî, Salon.com. Posted November 29, 2007. http://www.salon.com/news/feature/2007/11/29/grist_qa/. Accessed July 17th, 2008.

12 "Warming hits 'tipping point'", Ian Sample, The Guardian, Aug. 11, 2005. http://www.guardian.co.uk/environment/2005/aug/11/science.climatechange1

13 Mesozoic climate records available at http://www.palaeos.com/Mesozoic/Mesozoic.htm

14 Ibid Ian Sample.

15 The Independent (London), March 19, 2002.

16 Ibid Amanda Griscom Little.

17 Suzy Jagger and Carl Mortishead. ìIce Cream Makers Frozen Out as Corn Price Rises.î Times Online. Posted July 16th, 2007. http://business.timesonline.co.uk/tol/business/markets/united_states/article2080599.ece

18 Tonight Show with Jay Leno, January 7, 2008. http://www.youtube.com/watch?v=_-FTUfH4BPA

19 Eric Dondero interview with editor, July 2008.

20 "Angry White Man", The New Republic, James Kirchick, January 8, 2008.

21 Ibid.

22 Ibid.

23 New York Times Magazine, ìThe Antiwar, Anti-Abortion, Anti-Drug-Enforcement-Administration,

Anti-Medicare Candidacy of Dr. Ron Pauli, Christopher Caldwell, July 22,2007.

24 "Dissecting Ron Paul's New Hampshire Polls", USA Election Polls, Oct. 26, 2007. http://www.usaelectionpolls.com/2008/articles/ron-paul-dissection-new-hampshire-polls.html

25 "Sean Hannity Flees from Ron Paul Supporters", Jan. 7, 2008. http://www.crooksandliars. com/2008/01/07/sean-hannity-flees-from-ron-paul-supporters/

26 "Ron Paul Campaign Files Caucus Challenge with Louisiana GOP", retreived March 13, 2008. http://www.ronpaul2008.com/press-releases/175/ron-paul-campaign-files-caucuschallenge-with-louisiana-gop/

27 MTV-MySpace Debate, February 2, 2008. http://www.youtube.com/watch?v=knaxH_wYCVs

28 "Ron Paul, John McCain, MSNBC Debate: Explained", John Armstrong, Jan. 26, 2008.http://www.nolanchart.com/article1448.html

29 "Cuyahoga River Area of Concern", EPA. http://www.epa.gov/glnpo/aoc/cuyahoga.html

30 CNN Republican Debate, January 30, 2008.

31 Ibid Amanda Griscom Little.

32 "Worst polluted sites in Russia, China, India: study", Now Public, Sept. 12, 2007. http://www.nowpublic.com/environment/worst-polluted-sites-russia-china-india-study

33 "Free Market Solutions to Global Warming", John Stossel, The Atlasphere, Nov. 28, 2007. http://www.theatlasphere.com/columns/071128-stossel-market-solutions.php

34 Ibid Amanda Griscom Little.

35 "Ron Paul Launches Eight-State Ad Blitz", Los Angeles Times Blogs, retrieved March 8, 2008. http://latimesblogs.latimes.com/washington/2008/01/ron-paul-launch.html

36 "Ron Paul NH TV Ad Runs Despite Outcry", Oct. 30, 2007. Free Market News Network. http://www.freemarketnews.com/WorldNews.asp?nid=50871

37 Results for Montana, CNN Election Center, June 3, 2008. http://www.cnn.com/ELECTION/2008/primaries/results/state/#MT

38 "Barack Obama Raises $7 Million Since Super Tuesday", Charles Babington, Feb. 7, 2008. http://www.huffingtonpost.com/2008/02/07/barack-obama-raises-7-mi_n_85500.html

CHAPTER 27

1 As of press time for this book, no official estimate for the march has been reported, but observers have put it in the 10,000 range, and a video clip on YouTube showing the march seems to confirm these numbers. http://thebivouac.wordpress.com/2008/07/15/ron-paul-and-the-july-12th-washington-dc-march/http://www.youtube.com/watch?v=rFpJGLOjIjl

2 Chris Peden for Congress list of receipts http://query.nictusa.com/cgi-bin/dcdev/forms/C00435776/319077/sa/ALL

3 "ImPeden Reality", Johnny Kramer, March 6, 2008. http://www.lewrockwell.com/kramer/kramer11.html

4 Galveston County Daily News, iOur Congress vote must go to Pedeni, February 22, 2008. http://galvestondailynews.com/story.lasso?ewcd=3e97f1c7650d079f

5 David Benzion, "Can Chris Peden Beat Ron Paul", Lone Star Times, Feb. 29, 2008.

6 "Ron Paul vs. Chris Peden", Free Republic. Feb. 28, 2008. http://www.freerepublic.com/focus/f-news/1977846/posts

7 2008 Republican Primary Election Results, Office of the Secretary of State. http://enr.sos.state.tx.us/enr/mar04_135_race4.htm

8 Washington Times, March 19, 2008. iPaul slighted by the ëneoconservativeí GOP http://www.washingtontimes.com/news/2008/mar/19/paul-slighted-by-the-neoconservative-gop/

9 "McCain's dream team: Paul, Huckabee, Buffet", Howard Richman, Raymond Richman and Jesse Richman, May 15, 2008. www.wnd.com/index.php?fa=PAGE.view&pageId=64309

10 Washington Times, March 19, 2008. iPaul slighted by the ëneoconservativeí GOP http://www.washingtontimes.com/news/2008/mar/19/paul-slighted-by-the-neoconservative-gop/

11 Permanent rEVOLution, David Weigel. Reason magazine, July 2008.

12 "How the Ron Paul Movement Looks to an American in Europe", Ben Novak, April 24, 2008. http://www.lewrockwell.com/orig9/novak-b1.html

13 "Nevada GOP's state convention shut down early", CNN Political Ticker, April 27, 2008. http://politicalticker.blogs.cnn.com/2008/04/27/nevada-gops-state-convention-shut-down-early/

14 Reno Gazette Journal. April 27, 2008.

15 "Paul supporters make mark", Geoff Dornan, Nevada Appeal, April 27, 2008.

http://www.nevadaappeal.com/article/20080427/NEWS/252102622

16 Night Talk interview with Bloomberg TV, April 29, 2008.

17 "Ron Paul Scheduled Event Not Recognized by Party", Reno Gazette Journal, June 3, 2008. http://blogs.rgj.com/inside-nevada-politics/2008/06/ron-paul-scheduled-convention-not.html

18 "Paul Slighted by the Neoconservative GOP", Washington Times, Page 3, March 19, 2008.

19 Reason Magazine, July 2008, ìPermanent rEVOLutionî, David Weigel.

20 ìItís Not a Campaign, Itís a Mission ì, New York Times, May 25, 2008.

21 Official Ron Paul announcement of Campaign for Liberty, June 12, 2008.

22 "In Loving Memory of Kent Snyder", Campaign for Liberty Blog. http://www.campaignforliberty.com/blog/?p=95 retrieved on July 19, 2008.

23 $400K medical costs. http://www.kentsnyder.com retrieved on July 19, 2008.

24 "Libertarian Legacy? Ron Paul's Campaign Manager, 49, Dies Uninsured, Of Pneumonia, Leaving family $400,000 Debt" http://www.huffingtonpost.com/rob-kall/libertarian-legacy-ron-pa_b_111079.html retrieved on July 19, 2008.

25 "Rep. Ron Paulís Gay Campaign Chair Dies, Leaving $400K in Hospital Bills Behind" http://www.gaywired.com/Article.cfm?Section=66&ID=19631 retrieved on July 20, 2008.

26 C-Span BookTV May 7, 2008

27 Eric Donderoís blogtalkshow, ìLibertarian Politics Liveî, retrieved June 2008. Guest David Weigel.

28 Ibid.

29 "Kurt Russell - Libertarian", Advocates for Self Government. http://www.theadvocates.org/celebrities/kurt-russell.html

30 Ronpaul2008.com official campaign video, Feb. 8, 2008

BIOGRAPHIES

David Bardallis is a freelance writer and editor with an interest in economics, Catholicism, great film and literature, and good beer and spirits. His writings have appeared in the Detroit Free Press, National Review Online, and Lewrockwell.com. He blogs at Suds & Soliloquies (tikilounge.blogspot.com) and lives in Ann Arbor, Michigan, with his two cats but frequently wishes he was in New Orleans, his spiritual hometown.

Trevor Bothwell is a freelance writer living in Maryland. He is also a contributor to LewRockwell.com and author of the cookbook, 50 Ways to Impress Your Girlfriend's Parents. He holds a bachelor's and master's degree in education from the State University of New York at Geneseo.

Thomas R. Eddlem graduated Magna Cum Lousy from the I Can Read The Constitution School of Law and has been admitted to bar at pretty much any place he can afford to buy a round. He has been published in more than 20 periodicals, and his essays have been re-published in five books.

Benjamin Fenton is an undergraduate studying economics and political science at the University of Colorado at Boulder

Rick Fisk is a 45-year-old software developer and entrepreneur. He is married, has three children and resides in Austin, TX.

Dr. James N. Herndon is a media psychologist with Media Psychology Affiliates. He specializes in naturalistic research and media design for the worlds of politics and entertainment.

Christopher Horner is the author of The New York Times bestseller The Politically Incorrect Guide to Global Warming. He is an attorney and senior fellow at the Competitive Enterprise Institute, and makes frequent appearances on radio and television, including BBC, CNN, Fox News Channel, MSNBC, and The News Hour with Jim Lehrer. He lives in Virginia.

J. H. Huebert, an attorney and law professor, has lectured on legal and academic issues in the United States and Europe; his opinions have been solicited by both the print and the electronic media; he has appeared on television, been interviewed in academic journals and has provided his comments for front-page news stories. His writings are published in professional periodicals as well as the popular press.

Kyle Jones is an undergraduate in the Honors program at Spring Hill College in Mobile, AL, majoring in Political Science & Law and double-minoring in Pre-Law & Spanish. He is currently involved on campus with College

Republicans, College Libertarians, Students for Life, Honors Program Committee and works as a Resident Assistant. He volunteers at Legal Services Corporation of Alabama, which provides free and low-cost civil legal services state-wide, as a paralegal assistant to the Domestic Violence/Divorce staff and is the pianist at Snow Road First Baptist Church in Semmes, AL.

Johnny Kramer holds a BA in journalism from Wichita State University and is a columnist for LewRockwell.com. He is an admirer of former Libertarian candidate Harry Browne and keeps a blog at Johnnykramer.com.

Dr. Karen Kwiatkowski is a retired U.S. Air Force lieutenant colonel and has written on defense issues with a libertarian perspective for LewRockwell.com, and MilitaryWeek.com. She lives in Mount Jackson, Virginia.

Lucas Mafaldo is a Brazilian writer who blogs about philosophy, politics and economy. He is also one of the creators of Ron Paul Brazil, dedicated to introducing Brazilians to Ron Paul's ideas.

Stephanie R. Murphy, a University of Massachusetts summa cum laude graduate in Biochemistry and Molecular Biology, is currently an MD/PhD candidate at Dartmouth Medical School. Her scientific findings and medical research have been published in professional journals; her perspective as a member of LifeSharers has been published on human organ transplant public policy issues. Stephanie, the proud author of chapters nine and sixteen, resides in Lebanon, New Hampshire.

Michael Nystrom holds an MBA in international marketing from the University of Washington in Seattle. In the late 1990s he worked as a stockbroker during the bull market. In 2000, he took up web design and worked as a web designer and developer in Seattle until 2003. He moved to Taiwan for two years to teach English and started a financially oriented website, Bull! Not bull.

Geoffrey Pike resides in Florida with his wife and daughter. His interests include sports, music, investing, and studying libertarianism. He occasionally writes for LewRockwell.com.

Lasse Pitkaniemi is a 25-year-old English & Swedish-speaking Finnish political scientist and economist.

Brad Porter is a freelance writer and public policy fellow, as well as a blogger for The Crossed Pond, named one of the 10 best blogs for political coverage in 2007. He's been a director for The Free Assembly for Constitutional Thought and a longtime Republican activist. He currently lives in Pittsburgh.

Jason Rink is an independent political organizer and freelance writer. He is the founder of the Ohio Freedom Alliance, an organization dedicated to education and political action in Columbus, Ohio. He can be reached via email at jason@ohiofreedom.com.

An American Catholic son-in-law of Korea, **Joshua Snyder** lives with his wife and two children in Pohang, where he serves as an assistant visiting professor of English at a science and technology university. He blogs at The Western Confucian.

John Suarez has been a member of Young Americans for Freedom since 1992 and a lifelong conservative. He currently lives in Miami, Florida. He is a human rights activist who has spoken out in defense of civil and political liberties around the world with emphasis on Cuba, China, Tibet, Vietnam, and North Korea.

Vedran Vuk has a bachelor degree of economics from Loyola University of New Orleans, and was a 2006 Summer Fellow at the Mises Institute. He is currently pursuing a doctorate of economics at George Mason University.